LEGAL ISSUES IN SPORT

Tools and Techniques for the Sport Manager

Rachel Corbett

Hilary A. Findlay

David W. Lech

2008
Emond Montgomery Publications Limited
Toronto, Canada

Emond Montgomery Publications Limited
60 Shaftesbury Avenue
Toronto ON M4T 1A3
http://www.emp.ca

Printed in Canada.

We acknowledge the financial support of the Government of Canada through the Book Publishing Industry Development Program (BPIDP) for our publishing activities.

Acquisitions and developmental editor: Mike Thompson
Marketing director: Dave Stokaluk
Copy editor and indexer: Paula Pike, WordsWorth Communications
Proofreader: Francine Geraci
Text designer and typesetter: Tara Wells, WordsWorth Communications
Cover designer: Stephen Cribbin & Simon Evers

Library and Archives Canada Cataloguing in Publication

Corbett, Rachel, 1959-
   Legal issues in sport : tools and techniques for the sport manager / Rachel Corbett, Hilary Findlay, David Lech.

Includes index.
ISBN 978-1-55239-160-0

   1. Sports--Law and legislation--Canada.   I. Findlay, Hilary Anne, 1953-
II. Lech, David, 1956-   III. Title.

KE3792.C67 2008   344.71'099   C2007-904621-5
KF3989.C67 2008

Contents

CHAPTER 3   Violence in Sport: A Legal Perspective

CHAPTER 4   Administrative Law: Fairness in Decision Making

CHAPTER 5   Doping in Sport

CHAPTER 6   Discrimination in Sport

CHAPTER 7   Working Relationships

CHAPTER 8   Intellectual Property and Licensing Agreements

CHAPTER 9   Contracts

CHAPTER 10   Dispute Resolution Systems

CHAPTER 11   Risk Management

Preface

Over the past decade, sport management has grown into a well-defined profession, and the handling of legal issues has become an important and demanding part of the sport manager's responsibilities. To a certain extent, the law provides an underlying framework for most activities within all sport organizations, whether non-profit or commercial in nature. The majority of sport managers are not lawyers; nonetheless, to be effective in their jobs, they need a solid understanding of the legal principles that underlie many aspects of their day-to-day activities.

Existing textbooks, for the most part, provide information and knowledge on legal principles, but they do not demonstrate to the student or sport manager how to apply these principles to the situations they will encounter working in a sport milieu. Through this book we attempt to bridge the gap between legal theory and its practical applications. We provide the theoretical background but also show how legal principles are applied and, where possible, include samples of relevant documents.

Legal Issues in Sport has 11 chapters. Chapter 1 introduces the Canadian legal system, its tools of legal interpretation, and the significant issue of jurisdiction—which laws apply in particular circumstances. The areas of law that are of particular interest to the sport manager are then highlighted. This introduction lays the groundwork for the remaining chapters of the book.

Chapter 2 focuses on tort law with an emphasis on the common law principles of negligence and liability. Chapter 3 discusses violence in sport. It addresses both the criminal and the civil aspects of violence, and also examines violence from an organization's policy and internal regulatory perspective.

Chapter 4 deals with the principles of administrative law. Beginning with the basis of the authority of the private tribunal to make decisions that affect its members, the chapter reviews the fundamental principles of procedural fairness and their application in the sport context. Chapter 5 deals with the specific application of the principles of fairness in the area of doping from both national and international perspectives. Chapter 6 looks at the elements of discrimination and discusses how Canadian governments legislate against discriminatory practices.

Chapter 7 deals with the creation and termination of "working relationships." It looks at how the relationship of employer/employee is differentiated from that of employer/independent contractor, and the management implications of this distinction.

Chapters 8 and 9 focus on commercial interests for the sport manager. Chapter 8 identifies five categories of intellectual property (copyright, trade-marks, patents, trade secrets, and personality rights), discusses methods of protecting each kind of property, and describes the use of licensing agreements to maximize the economic value of the property. Chapter 9 focuses on contracts—the characteristics of a contract, special issues affecting contracts in the sport context, and the use of specific contracts in the sport industry.

Chapter 10 addresses systems of dispute resolution from a national and international perspective. The final chapter, chapter 11, takes a broad look at risk management by building on the principles addressed throughout the book, and offers various techniques for avoiding, deflecting, and transferring liability. We suggest that risk management is evolving into a comprehensive management tool that can help sport managers plan, organize, lead, and govern their organizations more effectively.

We hope you finish this book with an understanding that the law is not always complicated, with the knowledge that fundamental principles inform almost all legal issues and, finally, with the confidence to analyze and logically tackle the many legal issues that will arise in a sport manager's professional life. Our modest wish is that this book will become a useful resource for you.

Acknowledgments

Fifteen years ago we had the idea that sport managers needed to have a broader understanding of the legal issues that affected sport. We also believed that the law needed to be portrayed in a more accessible and relevant way to sport managers. At the time, we did not expect that our idea would become the Centre for Sport and Law, and that this little organization would grow to encompass four professionals living in three cities providing a range of legal services to local, provincial, and national sport bodies throughout Canada.

The idea for this book grew out of our awareness that there was no single Canadian resource on legal issues for either the sport manager or the student seeking to pursue a career in sport management or sport administration. We believed we could put together a single resource that could serve both groups. This book is the result.

We wish to thank Michael Thompson of Emond Montgomery Publications for suggesting that we could fill this void with this book. We also wish to thank all those we met over the Internet (Paula Pike and Tara Wells) and behind the scenes, for helping to bring the idea for this book to life.

This book is dedicated to the many people and organizations in the Canadian sport community who have invited us through their doors to make presentations, solve problems, and facilitate change and improvement. We also thank the students in the Department of Sport Management at Brock University who have kept us on our toes in lectures and in "Sport Court."

This book consolidates our body of writing over the past decade and a half as well as compiles new material for our readers. The Centre for Sport and Law celebrates its 15th anniversary this year, and we think this book is an excellent way to recognize and share this milestone.

With few exceptions, sport provides individuals, families, and communities with positive experiences that provide a wide range of social, economic, and health benefits. We hope that this book will help all leaders in sport, and sport's future leaders, to be more effective as they deliver quality experiences to their members and their communities.

Rachel Corbett, Hilary A. Findlay, David W. Lech
St. Catharines and Ottawa
July 2007

The Law

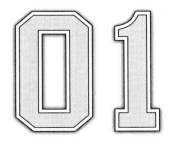

Introduction

The law can be a very useful tool for the sport manager: it sets out the rights and obligations of those subject to it, whether individuals, organizations, or businesses, and it provides a guide to decision making. However, determining what law or laws apply to the activities of a sport organization and the people operating within it can be a challenge.

The Canadian legal system is derived from two main sources of law: common law (also known as judge-made law) and statute law (laws created by provincial or territorial legislatures or the federal parliament).[1] In spite of these seemingly simple beginnings, the law can be complex and multifaceted. At any given point in time, an issue can be influenced by several areas of law. It is important for the sport manager to be able to sort through this landscape in order to make proper and appropriate decisions on behalf of the sport organization.

---

1 The Canadian legal system in all provinces and territories of Canada, except Quebec, operates within the common law tradition. Quebec follows the civil law system, derived originally from Europe, in which the courts look to a civil code to determine a given principle and then apply the facts of a particular case to that principle. Whereas the common law system extracts existing principles of law from decisions of previous cases, the civil law system draws guiding principles from an established code.

Sources of Law

Common Law

Common law is that body of law that has evolved over centuries of judicial decision making. The common law is a set of legal standards or principles that have developed over time as judges decide different cases. The common law is not static but continues to slowly evolve, often in response to changes in societal attitudes and community standards. Canadian common law has its roots in the British tradition but has slowly been developing a flavour of its own.

There are two key principles or doctrines that underlie the development and interpretation of the common law: *precedent* and *stare decisis*. The reasoning of a decision in a case may serve as a *precedent* for future courts to follow when deciding cases with similar sets of facts. *Black's Law Dictionary* defines "precedent" as "an adjudged case or decision of a court, considered as furnishing an example or an authority for an identical or similar case …" (Garner, 2004). In practice however, not every court must follow the decision of every other court. Essentially, a lower court must follow the decisions of higher courts in its jurisdiction. Although lower courts are not obliged to follow the decisions of higher courts from *other* jurisdictions, such decisions do have varying degrees of influence on the lower courts depending on the jurisdiction of the higher court. For example, a decision from a higher court within Canada would have more influence on a lower court than a decision from a higher American court. As well, a decision from a British court may have greater influence than one from an American court, given the similar roots of both British law and Canadian law. However, more recently, Canada's closer ties to the United States on many fronts (political, economic, and social) may have the effect of altering this balance.

This hierarchical application of the doctrine of precedence is known as the doctrine of *stare decisis* and is the second key principle underlying the development and interpretation of the common law. As a result of the operation of the doctrines of precedent and *stare decisis*, a body of case law has developed to guide judges hearing cases. As new fact situations arise and new cases are decided, the existing principles are broadened, exceptions are developed, and the case law is expanded.

Statute Law

The second main source of Canadian law is statute law. Canada adopted the British parliamentary system of governance under which Parliament is sovereign. Parliament can make or repeal any law, provided it does so within the limitations set out within the *Constitution Act, 1867*. The *Constitution Act, 1867* divided powers or domains of authority between the federal government and the provincial/territorial governments. Section 91 of the *Constitution Act, 1867* sets out the powers of the provinces/territories and section 92 of that Act defines specific areas of authority of the federal government and, as well, provides that all residual or unassigned areas come under the authority of the federal government. So, for example, education is within the domain of the provinces, whereas criminal matters, as set out in the *Criminal Code* of Canada, are within the federal domain of authority.

At times, from a practical perspective, the domains of authority are less clear or become blurred within various initiatives. Sport within the educational system falls clearly within the provincial domain. Some sport activities are carried out by municipal governments and local authorities and do not directly involve provincial or federal governments. International sport initiatives are clearly a federal matter. Both levels of government support sport initiatives and embrace sport as a governmental mandate through recognition within the governmental structure. That said, and as will become evident in the chapters ahead, sport organizations are not a part of the government structure, either federal or provincial. Nonetheless, to the extent they are reliant on government funding and government recognition of their status as a governing body of their sport, they must also incorporate government policy initiatives. Clearly, the interplay of policies between and among different levels of the hierarchy of sport governing bodies (provincial, national, and international) and different levels of government (municipal, provincial, and federal) is complex.

Within the federal domain, the *Physical Activity and Sport Act* is the prevailing federal statute embracing the federal perspective on sport policy. Provinces determine their own perspectives on sport policy and in all cases have some form of enabling legislation that addresses issues such as funding for sport. Sport exists in all communities and its subject matter permeates all levels of government. Each jurisdiction, whether federal or provincial, takes varying degrees of responsibility where each sees opportunity to advance its own political agenda.

Custom as Law

There are other sources of law but they play a much less dominant role than the two already identified. For example, "custom" is recognized as a source of law, but custom refers to a long-established course of conduct that has the explicit consent of the majority of the population. There are few examples of this—sportsmanship might be an example of accepted custom in sport.

Sport Rules and Regulations

Although not a formal part of the law in the way statute law and the common law are, the rules of a sport are a form of regulation. As well, sport organizations establish their own policies and rules to govern the activities of the sport organization and its members. The policies, rules, and regulations that apply to sport can be amazingly complex and multidimensional. This is why, as one will come to see, navigating through the jurisdictional landscape is challenging for the sport manager.

Jurisdiction

Jurisdiction refers to a body's legal authority over a particular matter—in other words, determining what rules apply, or do not apply, in a particular circumstance. Very often multiple sets of rules may apply and determining which rules will prevail can be tricky. For example, sport is organized in a hierarchical fashion from local club to regional league to provincial organization to national organization and finally to international organization. Each level has its own rules and regulations but is also subject to many of the rules and regulations of the organizations above it in the hierarchy. Simultaneously, other sport rules may also apply, such as anti-doping rules and regulations, or the rules and regulations of a major multisport event such as the Olympic Games, Pan-American Games, Commonwealth Games, Asian Games, Francophone Games, or Canada Games.

As an example of how multiple jurisdictions come to bear on a single incident, let us consider a doping case. Assume an athlete who plays rugby has been selected to represent Canada at the Commonwealth Games in Manchester, England. The athlete has taken a cold medication and is now concerned that the substance may be banned under anti-doping rules. What rules and regulations potentially apply in this situation? Figure 1.1 maps out the various organizations that may have some jurisdiction over this particular athlete. They include: Rugby Canada (the national governing body for the sport in Canada), Canadian Centre for Ethics in Sport (the anti-doping organization with the responsibility of managing Canada's anti-doping program), Commonwealth Games Canada (the national multisport organization that selects and sends the Canadian team, including the rugby team, to the games), the Commonwealth Games Federation (the international multisport organization responsible for the games in Manchester), the host committee for the Commonwealth Games (the local organization assembled to plan and deliver the games themselves), the International Rugby Board (the international governing body for rugby and the organization responsible for all rugby activity at the games in Manchester), and the World Anti-Doping Agency (the international agency overseeing anti-doping activities at the games). These seven bodies all have some jurisdiction in this one simple matter, although not all will necessarily have jurisdiction at the same time.

It is also important to keep in mind that acting as a backdrop to all this are the national laws of the jurisdiction within which the games or other sporting event

FIGURE 1.1   Application of Multiple Jurisdictions in a Doping Matter

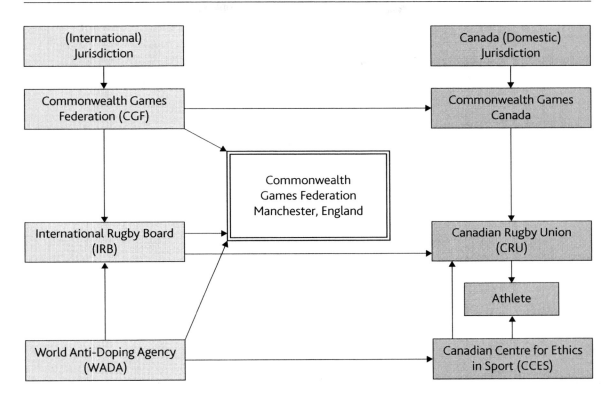

may be taking place. For example, although cocaine may be a banned substance in sport, its possession and use in Canada is also illegal under the *Criminal Code*. Thus, if the possession or use took place within Canada, not only could an athlete be sanctioned under applicable anti-doping rules, but he or she might also be charged criminally.

This jurisdictional interplay and complexity also comes into effect when dealing with human rights and discrimination matters. In Canada, both federal and provincial laws apply to human rights, and at times, these laws conflict with the rules of sport organizations. This issue is discussed more fully in chapter 6.

Not understanding this notion of multiple jurisdictions can result in unfortunate consequences. In *Garrett v. Canadian Weightlifting Federation*, Brent Garrett was not selected to the team competing in the Commonwealth Games in Auckland, New Zealand. He brought a legal action within Canada against the Canadian Weightlifting Federation, and was successful. What Mr. Garrett did not understand was that although the Canadian federation was responsible for nominating athletes to the Commonwealth Games team, it was not ultimately responsible for selecting the team. At a certain point in time, responsibility for the team passed from the national federation to Commonwealth Games Canada (as it was then called), but Garrett had failed to include this association as a named party in his lawsuit. Thus, although Garrett was successful in his lawsuit, the party that actually had jurisdiction was not named and was not required to comply with the court's order. As a result, Garret did not compete.

Areas of Law

There are many different areas of law, and there are also ways to categorize laws to make them more understandable. The first major division of law is that between public law and private law. Public law involves the interests of the "state" or the people. The criminal law is an obvious example of public law. The "Crown" represents the interests of the state against a private individual who may have breached the federal statute known as the *Criminal Code*. Criminal law is covered in chapter 3, where we discuss the topic of violence in sport. Tax and environmental legislation are two other examples of public law.

Private law refers to legal interests occurring between two or more private parties. The most well-known example of private law is in the context of personal injury matters where the injured party seeks redress from the party causing the injury. This is also part of the broader category of law known as "tort law," which is addressed in chapter 2. Employment law is another example of private law, even though the state regulates some minimum standards for the employment relationship through employment standards legislation. The two private parties are the employer and the employee. Employment law is addressed further in chapter 7 of this book.

Some areas of law can be broken down into subcategories. Tort law, as mentioned previously, is one particular area of law that can be further distinguished. There are intentional torts (where one person intends to cause injury to another person) and unintentional torts (where one party does not intend to injure but nonetheless does). There are different types of intentional and unintentional torts—for example, civil assault, recklessness, and defamation are intentional torts—while negligence is a well-known example of an unintentional tort.

Intellectual property law is another example of a broader category of law that can be broken down into subcategories. Intellectual property is one form of property and thus is part of property law. More specifically, intellectual property refers to particular types of "intangible" property of which there are a number of different types including copyright (copyright law), trade-marks (trade-mark law), and patents (patent law), to name a few. This area of law is dealt with in chapter 8.

BOX 1.1   Law and Sport

There are a multitude of areas of law that can affect sport, some more than others. Listed below is a sampling of different areas of the law. Think about how each one might apply to the business of sport.

tax law	human rights law	computer law
tort law	workers' compensation law	real estate law
criminal law	environmental law	immigration law
employment law	contracts	landlord and tenant law
labour law	bankruptcy and insolvency law	aviation law
corporate law	trade-mark law	maritime law
administrative law	copyright law	international law
agency law	communications law	education law
commercial and consumer law	entertainment law	competition law
debtor–creditor law	patent law	
constitutional law	trade secret law	

In summary, each chapter of this book addresses a different area of law as it applies to sport management. Two of these chapters stand out as being more substantial than the others because they cover areas of law that are particularly relevant to the daily work and activities of a sport manager: working relationships (chapter 7) and contracts (chapter 9). Every sport manager works with others, whether they are superior or subordinate employees or contractors, and every sport manager also deals on a daily basis with business contracts. It is our hope that this book will give the Canadian sport manager the knowledge and tools he or she needs to be informed and effective when dealing with the law.

Is Sport a Specialized Area of Law?

This is a growing debate. Legal practitioners and researchers take one of three positions:

- no separate identifiable body of sport law exists nor will it ever;
- although sport law does not represent a separate identifiable substantive area of law, recent developments suggest it will eventually warrant recognition; or
- there exists a separate identifiable body of sport law.

McLaren (2001) suggests that a *lex sportiva* (distinct, universal legal principles of sports law) is evolving from the body of decisions emanating from the International

Court of Arbitration for Sport (CAS), thus forming a distinct international sports law. While certain distinctive elements are emerging, a body such as CAS also operates to ensure that the fundamental legal principles of fairness, good governance, and equitable treatment are respected within the sport domain, and thus it is perhaps these principles, as opposed to a *lex sportiva*, that are reflected in CAS's body of jurisprudence (Foster, n.d.).

In any event, it is clear that an understanding of the legal principles underlying programs, activities, events, and business operations within the sport domain must now be an essential element of the sport manager's knowledge base. The areas of law addressed in this book represent the core areas of practice for the sport manager but are, by no means, the only areas of law pertinent to sport.

REFERENCES

Constitution Act, 1867 (UK), 30 & 31 Victoria, c. 3.

Criminal Code, RSC 1985, c. C-46.

Foster, K., "Lex Sportiva and Lex Ludica: The Court of Arbitration for Sport's Jurisprudence" (n.d.), 3(2) *Entertainment and Sport Law*, online: http://www2.warwick.ac.uk/fac/soc/law/elj/eslj/issues/volume3/number2/foster/.

Garner, B.A., *Black's Law Dictionary*, 8th ed. (Eagan, MN: West Law School, 2004), at 1059.

Garret v. Canadian Weightlifting Federation, unreported decision of Alta QB (Edmonton), Case no. 9003-01227, January 18, 1990.

McLaren, Richard H., "The Court of Arbitration for Sport: An Independent Arena for the World's Sports Disputes" (2001), 35(2) *Valparaiso University LR* 379-405, at 381.

Physical Activity and Sport Act, SC 2003, c. 2.

Negligence and Liability

Introduction

"Negligence" refers to behaviour or actions that fall below an expected standard of care. The law expects that everyone will behave in a reasonable, safety-conscious manner so that others will be safe from an unreasonable risk of harm. As with many legal standards, the standard of care is a somewhat flexible concept based on speculating what an average and ordinary person would do, or not do, when confronted with the same or similar circumstances. As adults, we are all credited with the same general level of intelligence and sensibility—or common sense. Given this common sense, the law expects all adults to perceive the potential dangers in a given situation and therefore to exercise the same degree of caution as any other reasonable adult would in similar circumstances.

Behaviour that does not meet this reasonable standard that the law expects may be deemed *negligent*, and when people are negligent they may also be *liable*. These two terms—negligence and liability—are legal terms with precise legal meanings. Legally, behaviour is negligent only when *all* of the following elements are present and can be proven:

- a duty of care is owed to someone;

- the standard of care imposed by this duty is not met;

- a harm or other loss is suffered; *and*

- the failure to meet the standard of care causes, or substantially contributes to, the harm or loss.

The existence of these four elements in a given situation will lead to a finding of negligence. "Negligence" refers to the conduct or behaviour that led to the injury or harm, while "liability" refers to the responsibility for that injury or harm. Often the person who is negligent may not be the same person who is liable. Many factors can reduce liability or eliminate it altogether, including a policy of *insurance,* a valid *waiver of liability* contract, *contributory negligence* on the part of the injured person, or *vicarious liability* on the part of an employer or organization who is ultimately responsible for the negligent acts of an employee or a volunteer, as the case may be.

Duty of Care

In order to be found negligent, people must first find themselves in circumstances that created a duty of care to ensure the safety of another person or persons. The circumstances that give rise to a duty to act responsibly toward another person stem from the presence of certain *relationships*—for example, a coach owes a duty to athletes, a teacher owes a duty to pupils, a parent owes a duty to a child, the directors of an organization owe a duty to members, a facility operator owes a duty to facility users, an event organizer owes a duty to event participants, etc. A second element that gives rise to a duty of care is the notion of *proximity.* Thus other circumstances outside a special relationship can also create this duty—for example, a golfer striking his ball owes a duty to those people near him on the tee box or on the adjacent fairway, even though the golfer might not share any special connection with those people. In essence, a duty is owed to anyone who we can reasonably foresee may be affected by our actions.

This principle of proximity is also referred to as the *neighbour principle*—when it is foreseeable that our conduct may cause injury to those in proximity to us, there is a duty to avoid that conduct. For example, coaches clearly owe a duty to the athletes on their team, but they also have a duty to act responsibly toward others involved in the game, including opposing players and coaches, parents, other users of the facility or field, and the sport organization or school for whom they work or volunteer. Even spectators and officials, who do not have a defined relationship with a coach, are owed a duty of care when it is reasonable to foresee that they could be affected by the coach's careless actions.

The principle of duty of care says that we must not act in ways that will create unreasonable hazards or put those to whom we owe a duty of care in unreasonable danger. The issue of whether or not a duty of care is owed is usually not complex. There is no dispute, for example, that teachers owe a duty to their students, or that coaches owe a duty to their athletes. But is there an *affirmative* duty—that is, a duty to take positive steps to save a stranger from harm even if we had nothing to do with putting that person at risk in the first place? The answer is, in most of Canada, "no." There is no legal obligation under common law to help someone with whom we have no special relationship and to whom we owe no duty as a result of the neighbour or proximity principle.[1] Therefore, the skilled swimmer can legitimately ignore the cries for help from someone drowning off the end of a dock, and a person trained in CPR and first aid can stroll right by a stranger having a heart attack on the sidewalk. Note that the concept of negligence refers to a legal duty, not the moral or ethical duty placed on a person to respond a certain way when someone else is in danger. However, once one does voluntarily offer assistance, then such assistance must not fall below the standard of care appropriate in the circumstances.

There are some relationships that do, by their nature, carry a responsibility for aid and rescue, even if the danger or hazard was created by someone or something else. For example, a program leader has a duty to rescue a participant who has been injured by whatever means, just as the driver of a car has a duty to care for his or her injured passengers, even when the accident may not have been the driver's fault. A duty to rescue also falls on the person who created the hazard or caused the injury—for example, the snowboarder who knocks a skier down has a responsibility to see whether that person is hurt and if so, to attend to his or her needs, as does a cyclist who collides with a pedestrian on a trail or a tennis player whose wild shot hits someone on an adjacent court.

Standard of Care

The second element of negligence refers to the standard of conduct or behaviour that emerges when there is a duty of care. This element of negligence operates as an objective standard, which means that it is based on what an average, ordinary, and reasonable person would do, or would not do, in the circumstances. This is different from a subjective standard, which would relate to what a specific person did, or failed to do, in the given situation. As an objective standard, the standard of care refers to what a person *ought to do* irrespective of his or her knowledge, intelligence, or general good judgment. These factors, or the lack of them, cannot be used as an excuse for failing to act in a certain way.

Specific knowledge, skills, or experience do become factors in influencing the legal standard of care if a person has greater than average awareness of a potential danger—in that event, the person will be expected to respond with extra care in

---

1   The Quebec *Civil Code* does impose a duty to help strangers.

BOX 2.1 Case Study: Crocker v. Sundance Northwest Resorts Ltd.

Crocker v. Sundance Northwest Resorts Ltd. is a leading Canadian case on negligence as it relates to risky sport activities. Crocker was a registered participant in a sliding race being organized by Sundance. The race was a sponsored promotional activity that involved two persons sliding down a steep mogul slope on an inflated inner tube. Crocker had entered the race two days earlier and had signed an entry form that incorporated a written waiver. On the day of the race he was visibly intoxicated. Two different representatives of the ski resort had suggested that he should not continue racing but neither took firm steps to stop him. On his second run, Crocker and his friend wiped out and Crocker sustained an injury that rendered him a quadriplegic.

The issue for the Supreme Court of Canada to determine was whether the ski resort had a positive duty at law to take steps to prevent a visibly intoxicated person from competing in its dangerous competition. The original trial judge had found the resort negligent and had allocated liability 75 percent against the resort and 25 percent against Crocker himself. The appeal court had overturned this ruling in a majority decision, finding that the resort had taken all reasonable steps to make the plaintiff aware of the risk of harm, including repeated warnings.

The Supreme Court of Canada's decision in this case opens with these comments:

> People engage in dangerous sports every day. They scale sheer cliffs and slide down the sides of mountains. They jump from airplanes and float down white water rivers in rubber rafts. Risk hangs almost palpably over these activities. Indeed, the element of risk seems to make the sports more attractive to many. Occasionally, however, the risk materializes and the result is usually tragic ... the broad issue in the present appeal is whether there is something to distinguish the situation here from the run of the mill sports accident.

This balance of the case then reads like an elegant textbook on negligence and liability. In its decision, the court worked through in detail each of the four elements of negligence and also addressed two further questions: Could the resort rely on the waiver that Crocker had signed when he entered the tubing event, and was Crocker contributorily negligent for his injuries?

Ultimately, the court concluded that the resort not only allowed, but indeed aided a visibly intoxicated person in participating in a dangerous sporting activity. Furthermore, the resort could not rely on the combined entry/waiver form signed by Crocker because it had not been properly brought to his attention, and he was, therefore, not aware that he was signing anything other than an entry form. The court did not alter the trial court's apportionment of liability, concurring that Crocker had contributed to his injuries by his own lack of care in deliberately getting drunk and participating in the tubing race.

the circumstances. Also, if a person represents himself or herself as having special skills or training, such as would be required to instruct gymnastics, coach a rugby team, or lead a scuba dive, that person will be held to the same standard as an average instructor or coach of gymnastics, rugby, or scuba diving. As such, if the person has represented that he or she is a skilled practitioner, the person will be held to the standards of such practitioners, whether he or she actually possesses those skills.

In summary, people with special knowledge or skills, who are operating within their area of expertise, are always held to a higher standard of care than ordinary people without such skills. As a general rule, professionals will be held to the same standard of competence as others in their profession. Therefore a coach, event manager, facility operator, or instructor will be expected to behave in the same manner as any other reasonably competent coach, event manager, facility operator, or instructor ought to behave under the same or similar circumstances. The same applies to those who serve on the board of directors or the executive of a non-profit organization: on legal matters, the lawyer serving on the board will be held to a higher standard than other directors, as would the accountant on financial matters, or the human resources professional on personnel matters.

Does the concept of the standard of care also apply to children? Not surprisingly, children are a special exception under the law—that is, unlike adults who are expected to meet an objective standard, children are held to a standard that is subjectively determined based on the child's age, ability, development, and experience. Because a child's sense of judgment and capacity to perceive and foresee risk are not as well developed as those of an adult, a lower standard of care is expected of children, and very young children will not be held responsible for whatever harm they cause. Because children are always held to a lower standard of care, it is important that parents, coaches, teachers, and program leaders take extra precautions to ensure the safety of children, as well as the safety of others who may be inadvertently harmed by the actions of children under their care.

In sport, a duty of care often exists between an instructor and pupil, which is very similar to the relationship between coach and athlete. In these relationships, someone is usually conveying knowledge or imparting a skill. Some leading cases from sport have shed light on the standard of care expected of those who are in such instructional situations.

In *Smith v. Horizon Aero Sports Ltd.*, a student in a parachuting course (Smith) was injured when she forgot how to steer her parachute and landed in a tree on her first parachute jump. In this case, the court very carefully examined the credentials of the instructor, and the content and delivery of the instruction Smith had received. In particular, the court inquired as to what steps the instructor took to test, either informally or formally, the student's understanding of the instruction and whether the instructor adequately considered the effects of stress on a student's ability to learn, retain, and repeat a skill. The court made a finding of negligence and both the instructor and the school were found 70 percent liable for the plaintiff's injuries. Smith was found 30 percent responsible for failing to clarify any misunderstandings she may have had about steering her parachute, for failing to give any indications that she was under extreme stress, and for ultimately sharing in the decision that she should jump from the aircraft.

Myers v. Peel County Board of Education is a Supreme Court of Canada case that examined standards for instruction, supervision, and protective equipment in the sport of gymnastics. Myers was a 15-year-old student who fell while executing a difficult dismount from the rings apparatus. Prior to the accident, he and a friend had been given permission by their teacher, the defendant in the case, who was supervising a double gym class of about 40 students, to go into an adjoining exercise room and practise. The friend had been spotting Myers, but believed that Myers was finished and turned away. Myers then executed the manoeuvre and in so doing fell to the floor and broke his neck. The court concluded that superior matting on the floor would not have prevented the injury, nor could it be presumed that the teacher's presence would have prevented it either. Nonetheless, the defendant was found negligent for failing to meet the standard of care of a "careful and prudent parent." This case reaffirmed an earlier case (*Thornton et al. v. Board of School Trustees of School District No. 57 (Prince George)*), which stated that it was not negligent for a teacher to allow children to do difficult manoeuvres in gymnastics provided that (1) the skill was suitable to the age and physical and mental condition of the athlete, (2) the athlete was progressively trained and coached to do the skill properly, (3) the equipment was adequately and suitably arranged, and (4) the activity, having regard to its inherently dangerous nature, was properly supervised. In this case Myers was found 20 percent responsible for his own injuries for having attempted a difficult manoeuvre that he had never done before, without the benefit of a spotter and in the absence of supervision.

How the Standard of Care Is Determined

It would be very convenient if one could look in a resource book and find out what the precise standard of care is in a given situation. However, the concept of a standard of care is necessarily ambiguous because it is always influenced by the specific circumstances. These circumstances will vary widely depending on the knowledge and skill of the person causing the harm, the nature of the sport, the setting of the activity, the age and skill level of participants, the extent of supervision of the activity, weather conditions if the activity is outdoors, and other unique circumstances.

Risk is inherent in sport activities and no one is expected to guard against all potential risks and dangers. Some risk is reasonable, acceptable, and unavoidable—falling while skiing or snowboarding, getting bruised in contact sports like football and hockey, or getting rope burns while rockclimbing, are all obvious and necessary risks of sport. The concept of negligence relates to how people perceive and deal with an *unreasonable* risk of harm. Therefore, the greater the likelihood of danger, and the greater the resulting harm should the danger occur, the greater the need to exercise caution to protect others from danger. In the end, the standard of care is a reasonable one where the risk is appropriately managed given the circumstances (see figure 2.1).

The standard of care required in a given situation is related to degree of risk and the foreseeability of harm. As a general rule, if the potential risk is great enough to cause a reasonable person to stop and question the safety of the situation, then precautions should be taken to guard against that perceived risk. Thus, although the duty to act responsibly is constant, the behaviour necessary to meet that duty will vary with the circumstances. The standard of care in any situation is influenced by four factors, of which no single factor is determinative: written standards, unwritten standards, case law, and common sense.

Written Standards

These include written and published standards such as those that exist in statutes and government regulations, building and facility standards, equipment standards such as those published by the CSA (Canadian Standards Association) or ASTM (American Society for Testing and Materials), industry guidelines for a certain activity, policy manuals for a certain facility or program, safety policies and protocols, written job descriptions, etc. The rules and regulations of a sport, facility, or organization are also written standards. These will specify not only the rules of the game

FIGURE 2.1   Standard of Care

Behaviour is **not negligent**	**Highest possible level of care** —risk is eliminated
- - - - - - - - - - - - - - - -	**Reasonable standard of care in the circumstances** —risk is appropriately managed
Behaviour **may be negligent**	**Failure to exercise any care** —risk is ignored

but may also provide standards for wearing helmets, protective padding, eye guards, and mouth guards, and may prescribe requirements for training and certification, ratios for supervision by staff, protocols for decision making in inclement weather, or schedules for inspection and maintenance of equipment.

Written standards, whether provided by government, industry, or the sport organization itself, promote responsible behaviour by telling people exactly how to behave before accidents happen. Disregarding a written standard may be strong evidence of a breach of the requisite standard of care, unless an argument can be made that the circumstances were such that the standard could not or should not have been followed. And, if an established standard is replaced with an alternative measure of risk protection, then there had better be good reasons for the replacement.

However, merely following written standards alone may not be sufficient in a particular situation. Even when a person does observe standards, that alone might be insufficient if the person is operating under unusual or risky circumstances—in these instances, extra measures should be taken over and above those measures advocated by the standard. In other words, written standards are minimum standards, and unique circumstances might require more stringent measures. Examples of situations that might require extra care include water-based sporting activities when conditions are windy or stormy, any outdoor sporting activity in either very hot and humid, or very cold conditions, or snow sports such as skiing or snowboarding in unusually icy or avalanche-prone conditions.

Delaney v. Cascade River Holidays Ltd. is an example of a case where meeting the minimum written standard was insufficient. Delaney was a participant on a rafting expedition on the Fraser River who drowned with two other people when their raft overturned. The rafting trip was occurring on a big river early in the season when waters were higher than normal and the operators were using standard life jackets that met government standards. However, negligence was ultimately found when it was established that although the trip organizers met minimum standards for flotation devices, these life jackets were not sufficient for cold water in a big river and, in fact, other rafting companies in the vicinity were using life jackets with more flotation. In this case, industry standards dictated that enhanced measures were necessary on large rivers at that particular time of year.

Unwritten Standards

These are standards that are common in an industry but might not necessarily be written or published. Examples of unwritten standards are the wearing of eye guards to play squash (although mandatory for junior players, eye guards are not mandatory for senior players, but the industry norm is for all players to wear them regardless of age), wearing helmets while cycling, or conforming to standard etiquette on the golf course or cross-country ski trail. It may be industry practice to bring sailors off the regatta course when there is a threat of lightning, to ring a bell to warn cyclists ahead of you that you are overtaking, or to suspend a softball game in rainy conditions that will make batting and base running less safe. Another example of an industry standard is to screen personnel using police records checks—although there may be no law or rule that this be done, it is nonetheless becoming a common practice within sport organizations that serve youth populations, thus achieving status as an industry standard.

The general practices of other members in the sport and recreation profession are usually a good indicator of appropriate behaviour because the standard of care derives from what a reasonable sport and recreation practitioner would do in the same or similar circumstances. Acting in line with common practice will often defeat an allegation that the standard of care has not been met because history has shown that the practice is an effective way to minimize the risk of injury.

Failure to act in accordance with generally accepted practice is often a clear sign of carelessness. But sport practitioners should be careful about following the crowd too closely—if following industry practice contains obvious risks that should be recognized, mere conformity with normal practice may not be sufficient to meet the standard of care. The standard of care always relates to what *should* be done in the circumstances, not what was done or what has been done historically. The Supreme Court of Canada case *Dyck v. Manitoba Snowmobile Association* is a case in point. In this case, an accident occurred when a race official stepped onto the snowmobile racing course to wave the checkered flag to signal that the winner had crossed the finish line. The result was that another racer had to swerve to avoid the official, resulting in a crash and injuries. The defendants argued that going onto the track to wave the flag was common practice; but the court found that even though this practice was the norm in snowmobile racing, it was nonetheless not reasonable. The official and the race organizers were found to be negligent in this case.

Case Law

This refers to previous court decisions about similar fact situations. Under Canada's legal system of law (except in Quebec), courts decide cases according to the doctrine of *precedent*. General legal principles have been developed over time, and judges are required to apply those principles to existing cases when the facts are similar. Because each case is always decided according to its particular facts, legal principles will always be expanded when new or unusual situations arise. In fact, in Canada, there is no general statute that deals with the concept of negligence and its four elements;

rather, these elements have emerged through case law (also termed "common law") over the years and now serve as a guide for judges, courts, and the rest of us.[2]

A second doctrine also comes into play in Canadian law—the doctrine of *stare decisis*. This doctrine says that a judge must apply the rulings of higher courts in the same province, and of the Supreme Court in all provinces. Higher courts can overturn decisions of lower courts within a province. Decisions from other provinces or even other countries may be followed at the discretion of the deciding court. Thus, although common law is applied in a uniform fashion across Canada, it is possible that cases with similar facts may be decided differently in different provinces. A more detailed discussion of these concepts is found in chapter 1.

The case of *Hamstra v. BC Rugby Union* is an interesting case from a number of perspectives, and shows how case law evolves and how a standard of care may also change as a result. Hamstra was a 17-year-old rugby player participating in a trial match. The match's purpose was to select players from the Fraser Valley under the age of 19 to go on to a final trial to select the BC under-19 representative team. As a result, players were being mixed up in different positions and on different sides and were being observed by coaches who were also serving as selectors. Hamstra was playing the position of "hooker" 10 minutes into the second period when the "scrum" collapsed, causing him to fall and sever his spinal cord. Hamstra sued the head coach, the rugby association, and the school board on whose field the match was being played, arguing that the coach had allowed mismatched and inexperienced players in the scrum and that this had caused its collapse and his eventual injury.

Ultimately, the court concluded that the coach had acted with the ordinary skill and care of a reasonable coach in the circumstances of that particular day, and had acted in accordance with the *Laws of the Game* as published by the Canadian Rugby Union and the instruction notes and guidelines that accompanied those laws. However, noting that there existed in other countries a number of articles and studies about the risks and safety aspects of scrums involving young players, the court did warn (at paragraph 23) that

> [t]he evidence shows that the rugby community's awareness of serious cervical spine injury is now much greater than what it was prior to the plaintiff's injury. I want to make it clear in these reasons that the standard of care as it relates to the risk of serious debilitating cervical spine injury in British Columbia in May 1986 is, in my opinion, a lower one than the Court would apply in British Columbia were the same injury to occur today in similar circumstances.

---

2   Most provinces and territories in Canada have passed an *Occupiers' Liability Act* to essentially "codify" the common law concepts of negligence and liability as they apply to owners and occupiers of buildings and other premises. See also the discussion of occupiers' liability below.

Clearly, the *Hamstra* case tells us that sport governing bodies do have a responsibility, within their means and their mandates, to stay current with new developments and best practices as they relate to safety and risk management, and to communicate this information to coaches and organizers. The various entities involved in promoting knowledge in the field of sport medicine also need to remain current. This case sends a strong message to coaches that it is important for safety and risk management that they keep informed on new technical information and emerging developments in their sport.

Common Sense

Intuition is a reflection of knowledge and experience. Trusting one's intuition is an excellent rule of thumb when a situation does not seem safe or right. Common sense is a very important part of the risk management tool kit, and sport practitioners should learn to rely on what their common sense tells them.

There have been several negligence cases in Canada that have revealed a defendant's total lack of common sense. The Alberta case of *Bain v. Calgary Board of Education* is one. Bain was a 19-year-old student at a vocational school for the learning disabled who was taking part in an out-of-province field trip organized by his teacher. The approved schedule for the trip called for the five students and their teacher to see a movie one evening. However, the students insisted on doing a hike up a local mountain instead, so the teacher drove them to the starting point for the hike and advised them that he would pick them up in a few hours. During the unsupervised hike, Bain fell from a rock ledge and sustained a serious head injury. The teacher and his employer, the school board, were found negligent and liable for the teacher's blatant failure to follow the written guidelines of both his employer and his profession, and for acting with complete disregard for the safety of his students who, although technically of adult age, were all of below average intelligence, were accustomed to receiving careful direction and constant supervision, and lacked any outdoor or hiking experience.

Cudmore Estate v. Deep Three Enterprises is another example of a defendant appearing to have acted without a shred of common sense. Cudmore and a friend enrolled in a scuba course being taught by an instructor who was also the owner of Deep Three Enterprises Diving School. Cudmore and his friend wanted to experience ice diving, so the instructor agreed to take them. After a two-hour lesson at a local pool, and an on-site demonstration in an ice-covered quarry, the instructor sent the two students under the ice with Cudmore attached to a dive line and the friend attached to Cudmore using a buddy line. During the dive the dive line became detached and the divers became lost. The instructor tried to locate them using a search line, but without success, and then in a panic fled the scene, leaving others to continue the search. The bodies of Cudmore and his friend showed up several days later.

The court in this case found the instructor negligent on many aspects: although he represented that he was qualified, in fact he did not have the required training and certification to lead ice dives; he had not instructed his students in emergency techniques or signals that should be used to communicate along a rope; the hook used to attach the dive line was not the type recommended for ice diving; the search rope he had used was too short and was of the wrong type; he should have sent the divers down on two dive lines as opposed to a single dive line and a buddy line; he should not have sent two inexperienced divers down together; and, certainly, he should not have fled the scene when the divers became lost.

Damages

The third element of negligence is that harm or loss must have occurred—in other words, that there are damages. Even if the first and second elements of negligence have been proven (there was a duty owed and a failure to meet the standard of care that this duty imposed), real harm must be suffered for a charge of negligence to be proven. Minor scrapes and bruises, fright, mental anguish, or hurt feelings usually do not represent damages and are not the basis for negligence. A teacher may owe a duty of care to a student and not have satisfied the requisite standard of care but if the student was not hurt in the resulting accident the teacher is not negligent—however, he or she was certainly lucky!

If, however, the injury is substantial and negligence is ultimately proven, courts will try to compensate the individual for the injury. Damage claims will include such things as pain and suffering, loss of earnings and future earning potential, loss of life expectancy, and the cost of future care, as well as direct costs arising from the injury such as medical care, special treatment and drugs, rehabilitation costs, transportation costs, costs of home care, tutoring (in the case of a child), etc.

Usually the issue of damages is the easiest of the four elements of negligence to establish. There is rarely a dispute about whether or not the harm or loss that has been suffered is serious.

Proximate Cause

The final element of negligence is proving whether or not the injury or harm was caused by the careless actions of the defendant or by other factors. The courts generally use the *but for* test to determine the proximate cause of an injury: but for the actions of the defendant, would the injury have occurred? The but for test determines the consequences of an action the way things generally happen—given the circumstances, was it reasonable to expect that the defendant's action or inaction would have led to the harm that occurred? The injury does not have to happen exactly as foreseen—as long as the general character of the damages was foreseeable and the causal element is present, the courts are concerned less with how the accident happened than with how severe the damages were. On the other hand, if something completely unexpected results, the courts will usually not find a defendant negligent because the result was so completely out of the norm that the damages were not foreseeable. In ordinary language, such an event might be referred to as a "freak accident." The law does not hold a person responsible for any and all harm that ensues, only for that harm that a person can reasonably foresee and therefore take steps to guard against.

This final element of negligence is perhaps the most complex of the four elements. Arguments about direct and indirect causation are sophisticated and subtle and usually unfold in the litigation setting. A negligence case may find its way through the first three elements only to eventually founder on the issue of causation. An example of this is the case of *Resurfice Corp. v. Hanke*, a product liability case involving ice-resurfacing machines used in ice rinks. In this case, Hanke was an operator of such a machine and was horribly disfigured when an explosion occurred after he put water into the gasoline tank of the machine. He claimed that the water tank and gas tank were too close together and looked too much alike, and that the defendant manufacturer should have foreseen the risk of an operator mistaking the two tanks. The Alberta Court of Appeal agreed, and taking into account the horrific aspect of the injuries and the respective financial positions of the parties, found liability on the part of the manufacturer. The Supreme Court of Canada, however, applied the but-for test and found that the defendant's omission to distinguish the two tanks did not cause or substantially contribute to Hanke's injuries. Rather, the court found that Hanke was an experienced operator, knew the difference between the tanks, knew not to put water in the gas tank, and disregarded the warning on the gas tank that it was for "gasoline only."

This case, among others, suggests that even though a defendant might have been deficient in achieving the legal standard of care, it does not automatically follow that such deficiency can be linked to damages. Often, the injured person is himself responsible for his injuries, in whole or in part. The case of *Scurfield v. Caribou Helicopter Skiing* examined the proximate causes of Scurfield's death while backcountry skiing in the Canadian Rockies. A guide had taken a group to a slope that proved to be hazardous for avalanches. The skiers were then given careful instructions on how to cross the slope safely. Scurfield ignored these instructions and skied right into an oncoming avalanche. The court found that if the defendant guide had a duty to protect skiers from the unreasonable risk of an unavoidable avalanche, that risk was over once the avalanche hazard had become obvious and avoidable. Scurfield's death was found to have been caused by his failure to "ski alert"—that is, to heed the danger of which he had been amply forewarned, which he could clearly see ahead, and which others had brought to his attention.

Statutory Liability

The previous sections discussed the general principles of negligence and liability as they relate to the sport and recreation practitioner. These principles exist in the common law—that is, they are derived from cases as opposed to statutes, and are often referred to as principles of "tort" or general liability. There are other areas of liability codified in statutes that are relevant to sport practitioners, including *occupiers liability*, *product liability*, and *directors and officers liability*. These are each discussed below.

Occupiers' Liability

A person in control of land or premises has a duty to protect from harm all those who enter onto the land or premises. This duty is described in legislation known as the *Occupiers' Liability Act*, which exists in provinces and territories throughout Canada. Under this statute, an "occupier" is defined as a person who is in physical possession of a premises, or a person who has responsibility for and control over the condition of the premises, the activities conducted on the premises and the persons allowed to enter the premises. Having responsibility and control of a premises refers to the power to permit or prevent people from entering the premises, and usually includes some degree of active participation in the management and operation of the premises. Being an occupier is not restricted to exclusive ownership or possession of a premises: in fact, many premises can have more than one occupier. For example, the owner of a sports facility as well as the user group that is renting the facility for an event would both be deemed to be occupiers. On the other hand, trip leaders conducting activities on land that they do not control, such as public parks, trails, or Crown land, would not be considered occupiers.

The standard of care of an occupier is written into the *Occupiers' Liability Act*. This standard is to take such care as is reasonable to ensure that the visitors on the premises will be reasonably safe. This standard does not extend to every risk that might face a visitor to a premises, because under law, an occupier must only guard visitors against those risks that are unexpected or unusual. Occupiers must turn their attention to three aspects of their premises:

The *physical condition* of the premises—the occupier must take care to protect visitors from unreasonable harm caused by physical characteristics or defects of the premises. Consequently, the premises must be properly constructed and maintained and defects should be promptly repaired. On a ski hill, for example, the occupier has a responsibility to ensure that hazards are adequately marked and that grooming techniques do not leave behind unusual hazards in the slope's snow cover.

The *activities* that take place on the premises—the occupier must see to it that activities conducted on the premises properly consider the safety of visitors. Consequently, a ski resort holding a race has a duty to protect others on the hill from dangers related to the race.

The *behaviour of third parties* using the premises—because the occupier has control of the facility, he or she also has an obligation to monitor the conduct of the people who use the facility. The occupier is not responsible for dangers inherent in the activity, but is responsible to take precautions to protect users from unnecessary and foreseeable dangers. Consequently, the ski resort operator would be acting properly if he or she revoked the skiing privileges of a reckless skier who was putting other skiers in danger.

The courts do not expect an occupier to remove every risk to ensure the safety of customers and visitors. Rather, the courts will balance the magnitude of the risk with the burden on the occupier to eliminate the risk—in other words, trade off the cost and benefit of safeguarding a visitor against a certain hazard. Thus, while an occupier must supply an adequate barrier to protect spectators at sporting events, what is adequate will depend on the degree of risk posed by the situation. A wooden barrier below knee height would be adequate at a field hockey match, while a high Plexiglas barrier and netting would be required in a hockey arena.

As with the standard of care in general negligence, common practices in an industry, a sport discipline, or a similar facility will go a long way toward helping occupiers determine the minimum safety measures they should implement on their own premises. Prudent occupiers would be familiar with any peculiar or unique features of their land or premises, and should make frequent inspections and prompt repairs to ensure that their premises remain safe.

The standard of care discussed above relates only to those members of the public who are legally entitled to be on an occupier's premises, either by virtue of having paid an admission ticket or because the premises is available to the general public. A trespasser is someone who enters a premises without permission, or someone who enters a premises lawfully but then does not stay where he or she is supposed to stay. Adult trespassers are owed a lesser duty of care than others, although an occupier cannot set out to harm a trespasser or otherwise behave recklessly with regard to the trespasser. A child trespasser is owed a higher duty of care, and occupiers must be aware that children are, by nature, curious and that they lack an appreciation of inherent risks and dangers. As a result, occupiers must take reasonable steps to protect a child trespasser, and need to be aware of, and protect against, any unusual features of their premises that might attract or lure children. Open water, exposed equipment, dirt piles, pits or trenches, and other hazardous features may in fact lure children onto a premises, and as a consequence, these hazards require special precautions.

Product Liability

Manufacturers, suppliers, distributors, and retailers have a legal duty to ensure the safety of consumers using their product. Injuries in sport are often linked to defective or dangerous equipment. Products that are seriously flawed as a result of production defects are not typically the source of injuries, because these flaws are easily detected before the product is sent to market. Most product liability claims against manufacturers stem from poor product design, which may reveal itself only after the product has been used for some time.

All products on the market must be safe for the purpose for which they are intended. If the product has some dangerous aspect, the product must come with the appropriate warnings. The supplier or retailer also has a responsibility to provide instructions about installation and maintenance of the product. Consumers share responsibility for their own safety, and are expected to use the product properly and for its intended purpose. A product is not defective if it does not stand up to a test for which it was not manufactured or designed.

The case of *Moore v. Cooper Canada* is an example of an unsuccessful case against a helmet manufacturer. Moore was a young hockey player using a Cooper hockey helmet, who slid headfirst into the rink boards and sustained a spinal injury. He sued the manufacturer of the helmet, claiming it had failed to protect him from his injury. The court reasoned that the helmet was intended to protect the wearer from head injury only: no other protection was promised to the consumer. Because the helmet had, in fact, protected the player's head, the product was fit for the purpose for which it was manufactured and sold.

Directors and Officers Liability

The duty of care of the directors and officers of a non-profit organization arises out of the relationship of *fiduciary trust* between the directors and the organization's members. Under common law, a director's fiduciary responsibility has evolved into three distinct duties:

- The duty of *diligence*—this is the duty to act reasonably, prudently, in good faith, and with a view to the best interests of the organization.

- The duty of *loyalty*—this is the duty to place the interests of the organization first and to not use one's position as a director to further private interests.

- The duty of *obedience*—this is the duty to act within the scope of the governing policies of the organization and within the scope of other laws, policies, and regulations that apply to the organization.

This duty and standard of care has been codified in provincial and federal statutes that govern the creation and oversight of corporations. The breach of this duty by a director is typically referred to as a "wrongful act." Wrongful acts relate primarily to how directors and officers behave in governing the organization, managing its funds, overseeing its staff and contractors, and making decisions that affect employees, members, and the public.

Examples of directors' wrongful acts might include managing the organization's finances carelessly so that payroll obligations cannot be met, directing the proceeds from a casino fundraising campaign to a purpose other than that required by a gaming licence, or writing a blog or newsletter piece that falsely questions the competence of a former director or employee. When a sport organization makes decisions affecting the rights and privileges of members, such as a selection, carding, or discipline decision relating to an athlete, the directors of the organization may be found liable if it can be shown that they arbitrarily or unfairly authorized, rendered, or implemented a decision.

As when considering the negligent behaviour of others, directors are not held to a standard of perfection—they are expected only to act with the care, diligence, and skill of a reasonable director. It is also important to note that directors of corporations, in their capacities as directors, may be held personally liable for unpaid wages, salaries, vacation pay, employee benefits, and taxes. This is an important consideration for directors of organizations experiencing financial difficulties while also having large numbers of paid employees. Should the organization be unable to pay those employees, or to pay adequate severance pay to employees who have been terminated, this burden may fall to individual directors.

The case of *Moose Jaw Kinsmen Flying Fins v. Minister of National Revenue* ended badly for the directors of a small swimming club in Saskatchewan. The Flying Fins engaged a coach for an annual stipend of $12,000. Both the club and the coach believed that the relationship between them was one of independent contractor, not employer–employee and as a result, the coach was paid in lump sums and no deductions were withheld. The government eventually became aware of this arrangement and determined that the coach was really an employee and not a contractor, and demanded that taxes, employment insurance premiums, and Canadian pension payments be remitted, going back over several years. The club went to court to appeal this decision, but lost. The unpaid taxes, withholdings, interest, fines and penalties, and legal costs put the club into bankruptcy and the directors, in their individual capacities, were required to cover these costs, which were significant. Unpaid wages and taxes are two areas of debt for which directors and officers may be personally liable.

Deflecting Liability

As noted previously, negligence refers to conduct while liability refers to responsibility for negligent conduct. Even if all four elements of negligence are proven (there was a duty, the standard of care was breached, serious harm resulted, and the breach of the standard of care was shown to have caused the harm), liability does not automatically follow. There are many factors that can limit liability or discharge it completely. For example,

- *contributory negligence* means that the injured person is forced to assume some responsibility for his or her own injuries, thus lessening the proportionate liability of the defendant;

- *voluntary assumption of risk* means that the injured participant voluntarily accepted the inherent risk and assumes responsibility for all of it;

- *indirect* or *vicarious liability* means that a different party assumes responsibility for the actions of another by virtue of their special relationship;

- an *insurance policy* transfers the financial responsibility for negligence to an insurance company; and

- a valid *waiver of liability contract* means that even though there was negligence, the injured person contracted beforehand not to sue for compensation.

These limits on liability are discussed further below.

Contributory Negligence

The law expects prudent behaviour from everyone, including the person who was harmed. In determining liability, the courts will also examine the conduct of the plaintiff to see whether he or she took reasonable steps to protect against harm. If this person's inattention, carelessness, or stupidity contributed in some way to the injury, then he or she may be held contributorily negligent. In such cases, liability will be apportioned according to the percentage of fault of the parties. Often, an injured person will be found from 10 to 25 percent responsible for his or her own injuries. If the cyclist hit by the car should have been wearing a helmet, if the squash player hit in the face should have been wearing eye guards, if the injured participant was intoxicated, if the rugby player disregarded safety instructions in the scrum, if the skier was not paying close attention to his speed or course—in these cases the plaintiff might be held partially, but not fully, responsible for the injuries. Two cases mentioned previously (*Myers v. Peel County Board of Education and Smith v. Horizon Aero Sports Ltd.*) both involved the courts assigning a portion of liability to the plaintiffs for having behaved recklessly and contributing to their own injuries.

It is also possible that liability may be apportioned among multiple defendants in a case. The case of *Lam v. University of Windsor* is an interesting study on the apportionment of liability. In this case, the relevant insurer had already agreed to compensate the injured person, but a trial was conducted to determine how liability should be allocated among several defendants, including the defendant university, which was covered by the insurer. This case turned on the issue of supervision, and the court's task was to determine who had failed in their supervision and oversight responsibilities.

Lam was an experienced judo athlete taking part in a judo class in a multipurpose room at the University of Windsor, held under the auspices of the university judo club. Because the regular instructor was ill, another person without coaching certification, but with judo experience, filled in. The substitute instructor "bowed out" the class to indicate the instruction had ended and then left the room. He stated later that he did not feel he could insist that the students also leave the room, because the premises was an unsupervised space open to student use at all times. Lam remained in the room and asked another student from the class to spar with him. This other student had very limited judo experience and was at least 40 pounds heavier than Lam. During the sparring, a tragic accident occurred which rendered Lam a quadriplegic.

The court determined that had the two sparring individuals been supervised, the accident would likely not have occurred. The court found that the substitute instructor ought to have known that it was inappropriate to leave the class unsupervised, notwithstanding the nature of the venue in which the class took place. The court found that the regular instructor had a duty to inform the substitute instructor that he should not leave the class unsupervised, and in this respect found him negligent for failing to properly instruct his replacement. Finally, the court found that the university, as occupier of the premises, had responsibility and control over the condition of the premises, the activities conducted there, and the conduct of persons allowed to be there, and had failed to put in place measures to ensure that entities like the judo club provided competent supervision of their activities. Ultimately, liability was spread equally over the three defendants, with each one being 33 percent responsible for a total damage award of $2,750,000.

Voluntary Assumption of Risk

The legal doctrine of *volenti non fit injuria* (harm does not come to one who consents) makes it possible to excuse another person of the duty of care he or she owes. To voluntarily assume risks in this fashion, the person must understand and appreciate the potential risks and then, either expressly (by means of a written contract) or impliedly (by means of voluntary participation) consent to those risks and give up the legal right to sue in the event of harm or injury. This doctrine forms the basis of many risk management techniques including educational materials, signage, waivers, and informed consent agreements.

At one time, this doctrine was a powerful and complete defence against liability. Until the 1950s, the simple act of participating in risky activities was evidence that a person consented to all the risks, including the risk that organizers would be negligent. Today, courts are reluctant to absolve a negligent party from liability unless there is very strong evidence of the *volenti non fit injuria* principle. Generally, while the courts now accept that a person can consent to the obvious and necessary physical risks of a sport activity simply by participating, they do not accept that a person can consent to the legal risk of negligence at the same time. Such consent can be given only through a written agreement such as a waiver of liability contract.

Because organizers of sporting events and activities are not expected to reduce or eliminate the risks that are a normal and necessary part of that activity, those who are injured in the normal course of sport rarely are able to make out a claim of negligence. It is the failure to take steps to protect against unusual or unexpected risks that are foreseeable that usually leads to negligence and liability against a defendant.

Vicarious Liability

Unlike the limits of liability just described, indirect or vicarious liability has nothing to do with the conduct of either the plaintiff or the defendant, but has everything to do with the relationship between two parties. A person or entity will be held responsible for the actions of another by virtue of this relationship—such as the relationship between employer and employee, or between organization and volunteer. Typically, therefore, the employee or volunteer who is carrying out authorized activities and who nonetheless acts negligently can be absolved of liability through the vicarious liability principle. Interestingly, from the perspective of vicarious liability, the law considers employees and volunteers to be in the same relationship with respect to the employer/organization, even though one is paid and the other is not.

When such a special relationship exists, proving vicarious liability requires that

- the harm or damage must have occurred as a result of the negligence of the employee or volunteer; and

- the employee or volunteer must have been acting within the normal scope of his or her duties.

The latter aspect is not always straightforward. A written job description cannot describe virtually every task or duty that a job involves. Therefore, it may be necessary to infer that in order to complete a stated task an employee or volunteer would have to do other related tasks as well. Clearly, an employer will not be held vicariously liable for the employee who behaves criminally while on the job, or who commits wrongdoing intentionally or deliberately. The boundaries may be less clear, however, when the issue is whether or not the employee or volunteer's conduct can be linked either directly or indirectly to the job being performed.

Two 1999 Supreme Court of Canada cases have shed further light on the issue of the responsibility of employers for the wrongful actions of employees and volunteers (*Bazley v. Curry* and *Jacobi v. Griffiths*). In both these cases, employees committed sexual offences against children who were in the care of their employers. Prior to these cases, the test for determining vicarious liability was to ask whether the wrongful act of the employee was authorized or was sufficiently connected to an authorized act to be considered an alternative way of performing that act. The new test emerging from these cases is whether, in planning and delivering the program or activity, the employer has either created or enhanced the potential for harm to occur, regardless of the employer's wishes or desires. In other words, the way the program is set up and run must significantly increase the risk of harm through one or more of the five following factors:

- the opportunity for the employee or volunteer to abuse his or her power (for example, by being alone with the victim);

- the extent of power over the victim that is conferred to the employee or volunteer (for example, is the employee or volunteer acting in a supervisory role, like a parent);

- the vulnerability of the victim (for example, as a result of age or disability);

- the nature of the employer's activity or enterprise (for example, is the program daytime only or does it involve a residential component); and

- the degree of intimacy, confrontation, or friction in the environment.

In the *Bazley* case, it was not difficult for the court to make a link between the risk created by the employer and the wrongful act of the employee. Curry, the employee, worked in a residential environment with troubled children and was expected to act with the authority typical of a parent. The environment conferred parental authority and allowed intimacy between Curry and the children. In the *Jacobi* case, on the other hand, the employee Griffiths worked at a Boys and Girls Club providing an after-school recreation program for children. His role was not to act as a parent, he was not expected to be alone with the children, the children participated voluntarily and were free to leave at any time, and the situation itself did not create any degree of intimacy. The basic enterprise of the Boys and Girls Club did not significantly increase the risk of harm to participants at the hands of the club's employee.

The gist of these two decisions is that a sport organization can make decisions that so enhance the risk of harm as to make the organization vicariously liable for such harm should it occur, regardless of everything the organization might otherwise have done to supervise and direct the employee or volunteer. The onus is thus on the organization to first, systematically make decisions about the nature of its programs and the extent of risk each activity introduces; and second, institute risk management measures in the areas of recruitment, screening, and supervision of employees and volunteers.

Insurance and Waiver of Liability Contracts

These are two risk management techniques that allow liability to be directed to a party other than the negligent person through a business contract. Liability insurance is a contract that transfers the financial responsibility for damage or loss to an insurance company. This contract involves the insured sport organization paying a modest sum of money in regular intervals (a "premium") to an insurance company in return for protection against a possible future obligation to pay out a very large sum of money all at once.

A waiver of liability agreement stems from the doctrine of *volenti non fit injuria* and involves a participant voluntarily assuming certain legal risks. A waiver is a strict business contract through which a participant expressly agrees to assume all responsibility for risks, both those physical risks that are inherent in the sport activity as well as the risks that are not inherent, including the risk of negligence. As such, a waiver is an onerous contract, because through this contract a person agrees to waive a very basic legal right—that is, the right to be compensated for an injury caused by negligence. In other words, asking participants to sign a waiver of liability for negligence is similar to asking them to condone negligence. Although legally this may be an acceptable course of action, it also presents moral and ethical issues that should be understood and discussed by the organization that uses waivers. As well, the courts review waivers very carefully and where it is possible to do so, will typically interpret them in favour of those who stand to be adversely affected by them (the sport participant) and against those who stand to benefit from them (the sport organization).

There is, however, a place for waivers in sport. Experienced, skilled, and informed adults pursuing risky activities in uncertain environments typically have no ethical or legal issue with signing waivers. For example, waivers are now commonplace in the ski industry and have been perfected over time in this sector such that most of them withstand the court's scrutiny and as intended, relieve the operators of all liability for injuries and accidents on the ski slope (*Karroll v. Silver Star Mountain Resorts Ltd.* and *Blomberg v. Blackcomb Skiing Enterprises Ltd.*). Much work has gone into ensuring that these waivers are properly worded and properly executed, and the participants who sign them are informed as to their nature and importance. Like all strong waivers, these waivers and releases include explicit reference to the legal risk of negligence as one of the risks that the waiver is intended to guard against.

In the case cited earlier, *Delaney v. Cascade River Holidays Ltd.*, although the rafting company was negligent for failing to use adequate life jackets, it was nonetheless relieved of liability through the waiver that Delaney had signed before embarking on the rafting trip. Given the hazardous nature of rafting on the Fraser River, the court found that the use of a waiver was appropriate in this instance. Moreover, the court found that the waiver was complete in scope, covering the defendant and its employees, agents, and representatives, during travel to the trip location, during the trip, and after the trip. The waiver clearly relieved the defendant of liability, including liability for negligence, which was specifically mentioned. Finally, Delaney had been advised ahead of time that he would have to sign a waiver, and had been given an opportunity to read and fully comprehend the waiver before embarking on the river excursion.

The use of waiver contracts in sport is a complex subject, discussed more fully in chapter 9 (Contracts) and chapter 11 (Risk Management).

REFERENCES

Bain v. Calgary Board of Education (1993), 14 Alta. LR (3d) 319, 146 AR 321, 18 CCLT (2d) 249, [1994] 2 WWR 468.

Bazley v. Curry, [1999] 2 SCR 534.

Blomberg v. Blackcomb Skiing Enterprises Ltd. (1992), 64 BCLR (2d) 51 (SC).

Crocker v. Sundance Northwest Resorts Ltd., [1988] 1 SCR 1186.

Cudmore Estate v. Deep Three Enterprises (1991), 28 ACWS (3d) 985 (Ont. Ct. (Gen. Div.)).

Delaney v. Cascade River Holidays Ltd. (1989), 44 BCLR 24, 24 CCLT 6 (CA).

Dyck v. Manitoba Snowmobile Association, [1985] 1 SCR 589.

Hamstra v. BC Rugby Union (1989), 1 CCLT (2d) 78 (BCSC).

Jacobi v. Griffiths, [1999] 2 SCR 570.

Karroll v. Silver Star Mountain Resorts Ltd. (1988), 33 BCLR (2d) 160, 47 CCLT 269 (SC).

Lam v. University of Windsor, unreported decision of Ontario Court of Justice, file no. 97-GD-39502, March 9, 2001.

Moore v. Cooper Canada (1990), 2 CCLT 92d) 57 (Ont. HCJ).

Moose Jaw Kinsmen Flying Fins v. Minister of National Revenue, 88 DTC 6099 (FCA).

Myers v. Peel County Board of Education, [1981] 2 SCR 21.

Occupiers' Liability Act, 1991, SO 1991, c. 33.

Resurfice Corp. v. Hanke, 2007 SCC 7.

Scurfield v. Caribou Helicopter Skiing (1993), 74 BCLR 225, [1193] 3 WWR 418 (CA).

Smith v. Horizon Aero Sports Ltd. (1981), 19 CCLT 89, 130 DLR (3d) 91 (BCSC).

Thornton et al. v. Board of School Trustees of School District No. 57 (Prince George), [1978] 1 WWR 607, [1978] 2 SCR 267.

Violence in Sport: A Legal Perspective

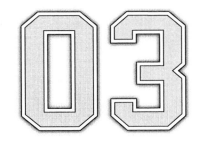

Introduction

Reports of violent sport incidents are becoming startlingly frequent. In recent years, the criminal convictions of National Hockey League (NHL) players Todd Bertuzzi for his assault on Steve Moore, or of Marty McSorley for his attack on Donald Brashear, are well known. There are others, perhaps less well known. For example, in 2006, Julia Tropea, a 21-year-old Canadian university student, received a suspended sentence and two years probation after she was convicted of assault for kicking an opposing hockey player in the head while she lay on the ice. Her sentence was more severe than either Bertuzzi's (conditional discharge and one-year probation) or McSorley's (18 months conditional discharge).

Less publicized incidents in Canada include a swarm of University of Moncton hockey players and their assistant coach attacking a hockey official over what they perceived to be a controversial goal at the end of a game in 1996. Or a grade 4 student filing a $10,000 lawsuit against his hockey coach in 2002, for allegedly threatening to "put a bounty on his head" during a violent post-game tirade. The coach denied the allegation, saying the boy was simply seeking revenge for being cut from the team. He also claimed that the boy hit his son in the stomach with the butt of his stick at the end of a game.

There are also some notable international examples of violent outbursts on the playing field. At the conclusion of a field hockey game during the 1998 Commonwealth Games in Kuala Lumpur, the Canadian goalie allegedly kicked an opposing

Pakistani player who was kneeling on the turf in prayer. At the end of a 2006 World Cup match, the French soccer player, Zinedine Zidane, head-butted an Italian player, Marco Materazzi, for allegedly making derogatory comments.

Finding examples of behaviour in sport that we would acknowledge as violent is not difficult. Violent incidents occur across a range of sports—soccer, football, basketball, and figure skating have all seen their share of violence, although the greatest offender likely remains professional hockey in North America. Furthermore, it is not just players committing acts of violence; coaches and spectators have also been involved.

A Legal Framework to Examine Violence in Sport

Violence in sport can be examined from a number of perspectives. First, it is useful to distinguish between violent acts that occur on the field of play and those that occur off the field. Off-field incidents are no different from violent acts that occur in any setting and should be dealt with just as any other violent act would be—according to the laws of the land. Violent acts that occur on the field of play are different: in many sports, a certain level of violence is desirable from a spectator appeal perspective, and in some sports a certain level of physical violence and aggression is an inherent part of the game. Football and boxing are obvious examples of such sports. When an athlete participates in these and other contact sports, it is done with the knowledge and understanding that a certain amount of violence will take place and that injury may result. However, by simply participating in a sport, an athlete does not consent to all forms of violent activity. There are limits on what one may consent to under Canadian law.

Violence in sport can be controlled using three different "legal" methods. First, there are the sport organization's own rules, regulations, and policies. Second, control is possible through the enforcement of criminal law (by laying a charge of criminal assault). Third, control is possible through a civil action (by bringing a lawsuit alleging negligence or civil assault). None of these three approaches is mutually exclusive, and in fact in some cases, all three may be pursued—the sport organization or sport league imposes player discipline, the police lay a criminal charge against the aggressor, and the injured player launches a civil lawsuit against those he feels are responsible for his injuries. In both the Bertuzzi and McSorley examples at the opening of this chapter, the NHL as a league imposed strict discipline on the offending players, and in the Bertuzzi matter specifically, injured player Steve Moore has also launched a civil lawsuit.

The internal rules, regulations, and policies of a sport organization or professional sport league fall under an area of law known as "administrative law." Administrative law governs the conduct of tribunals, and a very common type of tribunal is a voluntary association having members. Virtually all sport organizations are such voluntary associations and are thus tribunals. The legal obligations of tribunals are discussed fully in chapter 4 of this book. Although that discussion does not specifically refer to violent incidents, punishment for violent acts falls within the general area of discipline, and organizations that impose discipline on members are subject to the requirements of procedural fairness under administrative law.

On the other hand, "criminal law" deals with matters of public interest between individuals and the state as set out in the *Criminal Code* of Canada. "Civil law" handles matters between private citizens and, when violence occurs in sport, that typically means matters of unintentional torts (negligence) and intentional torts (civil assaults). There are significant differences in how these two types of law (criminal and civil) are interpreted by the courts, as shown in table 3.1 below. For example, the onus of proof and burden of proof are distinctly different, which is why some assault/violence cases may succeed under one type of legal analysis but not under another.

How the issue of violence is treated under these three areas of law is discussed more fully below.

Internal Rules, Regulations, and Policies

Sport organizations play an integral role in controlling the game through the rules, regulations, and policies that they establish for themselves, as well as the rules, regulations, and policies of their superior governing bodies that in nearly all circumstances will apply to them. A sport organization has significant, if not ultimate, control

TABLE 3.1 Differences Between Criminal Law and Civil Law

	Criminal Law	Civil law
Onus of Proof (Person with the responsibility to prove the case)	The State (Crown prosecutor)	The Plaintiff (Injured party)
Standard of Proof (Level of proof that is needed)	Beyond a reasonable doubt	Balance of probabilities (more likely than not)

over the level of violent conduct tolerated within its purview and it exercises this control (or in some cases, fails to do so) through enforcement of its own rules, regulations, and policies. Where a sport organization abrogates control, other remedies may be available through judicial intervention, although as noted in chapter 4 the courts are usually reluctant to step in and regulate the activities of voluntary associations.

The vast majority of Canadian sport organizations and clubs are "private tribunals," as are professional sport leagues and teams, as described in chapter 4. They are autonomous and self-governing associations and have the power to make rules, regulations, and policies that affect people engaged in their activities.

One of the key obligations of a sport organization is to ensure a safe sport environment—for both participants and spectators. The main tool that a sport organization uses to meet this mandate is through the use of rules, regulations, and policies. Codes of conduct and associated sanctioning provisions are key to an organization's control and reflect an organization's philosophy and commitment to provide a safe environment. It is interesting that after being criticized for its slow response under its own regulations in the McSorley/Brashear incident, the NHL moved much more swiftly after the Bertuzzi/Moore attack—immediately suspending Bertuzzi pending a hearing, and shortly thereafter, convening a disciplinary hearing that imposed a heavy fine and a further suspension of 20 games.

Detailed safety rules have been incorporated into a number of sports such as football and hockey, or have been implemented at different age or skill levels within a particular sport, such as rugby and boxing. Many sport organizations have adopted "zero-tolerance" codes of conduct for players and parents, and others have required all participants, including parents, to sign "fair play contracts." These measures have typically come as a reaction to specific safety and conduct problems. And although well intentioned, at times these internal rules and regulations can be inconsistent in their application or can lead to unintended results. An example of this is seen in the sport of minor hockey in Canada, where some leagues will impose a suspension on a coach who removes a team from play (thus inconveniencing those in charge of competition schedules), even though there are instances where a responsible coach has felt a compelling need, for safety reasons, to remove a team from a particularly violent, mismatched, or poorly refereed game.

On the Canadian national scene, some attention has been given to advancing a more comprehensive approach to policy as it affects the incidence of violence in sport, through the publication of a discussion paper by the Canadian Centre for Ethics in Sport (CCES) in 1999 entitled *Building a New Brand of Sport—What About Violence.* Although there may not be consensus on the points advanced in the paper, it has represented a starting point for discussion by the Canadian sport community at large around organizational philosophy and values. In 2001, all 14 provincial, territorial, and federal sport ministers reached a unique consensus embracing the view that "Canadians share a vision that ethics and ethical behaviour are integral to Canadian sport." Termed the "London Declaration" because it was endorsed at the 2001 Canada Games in London, Ontario, the declaration illustrates the ministers' commitment to the importance of ethics in sport and reflects their expectation that sport can help to bring about significant changes in attitudes, values, and behaviours in society. Following the declaration, the ministers directed their officials to prepare a comprehensive Canadian strategy on ethical conduct in sport, which over time has come to be known as the *True Sport Strategy* (Sport Canada, 2002). This strategy is gaining traction in the Canadian sport community and has raised awareness of issues such as bullying, violence, harassment, and parental conduct in sport.

Notwithstanding the initial success of the true sport movement in promoting fair play in sport, the NHL remains alone as a professional league that publicly professes it has no intention to curb fighting, and hence violence, in the game. Other jurisdictions, meanwhile, have taken legislative approaches to the issue of violence in sport. For example, a number of American jurisdictions at the state level have taken specific steps through legislation to punish the player, coach, or spectator who assaults a sport official (Cross, 1998).

Criminal Law

Some violent acts occurring within sport competitions do, at times, attract criminal charges. The most usual criminal charges are those of assault causing bodily harm, or the more serious form of assault, assault with a weapon. Other criminal charges are also possible, including criminal negligence and criminal recklessness.

A criminal charge has very serious ramifications, which include the possibility of incarceration, social stigma, limitations on cross-border travel, and possible restrictions on future career opportunities, especially in those professions or careers that require a clean police record. A criminal conviction is usually a reflection of a serious level of violence that is perceived to be against the public interest and thus against public policy. A sport organization's internal rules and regulations may not supersede the laws of the land, and where it is perceived that a sport organization is ignoring a situation or not responding sufficiently quickly, or if certain conduct is seen to be particularly serious, the Crown may intervene. In general, criminal courts in Canada are slightly more inclined to intervene than their counterparts in the United States, and generally in both countries, there is less hesitation to intervene in the disciplinary affairs of non-professional sport organizations than in professional sport leagues and teams.

Assault

The two most common criminal charges in a sport context are assault causing bodily harm and assault with a weapon. Section 265 of the Canadian *Criminal Code* defines assault:

> s. 265(1) A person commits an assault when
> (a) without the consent of another person, he applies force intentionally to that person, directly or indirectly;
> (b) he attempts or threatens, by an act or a gesture, to apply force to another person, if he has, or causes that other person to believe on reasonable grounds that he has, present ability to effect his purpose; or
> (c) while openly wearing or carrying a weapon or an imitation thereof, he accosts or impedes another person or begs.

Section 267 of the *Criminal Code* defines assault with a weapon causing bodily harm:

> s. 267 Everyone who, in committing an assault,
> (a) carries, uses or threatens to use a weapon or an imitation thereof, or
> (b) causes bodily harm to the complainant,
> is guilty of an indictable offence and liable to imprisonment for a term not exceeding ten years or an offence punishable on summary conviction and liable to imprisonment for a term not exceeding eighteen months.

The two key elements in proving an assault charge are *intention* to inflict the force and *lack of consent* to the force. These elements must be proved by the state (which in Canada, is also referred to as the "Crown") and must be established to the criminal standard of proof, which is one of "beyond a reasonable doubt." These two elements can be difficult to prove as they both relate to mental conditions and are thus not capable of being proved directly. One must, therefore, look to the surrounding factual circumstances to draw inferences for mental elements, which is why most criminal cases turn on the particular facts of a given situation.

Intention

In *R. v. McSorley*, Marty McSorley struck Donald Brashear in the head from behind with his hockey stick. McSorley maintained that he had meant to hit Brashear on the shoulder but had missed. The judge hearing the case set out the test for intent at paragraph 76:

> I must first determine if the blow to the head was deliberate. If not, was it an unacceptable risk of what was intended? If so, was McSorley aware of the risk?

If the blow to the head was intentional then, all things being equal (that is, if Brashear did not consent to the act and such an act was not permitted within the written or unwritten rules of the game), the violent act was an assault. An act is considered intentional if it "achieves a desired purpose or involves a consequence that is substantially certain" (Barnes, 1996: 270). If, however, the act was not deliberate, but was so extreme as to be inherently dangerous, then it is seen to have gone beyond what one could reasonably consent to. If this had been the case in *McSorley*, any consent, implied or otherwise, would be negated and McSorley could have been found *criminally negligent*. Finally, if McSorley was aware of the probable consequences of his act but went ahead anyway, indifferent to what were the reasonably foreseeable consequences, then his conduct could be classified as *criminally reckless*. These three types of conduct represent varying degrees of intent, as shown in table 3.2 below.

Consent

Most of the Canadian criminal cases involving violent incidents in sport ultimately turn on the issue of consent—that is, did the injured person consent to the level of violence that ultimately led to his injuries? Certain sports are often characterized by some degree of violence and the simple act of participating implies consent to a degree of violent conduct. However, in determining whether the conduct exceeds the scope of an acceptable level of implied consent, it is often necessary to look to external factors.

The court in *R v. Cey* set out a number of objective criteria that can be used to examine the issue of consent. The list includes: the setting of the game; whether the game is part of league play and the nature of such a league; the age of the players; conditions under which the game is played; the extent of force employed; and finally,

TABLE 3.2   Degrees of Intent

Assault	Person had clear foresight of the consequences
Recklessness	Person acted without regard to the probable consequences or knowingly proceeded in the face of reasonably foreseeable consequences (there existed an intent to act but not with regard to the consequences)
Negligence	Person failed to use care to avoid a reasonably foreseeable risk of harm (intent not relevant)

the degree of risk and probability of serious harm occurring. These criteria were used to determine the likelihood of injury and the severity of potential injury.

The reasoning in *Cey* was applied in the subsequent cases of *R v. Leclerc* and *R v. Ciccarelli*. In *R v. Leclerc* the court stated at paragraph 25:

> The weight of judicial authority appears to be that a player, by participating in a sport such as hockey, impliedly consents to some bodily contact necessarily incidental to the game, but not to overtly violent acts, all of which should be determined according to objective criteria.

Conduct that reflects a deliberate purpose to inflict injury will generally be held to be outside the immunity of the scope of implied consent in the sports arena. The ultimate question of implied consent, as in *R v. Cey* at paragraph 35, is "whether the crosschecking or push of the complainant across the neck ... in close proximity to the boards *was so inherently dangerous as to be excluded from the implied consent*" [emphasis added]. In *Ciccarelli*, applying the standard determined in *Cey*, the court set out the test of consent as follows at paragraph 12:

> [There is] such a high risk of injury and distinct probability of harm as to be beyond what, in fact, the players commonly consent to, or what, in law they are capable of consenting to.

Subsequent court decisions have gone on to apply the perspectives of *Cey* and *Ciccarelli* and have provided further guidelines for determining whether there exists implied consent in a given situation, including

- conditions under which the game is played (professional or recreational game, is the game fast, skilled, competitive?);
- nature of act (high-sticking, striking head);
- extent of force used;
- state of mind (was the act retaliatory or intimidating?);
- the degree of risk of injury and the probabilities of serious harm;
- whether the rules of the game contemplate contact (such as rules to permit body-checking or tackling);
- whether the action was an instinctive reflex reaction;
- whether the action was closely related to play (did it occur after the whistle?); and
- whether the action fell within the customary norms and rules of the game.

Courts now recognize that even where a particular level of violence is expected in a sport discipline or event, and may even have been consented to, conduct may be so inherently dangerous as to preclude such consent.

Defences to a Charge of Assault

If one must prove both intent and a lack of consent to sustain a charge of assault, then defences to such a charge include a lack of intent to inflict the harm or consent to the harmful conduct complained of. There are also a number of other defences one can rely on. For example, sections 34 to 37 of the *Criminal Code* allow a person to defend himself or herself from an attack, provided the force used defending oneself is no more than reasonably necessary under the circumstances. *Self-defence* is thus a full defence to a charge of assault.

Where an act can be characterized as an *instinctive reaction* or an *involuntary reflex*, it lacks the intent needed to prove an assault, and thus can also act as a full defence to a charge of assault. Although not invoked often, this defence was successfully argued in the 1971 case of *R v. Green*, where the court accepted Green's argument that the swing he took with his stick at Wayne Maki's head came as a result of an instinctive reaction to an earlier punch to his head made by Maki.

The excuse of *provocation*, wherein a defendant's actions are characterized as retaliation for some earlier wrongdoing, is not an accepted defence in most jurisdictions, including Canada.

Civil Law

An increasing number of violent acts occurring during competitive sport events, including professional sport events, are being addressed using tort law. For example, notwithstanding the criminal charges laid against Todd Bertuzzi and the suspension and fine imposed by the NHL for the assault by Bertuzzi, Steve Moore nonetheless filed a civil lawsuit against Bertuzzi seeking damages for the injuries he sustained. Moore also named Mark Crawford, coach of the Canucks at the time, the Vancouver Canucks Hockey Club, and the Canucks' parent company, Orca Bay, as co-defendants in the lawsuit (CBC, 2006).

Through the use of such lawsuits, the plaintiff is typically seeking compensation for injuries sustained as a result of the defendant's conduct. The legal framework for such recovery rests on establishing that the defendant owed a duty to the plaintiff, that duty was breached, and serious injuries resulted such that the victim is entitled to be compensated financially for the damages. This area of law, whereby a person seeks compensation for personal injury, is known as tort law. Broadly speaking, three categories of tort law are addressed in the context of sport-based injuries: unintentional torts (negligence), intentional torts (civil, as opposed to criminal assault), and recklessness.

Unintentional Tort: Negligence

Negligence refers to a person's conduct. Once a duty of care is established between parties, the court must determine whether the appropriate standard of care has been met in the circumstances, and if such a standard was not met, did that failure cause or contribute to serious injury? The court in the appeal decision of *Unruh v. Webber* adopted the following standard of care (at paragraph 31) in the context of a junior hockey game:

> The standard of care test is—what would a reasonable competitor, in his place, do or not do. The words "in his place" imply the need to consider the speed, the amount of body contact and the stresses in the sport, as well as the risks the competitor might reasonably be expected to take during the game, acting within the spirit of the game.

It should be noted that the test is an "objective" test established after the fact. It is not what the player thinks but what a reasonable person in similar circumstances would think.

Liability refers to taking responsibility for the injury or damages caused by the negligent act of the defendant. Liability can be direct or indirect. That is, a party may be held responsible for his or her own negligent actions—this is known as direct liability. Alternatively, a party or parties may be held responsible for the conduct of others. For example, parents can be held responsible for the negligent conduct of their children, and sport organizations can be held responsible for the negligent conduct of their employees or volunteers, including coaches and officials. This is referred to as indirect, or vicarious, liability. The concepts of negligence and liability are discussed more fully in chapter 2 of this book. Readers are advised to review that chapter in order to understand the legal basis of the tort of negligence.

The issue of consent is important in determining civil liability, just as it is in determining a criminal assault. It is possible for an injured player to have consented to the violent act that led to his injury. This is the defence of *volenti non fit injuria* (harm does not come to one who consents). As in the case of criminal assault, the question is this: What was consented to under the circumstances? In the case of *Dunn v. University of Ottawa*, the court accepted that by participating in the intervarsity game of football, Dunn, a punt return specialist, had consented to a certain degree of violence, but that the consent covered only what might reasonably be expected under the circumstances of the intervarsity game and within the rules of university football.

In that decision, the court wrote at paragraph 36:

> Not every breach of the rules, by any stretch of the imagination, will result in a finding of negligence within the context of a game such as football. Such non-compliance is but one factor in any judicial determination. Only when there is a deliberate intention to cause injury or a reckless disregard for the consequences of one's actions in an uncontrolled and undisciplined manner will a finding of negligence result.

The court found that although a punt return specialist consents to being hit hard by a tackler, he does not consent to "being head-butted or speared in the face by an onrushing 225-pound linebacker while in that vulnerable position [that is, looking up to track the ball within the five-yard no-tackle zone]." The court found that the actions of the defendant in this case fell far below the standard that might reasonably have been expected of a university football player.

In this case the coach of the defendant's team, as well as the university, were also sued. The plaintiff alleged that the coach "failed to prevent his staff and players from embarking upon unreasonably dangerous activities during the course of a football game" and that the university, as the employer of the coach, was vicariously liable for the coach's negligent actions. The court examined the coach's responses to past incidents of violent activity and in this instance found that the coach had taken reasonable steps to deal with unruly actions and "trash-talking" by players. The court did point out (at paragraph 13) that "without any doubt, at the university intercollegiate level, it is the responsibility of the coach to encourage and teach fair play and good sportsmanship. The game is played to win, but it is not played to win at all costs." From this case it can be seen that there might well be circumstances under which a coach could be held responsible for the actions of an aggressive or violent player.

Those in positions of authority within the sport organization need to be concerned about their own actions, but also about the conduct of those for whom they have some responsibility. In particular, sport managers need to be concerned with the conduct of program participants, coaches, and officials. The level of violence seen in many competitions has as much to do with coaching technique and attitude and officiating behaviour as it has to do with the actions of a handful of players. Ultimately, the sport organization is responsible for the "tone" set by those controlling the competition.

It is important to note that when courts examine the issue of consent (whether in the criminal or civil context), they have considered whether a rule of play has been breached, and the nature and origin of that rule. The courts recognize that some rules have been implemented as a direct response to safety concerns, arising usually out of a historical analysis of injury trends. For example, between 1966 and 1987 in the game of hockey in Canada, there were 117 cervical spine and spinal cord injuries. Twenty-six of these injuries resulted from hits from behind near the boards.[1] In response to these statistics, the Canadian Amateur Hockey Association (as it was then named) introduced the "no checking from behind rule" in 1984. It is notable that the courts in the *Cey* and *Leclerc* cases both recognized this rule and differentiated it from other rules of the game as a "safety rule."

A similar distinction has been made by the courts involving other sports. For example, in the case of *Dunn* described above, the court recognized the "five-yard non-encroachment rule" on punt returns as a safety rule. In the case of *Hamstra v. BC Rugby Union*, which involved the collapse of a "scrum" in a game being played by junior rugby players, the court noted that other jurisdictions had modified the scrum rules for junior players for safety reasons. The courts clearly take a different view of those rules established for safety purposes, and the breaches of such rules, than they do of other general rules of the game. Similar discussions about rules and regulations directed toward safety have occurred in the sport of squash (eye guards), in equestrian sport (helmets), and in soccer ("heading" the ball).

Although the courts are prepared to give substantial deference to the internal rules and standards governing a particular sport or event, they are not prepared to blindly accept any standard. In *Dyck v. Manitoba Snowmobile Association*, the court stated that, even where an association might follow its usual procedures and these procedures are common practice within the sport, if the procedures are unreasonable, given the circumstances, the court will not hesitate in finding the resulting conduct negligent. Similarly, in the *Hamstra* case, the court took note of rule modifications made in other Commonwealth jurisdictions for safety reasons, but that were not implemented in the province of British Columbia or elsewhere in Canada. The court warned the British Columbia Rugby Union that, now having knowledge of the institution of rule modifications in other jurisdictions, if a similar rugby accident were to occur in British Columbia in the absence of such modification, the court would view the matter much differently, suggesting that a court could find the organization negligent.

---

1   The court in the civil case of *Unruh v. Webber* quoted hockey-related injury statistics kept by the Canadian Sports Spine and Head Injury Research Injury Centre at the University of Toronto. Between 1975 and 1987, that institution documented 107 spinal injuries, 99 percent of which occurred in organized games; 87 percent were injuries to the neck, and 81 percent came about as a result of the injured player hitting the boards.

Intentional Tort: Civil Assault

Just as the Crown may charge a person with a criminal assault, an injured person may bring an action against another person for *civil assault*. As in the case of criminal assault, a civil assault involves a deliberate use, or threat of use, of force against another person. A kick, a punch, or a stick swung at another person on purpose may be an assault. It doesn't matter that the individual did not mean to cause the exact damages that ensued, or even that the intended target was actually another person—it is the intent to use force and the final contact that matter.

An assault is distinguished from negligence by the notion of *intention*, whereby an assault is in the category of intentional torts along with defamation and invasion of privacy, while negligence is in the category of unintentional torts. In an assault (whether criminal or civil), the perpetrator must be shown to have *intended* the violent act. The high speed and legitimate physical contact that characterizes many sports in which violent actions occur make it difficult in many cases to prove the element of intent.

The same defences that apply in a criminal case of assault would also apply in a civil case of assault—consent, self-defence, and involuntary reflex.

Recklessness

Somewhere in between the unintentional act of negligence and the intentional act of an assault is the notion of *reckless* behaviour. A person is reckless where he or she knew, or ought to have known, that the conduct would likely cause serious injury to another, but the person was nonetheless indifferent to that risk and carried out that conduct anyway. The difference between reckless conduct and negligence is the degree of foreseability of harm, while recklessness differs from an intentional wrongdoing such as assault by way of the issue of intent.

As noted by Citron and Abelman (2003: 206):

> A reckless individual has the intent to act, but does not intend to cause the harm which results from the act. In the context of recklessness, it is sufficient that the individual realize, or from the facts that he knows, should realize that there is a strong possibility that harm may result (as opposed to substantial certainty, without which there can be no intention).

In the United States, recklessness appears to be the appropriate minimum standard of liability in sport injury litigation cases. In Canada, the courts tend to use a negligence framework for analyzing liability but may require a level of recklessness (thus needing a degree of knowledge—whether actual or implied), or even the establishment of actual intent, in order for the plaintiff to recover damages (Citron and Abelman, 2003: 208). For example, in *Dunn v. University of Ottawa*, the court stated (at paragraph 26): "[O]nly when there is a deliberate intention to cause injury or a reckless disregard for the consequences of one's actions in an uncontrolled and undisciplined manner will a finding of negligence result."

In conclusion, violent activity as perceived from a civil perspective occurs along a continuum (see figure 3.1). At one end is the tort of negligence where there was no intention to cause harm (although harm may have been the result), while at the other end is civil assault, where there was intention to harm. Recklessness lies somewhere in between the two ends of the continuum.

FIGURE 3.1   Continuum of Torts

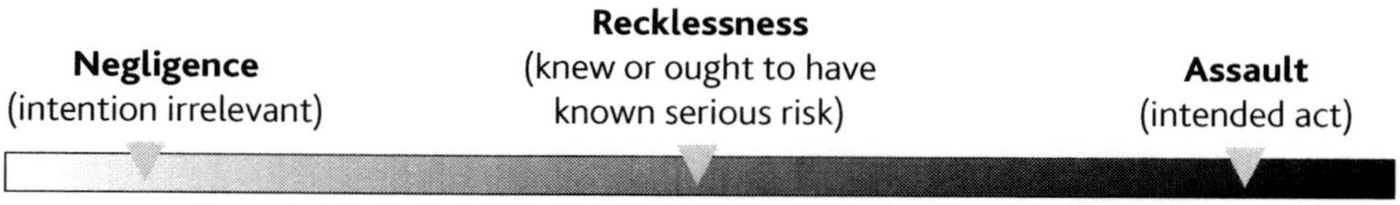

Negligence
(intention irrelevant)

Recklessness
(knew or ought to have
known serious risk)

Assault
(intended act)

REFERENCES

Barnes, J., *Sports and the Law in Canada*, 3rd ed. (Markham, ON: Butterworths, 1996).

CBC, 2006 report of Bertuzzi lawsuit: http://www.cbc.ca/olympics/sports/ icehockey/stories/index.shtml?/story/olympics/national/2006/02/15/Sports/ bertuzzi060215.html.

Citron, Jeffrey A. and Mark Abelman, "Civil Liability in the Arena of Professional Sports" (2003), 36(2) *UBC Law Review* 193-230.

Criminal Code, RSC 1985, c. C-46.

Cross, T., "Assaults of Sports Officials" (1998), 8(2) *Marquette Sports Law Journal* 429-54.

Dunn v. University of Ottawa, [1995] OJ no. 2856 (QL) (Ct. J. (Gen Div.)).

Dyck v. Manitoba Snowmobile Association, [1985] 1 SCR 589.

Hamstra v. BC Rugby Union (1989), 1 CCLT (2d) 78 (BCSC).

R v. Cey (1989), 48 CCC (3d) 480, 75 Sask. R 53, [1989] 5 WWR 169 (CA).

R v. Ciccarrelli (1989), 54 CCC (3d) 121 (Ont. Dist. Ct.).

R v. Green, [1971] 1 OR 591, (1971), 16 DLR (3d) 137 (Prov. Ct.).

R v. Leclerc (1991), 7 CR (4th) 282, 4 OR (3d) 788, 67 CCC (3d) 563, 50 OAC 232 (CA).

R v. McSorley, [2000] BCJ no. 264 (QL) (BC Prov. Ct.).

Sport Canada, *The Canadian Strategy on Ethical Conduct in Sport* (Ottawa: Department of Canadian Heritage, 2002).

Unruh v. Webber (1994), 88 BCLR (2d) 353, 112 DLR (4th) 83 (CA).

Administrative Law: Fairness in Decision Making

Introduction

The vast majority of Canadian sport organizations are "private tribunals"—that is, they are autonomous, self-governing, private organizations that have the power to write rules, make decisions, and take actions that affect their members, participants, and constituents. A body of law called "administrative law" prescribes the rules by which tribunals must operate in Canadian society and allows for legal remedies when these rules are not followed and someone is disadvantaged or harmed as a result. This chapter examines the sport organization's status as an administrative or private tribunal and its corresponding "duty to be fair" in its decisions and actions as they relate to members.

Historically, the courts have been reluctant to interfere in the affairs of private tribunals. The relationship among the members of an association was viewed as personal, particularly where membership was voluntary. Within such associations, membership rights had to somehow be bound to property rights in order for the courts to intervene. Lord Denning's decision in *Lee v. Showmen's Guild of Great Britain* precipitated a radical departure from this hands-off approach. The Court of Appeal in the *Lee* case unanimously held that it had the jurisdiction to review any decision of an association that involved a question of law, including any question of interpretation of the association's constitution.

In Canada, *Lee* is viewed as a starting point when considering the legal context for decision making within sport organizations. Athletes and others seeking legal remedies for the adverse decisions of their sport governing bodies have, almost without exception, relied on the principles set out in *Lee*. These principles are

- that an association's governing documents represent a *contract* among the association's members, enabling the association and its members to clarify their rights, privileges, and obligations in order to better regulate the association's affairs; and

- that the rules of *natural justice* apply to the internal decisions of private tribunals. Lord Denning in *Lee* wrote at page 342: "Although the jurisdiction of a domestic tribunal is founded on a contract, express or implied, never-theless the parties are not free to make any contract they like. There are important limitations imposed by public policy. The tribunal must for instance observe the principles of natural justice."

The court in *Lee* also observed that different types of associations had different thresholds for judicial intervention. *Lee* distinguished between memberships that could be linked to an individual's livelihood (such as a trade union or professional association) and those memberships that were voluntary and social in nature. This notion that the threshold of fairness is flexible has been important in sport, because sport occurs along a broad continuum, from the local club that is primarily recre-ational and social in nature to a national team of elite athletes who compete on the global stage.

These principles have been amplified further through several leading Canadian cases dealing with administrative tribunals. *Nicholson v. Haldimand Norfolk (Region-al) Police Commissioners* was a case brought by a police constable who was dismissed from his appointment without notice, without the benefit of a hearing, and with-out the opportunity for an appellate review. The rules in place at the time conferred on the commissioners the authority to "dispense with the services of any constable within eighteen months of his appointment to the force." Nicholson was released within the 18-month period, but argued that the commissioners had a duty to no-tify him of the reasons for his release and to give him an opportunity to respond. The Supreme Court of Canada ruled that although the appellant could not claim the procedural protections afforded to a constable with more than 18 months ser-vice, he should not be denied any protection, but rather should be treated fairly as opposed to arbitrarily.

Lakeside Colony of Hutterian Brethren v. Hofer asked the Supreme Court of Canada to rule whether the expulsion of members from a private association (in this case, a religious community) had been carried out according to the applicable rules and the principles of natural justice. Although not a sport case, like *Lee* and *Nicholson*, this case offers up guidance on a situation that is very typical in the sport world. As with *Nicholson*, this case confirmed that there exists a general duty of fairness within private tribunals. In this particular dispute within the Hutterite colony, the court noted that it was reluctant to become involved in a dispute over membership within a private, voluntary association, but acknowledged that the courts *will* exercise jurisdiction where property rights or civil rights turn on the question of membership. Of particular importance for sport organizations are these words from page 195 of the decision:

> The content of the principles of natural justice is flexible and depends on the circumstances in which the question arises. However, the most basic requirements are that of notice, opportunity to make representations and an unbiased tribunal.

This chapter examines more fully these basic fairness requirements, and how they play out within sport organizations and in sport disputes.

Organization–Member Contract

As private tribunals, sport organizations are self-governing and derive their authority from their constitution, bylaws, policies, procedures, and rules. Taken together, these are the governing documents of the organization and form a contract between the organization and its members. This contract provides the sport organization with the legal authority to establish the rights, privileges, and obligations of membership. As in any contract, the parties to the contract are expected to adhere to its terms and provisions, and failure to do so may result in a breach of the contract. In serious matters, such a breach of contract may give rise to disputes for which there may be legal remedies.

When an individual joins a sport organization, he or she accepts the inherent authority of the sport organization and the terms of the contract expressed in the organization's governing documents. In most cases, athletes, coaches, and officials are members of their respective sport organization and thus are parties to a contractual relationship with the sport organization. This contract works to the benefit of both parties by establishing and clarifying their respective rights and obligations. Occasionally, however, the contract may work to the detriment of the parties if the policies that make up the contract are poorly designed, vague, contradictory, or ill suited to the organization's needs, resources, or realities.

A sport organization's governing documents are critical as they provide the foundation of the organization's structure and authority and contain all the rules by which the organization and its members govern themselves. Typically, sport organizations pay too little attention to their governing documents and realize their importance only when the deficiencies in these documents land them squarely in the middle of a dispute with a member, such as an athlete. For many sport organizations, it is a sobering lesson to learn that policy is what's written on the paper and not what's in the mind of the drafters of the policy, or in the organization's collective memory.

If an organization and its members agree that they do not like the terms of their contractual relationship, then they can take steps to change the governing documents using conventional policy-making channels. If a group of members, such as athletes, takes the view that they do not like the terms of their contractual relationship with the sport organization, then they can take steps to influence the leaders and decision makers of the organization using conventional democratic procedures.

A group of members, or one member alone, cannot unilaterally rewrite the terms of the contract with the sport organization, and a court cannot do this either. As noted in the *Lakeside Colony* case, courts are very reluctant to interfere with the internal matters of private tribunals, and will not rewrite the governing documents and policies of private organizations. However, an individual such as an athlete or coach may apply to the court and the court may intervene if these policies are ignored, not followed, improperly interpreted, or wrongly applied, and such deficiencies have an adverse effect on an individual's property or civil rights. An individual may also pursue other avenues to resolve his or her dispute, such as those discussed in chapter 10.

In addition to the contractual relationship described above, there may also be explicit contracts between an organization and its members. All high-performance athletes who are members of national teams in Canada enter into binding contracts with their national sport organizations. The early rationale for these contracts was to set out the requirements and expectations of athletes who received financial assistance through the government of Canada's Athlete Assistance Program. Today, these contracts typically include commercial and dispute resolution provisions in addition to specifying the respective responsibilities and entitlements of the athlete and the national sport organization (Findlay and Ward, 2006). The rights and obligations outlined in an athlete's contract do not replace the rights and obligations that exist in the contractual relationship between the athlete and the sport organization, but rather incorporate, confirm, and clarify them.

The case of *Kelly v. Canadian Amateur Speed Skating Association* illustrates perfectly the obligations imposed by the organization–member contract. Kelly was a speed skater and a member of the Canadian Amateur Speed Skating Association (CASSA). Like many high-performance athletes, Kelly had entered into an athlete agreement with CASSA. This agreement formed a part of CASSA's governing documents, and stated that CASSA must publish selection criteria for national teams at least three months before the selection date. The agreement further stated that the selection process must conform to the generally accepted principles of natural justice. The original criteria provided for four athletes to be chosen at a trial event. One week before this trial, which was occurring outdoors in uncertain weather conditions, CASSA changed the criteria to specify that two skaters would be chosen at the trial and two more would be chosen at a later event occurring indoors in controlled conditions. All technical personnel, coaches, and athletes were in favour of this change but Kelly was not, because his training plan had been designed for him to make the team by finishing third or fourth, thus being in a position to "peak" at the international competition some weeks later. The court concluded that ordinary justice required the parties to fulfill their contractual obligations, and likened the change in criteria to "changing the rules of the game while the game is underway."

Procedural Fairness

The second fundamental legal principle highlighted by the *Lee* case is that private tribunals are subject to the rules of natural justice. Prior to *Lee*, a distinction was made between judicial or quasi-judicial decisions, and administrative decisions. Judicial and quasi-judicial decisions were subject to the rules of natural justice, while administrative decisions were not (where natural justice is taken to mean that decision makers should not only act in good faith and without bias, but should also grant a hearing to persons who stand to be adversely affected by a decision). Since *Lee* the law has evolved to impart a "duty of fairness" on those making administrative decisions, and this duty has replaced the rules of natural justice. As noted by Blake (1992: 13): "The distinction is now meaningless: every tribunal making decisions that could adversely affect individual rights or interests must proceed fairly." The sport organization that fails to proceed fairly will ultimately find itself in the middle of a nasty dispute that may end in either an arbitration hearing or a courtroom.

All of us generally have a good sense of what is fair and what is unfair. At law, the duty to act fairly, or *procedural fairness*, has a specific meaning. Being fair means following a minimum of two basic rules:

- the decision maker has a duty to give persons affected by the decision a reasonable opportunity to present their case (commonly referred to as the *right to a hearing*); and

- the decision maker has a duty to listen fairly to both sides and to reach a decision untainted by bias (commonly referred to as the *rule against bias*).

As well, it is presumed that the decision maker has the authority to make the decision in the first place, where this authority is identified in the organization's contractual relationship with its members, or its governing documents. This issue of authority can sometimes be confusing because many sport events occur under the auspices of more than one governing or organizing body, and every sport organization exists within a complex hierarchical structure of superior and subordinate organizations, with the result that any single issue may be subject to different layers of jurisdiction.

Right to a Hearing

It is a long-established rule of law that before an adverse decision can be made against a person, that person has a right to know the case against him or her and to be given a reasonable opportunity to respond on his or her own behalf. There are two obvious purposes for this rule: first, the person adversely affected by the decision has an opportunity to defend his or her interests or assert a claim and, second, by allowing the person to have input, the decision maker is better able to make a rational and informed decision.

Although all organizations have a duty to be fair and to follow these rules, the procedural safeguards that are required to satisfy the right to a hearing will vary with the circumstances. Such safeguards may be described as falling along a continuum from simple and relaxed at one end to complex and formal at the other (see figure 4.1). For example, in some circumstances, an opportunity to make written submissions may be appropriate, whereas fairness in other circumstances may require that the person be given the opportunity to make oral representations.

FIGURE 4.1 The Spectrum of Fairness as It Relates to a Hearing

◄──────Informal, simple──────────			──────Formal, complex──────►		
Oral interview and response	Review of written documents	Review of written submissions, response, and rebuttal	Documentary review supplemented by telephone conference call	In-person oral hearing	In-person hearing with court-like procedures (evidence from witnesses, cross-examination, legal arguments, recorded transcript)

Even within these two types of hearings (written submissions and oral presentations), there are ranges of formality and complexity. For example, written submissions can be as simple as a letter or series of letters stating one's position or as complex as a written application supported by documentary evidence and expert reports. Similarly, oral representations can be as simple as an interview or group discussion with the decision maker or as complex as a court-like proceeding with the examination and cross-examination of witnesses. A hearing can also be a combination of written submissions and oral presentations wherein the decision maker reviews documents and written arguments and then convenes a conference of the parties to ask questions and clarify any uncertain matters.

The case of *Fernandes v. Sport North Federation* reminds us of the range of circumstances that exist in the sport milieu and of the corresponding need for flexibility. This case involved a dispute about the eligibility of figure skaters who had qualified for the territorial team competing at the 1996 Arctic Winter Games. There was some concern about their residency, and thus their eligibility to compete, and the Sport North Federation resorted to its usual practice of asking the technical committee of the host organization for a ruling. The committee ruled they were Northwest Territories (NWT) residents and thus eligible. The governing body for figure skating in the NWT became concerned because if the skaters were later found to be ineligible, it could jeopardize the entire team's results. This body asked Sport North Federation to review the skaters' eligibility, which they did using ad hoc procedures, ultimately determining that the skaters were not eligible. The skaters went to court, arguing that the initial decision of the technical committee should stand, because it was the usual practice of the federation to rely on this committee for rulings. The court found that the process used by Sport North Federation, while ad hoc and improvisational, was not inherently unfair in the circumstances. The basic requirements of fairness had been met because the skaters were given notice and were allowed to make representations before unbiased decision makers. As well, Sport North Federation had not acted arbitrarily, in bad faith, or otherwise outside its jurisdiction. Thus, an organization that finds itself without a system for an appeal can put in place an ad hoc process provided it respects the basic principles of procedural fairness that are owed in the circumstances.

The rule of the right to a hearing has one additional element. In order for a person potentially affected by a decision to make a full and meaningful response, that person must know the details of the case to be met. Thus, in addition to an affected person having the right to be heard, he or she must also be afforded the right to be informed. Just as procedural fairness occurs along a continuum, what is required by the right to be informed will vary with the circumstances. In some cases it is sufficient to provide the affected person with a précis or summary of the details of the case, and in other cases the person may have a right to review original documents and cross-examine witnesses. Again, fairness will dictate the nature and extent of the disclosure, but to the greatest extent possible, disclosure should be as complete as possible, because transparency is always a good policy.

In any given case, the information on which a decision will be based may come from many sources. Some sources will produce more reliable information than others. It is critical that the parties affected by a decision have an opportunity to confirm, correct, or contradict any information contrary to their interests. This can happen only if the information is disclosed to them.

Sport organizations often promise confidentiality to individuals providing information about another individual, particularly if such information is negative in nature. Similarly, those providing information are often reluctant to do so unless it can be done anonymously. It is a very rare case where information should be withheld from an affected party. The details and completeness of the disclosure will depend on the complexity and seriousness of the case. At times, a summary of factual information may be sufficient, but where credibility is an issue, the identity of the source of the information and the context in which the information was given are typically necessary in order to allow the affected party to respond fully and completely.

A recent Canadian case, *Paterson v. Skate Canada*, illustrates nicely these principles of notice, hearing, and disclosure. The Patersons were a married couple who both earned their livelihood as figure skating instructors. Parents of some of their skaters made complaints about the Patersons, alleging dishonesty, harassment, and abuse of power. Skate Canada set in motion their complaint procedures, and two individuals carried out an investigation that involved interviewing the parents, the Patersons, and witnesses. The investigators also disclosed to the Patersons the written complaints. The procedure would continue with the investigators' report being provided to a discipline committee, who would review it, and nothing more, and make a decision. In essence, Skate Canada's policy called for the investigation to also serve as the hearing, and this is where problems arose.

The Patersons found themselves in a situation of being accused of serious misconduct but without any opportunity to challenge their accusers or to speak directly to the decision makers. They sought the intervention of the court. The court agreed that procedural fairness was not possible using a procedure that did not allow an accused to challenge the accusers, witnesses, or the investigation report directly. Nor could such unfairness be "cured" at the appeal stage, because Skate Canada's policies called for an appeal on the record only, meaning that no new information would be allowed and the appellants would not be able to scrutinize the existing information.

This case is informative because the complaint procedures of Skate Canada are very similar to those that exist in other Canadian sport bodies. The lesson from this experience is that a person facing disciplinary charges before a tribunal that is obliged to meet the standard of procedural fairness (as all sport organizations are obliged to do) is entitled to challenge the credibility of his or her accusers through cross-examination. The accused is also entitled, in such situations, to bring forward his or her own evidence to contradict the evidence of the accusers. If the original evidence comes forward through a written document, then a written response is sufficient. If the evidence comes orally, then the response needs to be done orally as well. If such a challenge poses a problem because complainants are not prepared to come forward for cross-examination, then there can be no complaint pursued and no disciplinary action.

Procedural Fairness as a Flexible Concept

There are a number of guidelines that can assist in determining what process and what extent of disclosure will meet the required threshold of the duty of fairness, given all the circumstances of the situation, and in light of the understanding that procedural fairness is a flexible concept. These guidelines are summarized below.

As a general rule, decisions relating to withdrawing rights or privileges *already conferred* require greater procedural safeguards than decisions relating to withholding rights or privileges *not yet granted*, where such rights or privileges are equivalent. In other words, decisions about awarding a benefit such as membership in a sport organization may be made using simple procedures. On the other hand, a decision to take away a benefit such as membership would require more complex procedures. In practical terms, this means that decisions about discipline often require more stringent procedural safeguards than decisions about eligibility for membership or team selection.

The guideline just described must be applied in conjunction with a second guideline, which is that procedural safeguards should be in direct proportion to the potential *consequences* of the decision—in other words, to what is at stake. Clearly, decisions that affect a person's livelihood demand very strict procedural safeguards. For the gifted amateur athlete, a great deal may also be at stake. A sport organization differs from many voluntary organizations in that membership is compulsory (not voluntary) for any individual contemplating athletic pursuits within that particular sport discipline. The failure to award membership, or once awarded, the loss of membership, precludes such pursuits entirely. Therefore, denying or revoking membership to an amateur athlete requires strict procedural safeguards.

Denial of competitive opportunities to athletes, particularly elite athletes, may also have the effect of denying other more significant opportunities, including future income, sponsorship, employment, and scholarship opportunities. Denial of these opportunities demands careful attention to procedural safeguards.

The choice of procedure depends on the extent to which a *decision is final and binding* on a person. Procedural safeguards are generally higher with respect to a final decision than they are with respect to an interim decision. Also, although expediency is not an excuse to override the principles of fairness, it may be a consideration in determining the nature of the process. Thus, issues arising during the course of a tournament or competition may be dealt with differently than those arising outside of competition, so long as the fundamental principles, or rules of fairness, are respected.

Where an appeal is not available, procedural safeguards must be more strictly observed because there is no opportunity for procedural errors to be corrected. For example, where a decision maker of last resort makes a procedural error during the course of the hearing, it may be possible to correct or cure the default as part of the decision-making process. But if the error is not corrected, then the only other recourse is litigation in the courts. If the decision being made is not absolutely final and there are opportunities for further appeal, it is not so critical that procedural errors be promptly corrected, because there will be subsequent opportunities to correct them.

The case of *McGarrigle v. Canadian Interuniversity Sport* is one where an initial error that might have easily been corrected was compounded further by the actions of other parties, landing this case ultimately in the courts. McGarrigle was a university basketball coach who was suspended by a Canadian Interuniversity Sport (CIS) discipline committee for "knowingly" playing an ineligible player. The CIS decision had been based substantially on a report from the athletic director at McGarrigle's university that McGarrigle was fully aware of the ineligible student's academic status. On appeal, all the parties agreed on certain facts: that McGarrigle had never seen a copy of the athletic director's report, that the athletic director had waived the notice period for a disciplinary hearing without McGarrigle's knowledge, and that pursuant to the university's privacy policies, McGarrigle was not authorized to access student transcripts. Nonetheless, the appeal was denied by an internal CIS appeal panel and McGarrigle sought judicial review.

The court established that the CIS had committed multiple and compounding errors. As McGarrigle's livelihood was at stake, the CIS had a high onus to "get it right," which it failed to do. The first error was not making the case against McGarrigle clear, as its policies required. McGarrigle was not informed of the specific charge under the rule, policy, or practice of the CIS operations manual that had been breached. Instead, the discipline committee relied upon the evidence of the athletic director, and did so without McGarrigle's knowledge or input, even though it was clear that the two would not necessarily have the same interests. A further error was that the discipline committee expanded the charge against McGarrigle— initially, the charge was breach of the eligibility rules, but the charge ultimately considered was ethical misconduct. A third error was that the appeal committee of the CIS, confronted with the parties' agreed statement of facts, which the court felt pointed to obvious errors, should have immediately granted the appeal so that the discipline charge could be heard again using fair procedures. A fourth error was that the appeal panel incorporated into its analysis knowledge that it possessed generally about the situation as well as inferences from incomplete information, instead of properly relying on information placed before it. Finally, the court found that the CIS had misinterpreted its own rules when it found against McGarrigle. The rules of the CIS make it the responsibility of an athletic director to ensure the eligibility of players. In reality, the athletic director, and not McGarrigle, should have been the subject of this discipline hearing.

This case urges those involved in tribunals to stay within their jurisdiction, inter- pret rules properly, and ensure that individuals in their own right have proper notice and opportunity to be heard. These are the minimum expectations of fairness, and these principles must be satisfied at all times even when the parties are all familiar with each other, when everyone knows everyone else's business, and when the out- come is certain. The Supreme Court of Canada in the *Lakeside Colony* case noted that voluntary associations are meant largely to govern themselves, and should do so flexibly. However, this does not mean that a tribunal can take shortcuts in its duty to be fair. "Natural justice requires procedural fairness no matter how obvious the decision to be made may be. Natural justice requires that notice be given of a meeting to consider the matter and that an opportunity be given to make representations concerning it. This may not change anything, but it is what the law requires" (at page 170).

Rule Against Bias

The second rule of procedural fairness relates to the impartiality, or bias, of those making decisions. There are two types of bias:

- The first type is *actual bias*, wherein a decision maker is predisposed to decide a matter in one particular way over any other. Such a decision maker is said to have a "closed mind" and is unwilling or unable to take into consideration any other perspective.

- The second type of bias is *apprehended bias*—that is, it may be possible to hold a reasonable belief, perception, or apprehension that the decision maker is or may be biased. This type of bias is much more common than the first type, and is also much more difficult to prove.

Clearly, where a decision maker has a direct material interest in the outcome of a decision or has publicly favoured one position over another, actual bias may be established and the decision maker may be disqualified. However, situations involving allegations or perceptions of bias are rarely so clear-cut or concrete. Bias arises from the state of mind of the decision maker, and as such there is rarely direct proof that it exists. It is necessary to draw inferences from surrounding factors in order to establish bias, and even so, the test is never definitive. While a previous or existing friendship, business relationship, or family relationship might be perceived as biasing a decision maker, it is important to note that it is not the relationship itself that creates the bias, or the apprehension of bias, but rather the extent to which the relationship influences or is perceived to influence the decision maker. As suggested, this is often difficult to prove.

For perceived bias to be found, the relationship must be direct, consequential, and influential. The test used by the courts in these cases is whether "a reasonable person, knowing the facts concerning the person [i.e., the decision maker] would suspect that the person would be influenced, albeit unintentionally, by improper considerations to favour one side in the matter to be decided" (Blake, 1992: 92). In other words, the test is an objective test: it is not what the person raising the allegation believes but rather what a reasonable and objective third party would believe, given all the circumstances.

Relationships and elements that may result in bias or a reasonable apprehension of bias can be grouped into a number of broad categories: relational bias, informational bias, attitudinal bias, institutional bias, and operational bias (Kligman, 1998). All categories have been alleged at various times in sport.

Personal relational bias includes personal relationships that might suggest favouritism such as friendship, kinship, or a coach–athlete relationship. It also includes personal relationships that might invoke animosity or prejudice such as personality conflicts, a history of strained relations, or involvement in a previous dispute. There are frequent examples from sport situations where this perceived bias comes into play because coaches who have a close relationship with an athlete are often also involved in making administrative decisions within the organization. Thus, it is not uncommon that a coach finds himself or herself in a position to decide in favour of the athlete with whom he or she has a relationship (see *Garrett, Depiero*, and *Kulesza*).

Non-personal relational bias typically relates to a commercial or business relationship between a decision maker and a party that might result in bias either in favour of or against a party. This might include an employee–employer relationship, competitors, or even one party's membership in a particular organization or interest group.

Informational bias involves situations in which the allegation of bias is made because a decision maker learns details about a person or a relevant issue as a result of some prior involvement, perhaps through a previous dispute proceeding. This typically arises where a decision maker has participated in an earlier hearing that involved the same person or similar issues. This type of bias is not uncommon in Canadian sport, because the community is relatively small and its volunteer participants often have overlapping roles and will typically have extensive knowledge of each other.

Attitudinal bias relates to whether a view or a position taken by a decision maker in the past, although not specifically directed to the matter under consideration, suggests a predisposition on the part of the decision maker toward one side or the other. This is a tricky issue. As noted by Kligman (1998: 31), "[a] person serving in an adjudicative role must have an open mind, but not necessarily a blank or void one." Clearly, decision-making bodies can make policies and general statements regarding various issues and how they intend to deal with them. But they cannot be so entrenched in a position as to have a "closed mind."

Institutional bias refers to the manner in which the organizational structure of an organization creates or builds in a bias or apprehension of bias. A classic case of such bias arises where a board of directors is authorized to make a certain decision and any appeal of such a decision is to be heard by the executive committee. In most sport organizations, the executive is a subgroup of the board and thus a portion of the board is in the position of hearing an appeal from its own decision. This is a clear example of actual bias. In this situation it can be reasonably expected that the original decision makers will be predisposed to uphold their original decision.

Another aspect of institutional bias is the degree of independence of the decision maker, or the degree to which those appointing the decision maker have a stake in the matter being heard. This occurs often in sport situations because directors of sport organizations are often parents of athletes. The case of *Kulesza v. Canadian Amateur Synchronized Swimming Association Inc. et al.* is an example of a case where an athlete alleged bias because an employee who was making selection decisions held her job as technical director at the pleasure of the board, which included among its membership the parent of one of the other athletes.

Operational bias arises from the manner in which a hearing is conducted. More specifically, operational bias may be alleged where the procedure adopted by the decision maker has created a situation of unfairness for one of the parties. Where a decision maker communicates with one of the parties in the absence of another, a reasonable apprehension of bias or preference to that party may arise. Any information discussed or exchanged with one party should always be discussed or exchanged with all parties, so that all parties have the opportunity to address the decision maker on the issues in dispute. While casual contact between a decision maker and a party may be logistically unavoidable, the nature of the contact should never relate to the subject matter of the hearing.

Operational bias may also be alleged where the decision maker becomes involved in the proceeding to such an extent as to appear to be an advocate for one side or another. Similarly, a decision maker who takes an overly adversarial position in the conduct of the hearing may give rise to a claim of this type of bias.

Having Proper Authority

As noted above, procedural fairness presumes that the decision maker is acting with appropriate and legal authority in the first place. This means not only that the proper persons or bodies are making decisions, and are doing so without bias, but also that the policies, procedures, and rules under which such decisions are made have been properly implemented.

Several notable Canadian sport cases have turned on this issue. In *Kane v. Canadian Ladies Golf Association*, then-amateur golfer Lori Kane challenged the decision of the Canadian Ladies Golf Association (CLGA) to add a subjective consideration into the selection criteria for the World Amateur Championship. Prior to the selection in question, the policy of the CLGA had been to select teams solely on the basis of golf scores in designated national and international tournaments over the previous two years. On this basis Kane had ranked among the top four golfers in the country in the five years leading up to the World Amateur Championships, including ranking second in the country in 1991 and 1992. However, early in 1992 the director of the teams committee altered the original selection criteria by adding a number of subjective elements, including *exceptional performances in provincial and national championships, international experience,* and *results from past performances.* These criteria resulted in Kane being selected as an alternative member, and not as a playing member, of the Canadian team. In court, Kane argued that the CLGA had failed to follow its own rules. The court agreed, finding no evidence that either the executive committee or the teams committee had approved the revised criteria, as the governing documents of the CLGA required.

Two other cases involved sport associations imposing discipline on athletes when they lacked the authority to do so. In *Omaha v. British Columbia Broomball Society*, three athletes were suspended from the society for roughhousing on a bus returning from a competition. However, the society had no code of conduct or policy relating to discipline and its bylaws were clear that members could be suspended only for non-payment of fees. In the case of *Lassen v. Yukon Weightlifting Association*, the sport body suspended Lassen from membership even though it lacked such authority in its governing documents. And even if the court was wrong in this determination, the association had breached at every turn its duty to be fair: Lassen was prohibited from attending both national and international competitions for which she had qualified, she had been suspended for reasons that were not factually supported, she had been given no notice of the decision to suspend her and no right to a hearing, and she was denied any avenue of appeal.

Administrative Appeals

This chapter so far has illustrated the legal responsibilities that a tribunal has, and what it needs to do to meet the duty of fairness in its decisions. What if it fails to do these things? At law, sport organizations have no legal obligation to offer individuals an appeal of their decisions. Nor do sport organizations have a legal duty to explain the reasons for their decisions. However, it makes good sense from a risk management and governance perspective to provide reasons and to make internal remedies available. And perhaps not coincidentally, an appeal mechanism is also a requirement attached to funding from provincial, territorial, and federal governments in Canada, and a prerequisite for disputing parties to use the services of the national arbitration program offered through the Sport Dispute Resolution Centre of Canada (SDRCC). Chapter 10 provides more information on dispute resolution systems and the SDRCC.

It is well established that members of associations cannot seek recourse to the courts until they have exhausted internal remedies. Internal appeals are a good idea because they are a disincentive to litigation and because they are private matters, whereas any appeal to a court is a public matter. All sport organizations are encouraged to implement a sound policy to hear appeals of decisions, and to ensure that these policies are flexible enough to accommodate the short timelines that are typically associated with disputes relating to eligibility and selection for sport competitions. This next section discusses common issues arising from appeals and shares some insights from appeal cases that have been heard in Canada.

Scope of Appeal

What decisions may be appealed? This is up to the sport organization to decide—provided, of course, that the matter under appeal lies within the powers that are vested in the organization through its bylaws and other governing documents. In other words, an organization cannot hear appeals on decisions over which it has no jurisdiction. It is important to distinguish between those matters for which a sport organization makes *recommendations* and those matters for which it makes *decisions*. It is important to note that a sport organization *recommends* athletes for carding and *recommends* athletes for selection to national teams competing in international multisport games. If a sport organization does not recommend an athlete for carding or selection, the athlete's recourse for appeal is to the sport organization. However, final *decisions* on carding are made by Sport Canada and final *decisions* for selection to international games are made by the Canadian Olympic Committee or Commonwealth Games Canada. If the final decision on carding or selection has already been made, then the athlete's appeal recourse is to these bodies, not to their sport organization.

Within its scope of powers, a sport organization may adopt either a narrow or a broad approach on appeals. A narrow approach would allow only appeals on decisions where the rules of procedural fairness require the greatest procedural safeguards. Thus, only decisions that result in the revoking of certain rights or privileges, such as disciplinary matters, would be open to appeal. A broad approach would allow appeals on decisions made by any committee or by the board of directors of the organization. Keeping in mind that an important purpose of administrative appeals is to resolve disputes internally, the broad approach is highly recommended. This doesn't mean that the organization will be inundated with appeals, because not all decisions being challenged will reach the threshold for an actual appeal hearing—that is, it may not be based on a necessary *ground* of appeal. Thus, although the *scope* of appeal may be broad, the permissible *grounds* for an appeal may be more limited, thus restricting the number of appeals.

Grounds for the Appeal

When may decisions be appealed—that is, on what basis may a decision be challenged? The organization's appeal policy should clearly set out the "grounds" on which a decision may be appealed. Typically the grounds of appeal relate to issues of proper authority and issues of procedural fairness, as discussed in the first part of this chapter.

Such grounds of appeal presume that decisions will be based on policy and that such policies reflect the will of the membership and have been properly approved and implemented. Underlying this approach is the presumption that decisions should not be appealed just because someone is dissatisfied with the outcome. To allow this would undermine the decision-making authority of individuals and committees properly entrusted with making decisions in the first place.

The practice of limiting grounds of appeal also assumes that the policies of the organization are clearly written and reflect a rational, workable, and fair approach to the subject matter in question—whether that be selection, discipline, or some other issue relating to the allocation of rights and obligations in sport. No individual should be able to appeal the *substantive* aspects of any policy that is properly made by an organization—that is, the substance of the policy. The normal and democratic method of making policy is the appropriate avenue for reviewing the substance of an organization's policy.

A selection dispute before the 1996 Summer Olympic Games in Atlanta nicely illustrates this distinction between procedure and substance (see *Roberge*). Leading up to these games, Judo Canada put in place a fairly complex point system for selection based on international matches. Part of the process anticipated that there could be a tie in accumulated points in any weight division and therefore, not one, but three tie-breaking procedures were incorporated. As it happened, it was necessary to invoke the third tie-breaking procedure, which gave rise to an unanticipated dilemma as higher-ranked athletes, who earned "byes" in competition, ended up being disadvantaged in the points calculation. An initial appeal panel found the tie-breaking policy to be unfair and essentially rewrote the tie-breaking process. The matter then went to independent arbitration where the appeal decision was overturned. The following rather extensive quotation from the arbitration decision of *Roberge v. Judo Canada* (at page 7) illustrates the rationale of the arbitration panel:

> What the [appeal panel] did, in effect, was to substitute its own decision as to who was the better athlete and accordingly manipulated the rules of the Handbook by reversing the order of the criteria to arrive at that conclusion. This is clearly inappropriate especially in a case such as this, where the tie-breaking formula contained criteria that were clear, concise, objective and non-discretionary. It is not within the jurisdiction of the [appeal panel] to intervene into the affairs of Judo Canada and re-write their selection rules based on what the [appeal panel] thinks is fair, or what it thinks the criteria should be in order to select the best possible athlete. The tie-breaking formula involved, in essence, the mechanical application of the criteria set out in the Handbook: adding up points, identifying the highest category of tournament and counting the number of wins. There was absolutely no room for the abuse of discretion, subjective evaluation or ambiguity. In such circumstances, it is not for the [appeal panel] to become involved in whether the selection criteria enable Judo Canada to identify the best possible athlete. It is up to the experts in the sport organization which, in this case, was the Technical Committee ... The tie-breaking formula was set out in the Handbook so that all athletes knew well ahead of time what the "rules of the game" were in the event of a tie ... Decisions with respect to clear and concise criteria cannot be appealed simply because an athlete does not like the outcome and feels they are a better overall athlete than the person who won the tie-breaker. [To do this] would be grossly unfair.

This decision highlights several important points. First, it recognizes the value of clear, objective criteria known by athletes well ahead of time. In so doing, it sets out those aspects of organizations' policies and procedures that typically cause problems and lead to appeals—the abuse of discretion, subjective evaluation, and ambiguity in policies and procedures. But the decision also goes on to emphasize that review panels should not rewrite the policies of organizations. Just as our courts do not have jurisdiction to rewrite legislation, policy is the sole prerogative of the duly elected, duly appointed, and properly authorized committees and boards of the organization.

A Review of Canadian Appeal Cases

The *Roberge* case was one of 25 selection disputes heard prior to the 1996 Summer Olympic Games in Atlanta. Some, but not all, ended up in the courts. In anticipation of the 2002 Winter Olympic Games in Salt Lake City, an ad hoc arbitration system was put in place in Canada to handle disputes relating to these games. To support this system, a study was done of 30 selection disputes that had been heard before Canadian courts and tribunals (Findlay and Corbett, 2002). The purpose of the study was to identify themes of potential interest to adjudicators, and to assist them in properly and consistently exercising their broad discretion in dealing with potentially complex disputes under short timelines. The themes that emerged from this study are summarized here.

The first theme is that a large number of appeals arise from the interpretation of the contract between the sport organizations and its members. Sport organization bylaws tend to be based on generic templates designed to accommodate a wide range of general interest associations, and are often ill suited to the needs of a body overseeing the competitive activities of elite athletes. Specifically, policies relating to team eligibility and selection are written by people who are technically knowledgeable but not skilled in draftsmanship. As a result, adjudicators will often have to interpret selection policies that are vague, incomplete, contradictory, and even silent on critical points. For example, there is confusion between the authority to *develop* criteria and the authority to *apply* criteria; as in the *Roberge* case, tiebreaker procedures do not actually work in breaking a tie; the vagaries of weather or other unforeseen circumstances are not accommodated; procedures for dealing with an appeal do not exist, requiring that an ad hoc procedure be improvised that is ultimately challenged; performance criteria based on national and international standards are supposed to mesh together but do not; criteria are not weighted relative to each other so those applying the criteria must make arbitrary decisions as to their relative weight; changes are made to the selection process and these are not communicated to athletes—the list continues. Adjudicators will find themselves having to make interpretations on those deficiencies that arise from the drafting of selection policies and criteria.

A second theme is that many selection disputes arise from allegations of bias. The sport community is small and many leaders within the community perform different roles at different times, and at times these roles may be in conflict. Athletes and coaches may have professional relationships that span many years, and coaches are often given responsibility to select athletes from among a group including athletes whom they coach currently or may have coached previously. As well, within sports that cater to small numbers, it is not uncommon to have a certain degree of parental involvement in leadership positions (such as board member), which may be perceived as having some influence over decisions affecting national team athletes, including selection. It has been accepted that a degree of bias is often inevitable within small associations, and it is not necessary to force all internal hearings to an external forum simply on the basis of a perceived bias under such circumstances.

A third theme is that the sport system is hierarchical and the issue of which entity has jurisdiction may not be straightforward. It is widely understood that national sport associations "select" national teams. For single-sport international competitions and championships this is true, but in the multisport games setting (Olympics, Commonwealth Games, Pan-American Games, World Student Games) this is in fact not true. Legally and technically, national sport organizations "nominate" athletes to the national team but it is the multisport organization (Commonwealth Games Canada, Canadian Olympic Committee, Canadian Interuniversity Sport) that actually "names" the team and has ultimate responsibility for the members of the team. Thus, depending on the timing of the dispute and the date of the *actual* selection, the authority to identify the team may rest with the national sport organization or with the multisport organization, or in the case of the Canada Games, with a provincial government.

A fourth theme observed from among the 30 cases reviewed is that many eligibility and selection disputes involve multiple affected parties. Selection disputes are not win–win scenarios: typically, only a finite number of individuals may be on a team (as determined by the rules of a national or international sport federation, or a national or international multisport organization), and the outcome of the dispute is invariably that one athlete will join the team and another athlete will not. If, in an appeal, an adjudicator's decision results in placing a previously non-selected athlete (the appellant) on a team, an athlete actually selected to the team will have to be removed. The athlete removed from the team may then have a right to appeal—thus potentially beginning a vicious cycle of appeals. This challenge is often addressed by extending the jurisdiction of the appeal to any athlete who might be displaced from the team if the appeal is successful. By giving the affected athlete this jurisdiction, however, the affected athlete is precluded from any other independent appeal of the matter.

A final theme is that the factual basis of many selection disputes is highly technical. Criteria to select athletes to individual sports are usually objective and straightforward: they include speed, time, placings, points, and rankings—criteria that are all easily measured. Selecting athletes to team sports, or to sports that have both individual and team components such as gymnastics, squash, or badminton, often involves subjective criteria and thus requires a certain amount of discretion on the part of the selectors. Both objective criteria and subjective criteria may be appropriate, depending on the circumstances, but they give rise to vastly different disputes. Disputes involving objective criteria tend to revolve around their application and are technical in nature, while disputes about subjective criteria and selection to teams tend to revolve around issues of bias and discretion.

Often, coaches are given broad discretion in selecting a team. As noted by the court in *Kulesza v. Canadian Amateur Synchronized Swimming Association*, coaches bring to this task their abundant technical knowledge and experience, as well as a thorough understanding of the strengths, weaknesses, and attributes of the athletes seeking to be selected. Many selection disputes have revolved around whether or not a coach properly exercised his or her discretion in applying the subjective criteria in making a decision. In an appeal over selection to the Canadian team competing at the 1999 Pan-American Games, a number of athletes argued that the coach, who was duly authorized to make selection decisions, had abused his discretion when he ignored one of the selection criteria incorporated into the selection process (see *Green and Ceresia*). In its selection policy, the association had set out nine criteria for the coach to consider; however, it had given the coach absolute discretion as to how he wished to weigh or rank the criteria. In other words, the coach could put whatever emphasis he felt appropriate on each criterion (although proportionally the same for each athlete) but he had to at least consider each criterion. The coach acknowledged he felt one criterion to be irrelevant and had not considered it. The athletes were thus successful in their appeal. The matter was sent back for a reconsideration correcting the error.

In another appeal the selectors were found to have prejudged certain athletes and applied the selection criteria in an uneven and ad hoc manner, if they applied them at all (see *Hall and Samuel*). The tribunal characterized the selection process as being entirely subjective, almost a "we know one when we see one" approach to team selection. It went on to say at page 18:

> Such subjective approaches to team selection are inevitably followed by allegations of bias, unfairness and impropriety ... Some criteria must be used to ensure that any

personal biases are eliminated, and some method of scrutinizing the selection process should be in place to ensure that even the subjective elements are fairly and properly applied.

Although there needs to be some flexibility in the selection process to deal with unexpected circumstances and the selectors should be afforded some degree of judgment, there is a danger that completely unfettered discretion can lead to arbitrary decisions. And if it does not lead to actual arbitrariness, it certainly can give the perception of arbitrariness. Arbitrary decisions are not fair decisions and are, without exception, open to review. Arbitrariness can be controlled by controlling discretion, using objective criteria, articulating subjective criteria as much as possible through the design and application of more objective factors, using more than one selector and providing reasons for selection, among other measures.

Since the 2002 Winter Olympics, the ad hoc arbitration program has become permanent in Canada and at the time of writing, some 75 sport disputes have been heard, decided, and published. There is now a significant body of sport case law emerging from this program. At present, the SDRCC offers its services only to national sport governing bodies; nonetheless, important principles are being clarified and communicated, which is benefiting the management of sport disputes at all levels within the Canadian sport system. Chapter 10 provides further information on this topic.

Judicial Review

A member of an organization is never barred from taking a matter to the courts. However, what the courts can or will do is very limited. As noted previously, courts are reluctant to interfere in private matters, and it is well established that a party must first exhaust his or her internal remedies before seeking an external remedy, unless such recourse is impossible due to time restrictions. This principle has been affirmed time and time again in the Canadian sport community. The case of *Trumbley v. Saskatchewan Amateur Hockey Association (SAHA)* is a perfect illustration. Trumbley was suspended for coaching a midget team in a tournament that was not sanctioned by the association—a penalty that was expressly permitted under its constitution. After being suspended, Trumbley brought a court action against the SAHA. A trial court ruled in Trumbley's favour, but ultimately the Court of Appeal determined that Trumbley could not seek judicial review of the association's decision until he had exhausted all other available remedies. Notably, the association had offered Trumbley an appeal, there was nothing to suggest that he would not have received a fair hearing in an appeal, and the appeal could have been conducted in a timely manner because the suspension had been imposed in the summer and the new hockey season was some months away. The court observed that an internal appeal hearing was clearly preferable to court action in terms of convenience, timeliness, and cost to the parties.

It must be noted that judicial review is not an appeal. The courts will not review the merits of a matter, nor will they review the *substantial* fairness of a matter. The courts will defer entirely to the expertise within the private organization and, as shown in numerous cases, will tend not to substitute their own decisions for those decisions more properly made by those with the necessary expertise. Courts will only review a procedural error. As well, the courts will not intervene where an organization has acted properly according to its policies and rules.

This reluctance to become involved in substantive matters is illustrated in a yachting case—*McCaig v. Canadian Yachting Association et al.* This case was brought by two athletes who argued that they were denied the opportunity to fully compete for selection to the 1996 Canadian Olympic Sailing Team. The selection procedure involved three regattas; however, weather conditions forced the cancellation of the third regatta shortly after its commencement. The selection process made no contingency provision for cancellation due to weather and the association argued there were no suitable alternative regattas available prior to the selection deadline. Selection to the team was thus made on the basis of the two completed regattas. The court stated at page 6:

> There was no provision in the agreement which provided for an alternative if, without fault on the part of either party, the event could not be completed … If the relief sought by the applicants were to be granted, it would, by necessary implication, require the court to write into the agreement a clause which does not exist. Apart from a claim for rectification, I know of no basis upon which a court can rewrite a contract by inserting a fresh clause into the agreement, no matter how desirable it might be.

Clearly, this case shows that the courts will not rewrite the agreements of sport organizations. The lesson from *McCaig* is that sport organizations need to incorporate contingency planning into their selection process, in order to deal with unforeseen issues such as changes to the event that are not within the organization's control, inclement weather, injuries, and the need to break a tie.

REFERENCES

Blake, S. *Administrative Law in Canada* (Markham, ON: Butterworths, 1992).

Depiero v. Canadian Amateur Diving Association et al. (1985), ACWS (2) 330 (Ont. HCJ).

Fernandes v. Sport North Federation, [1996] NWTR 118 (SC).

Findlay, H.A. and B. Ward, "Increased Commercialization of Athletics Requires Sophisticated Athlete Agreements" (October 2006), 26(48) *Lawyers Weekly* located at http://www.sportlaw.ca/articles/sophisticated_athlete_agreements .htm.

Findlay, H.A. and R. Corbett, "Principles Underlying the Adjudication of Selection Disputes Preceding the Salt Lake City Winter Olympic Games: Notes for Adjudicators" (2002), 1(1) *J Ent. Law* 109-20.

Garrett v. Canadian Weightlifting Federation, unreported decision of the Alta. QB (Edmonton), January 18, 1990.

Green and Ceresia v. Canadian Racquetball Association, internal appeal decision of the Canadian Racquetball Association, June 26, 1999.

Hall and Samuel v. Bobsleigh Canada, internal appeal decision of Bobsleigh Canada, August 19, 1999.

Kane v. Canadian Ladies Golf Association (1992), 11 CPC (3d) 260 (PEI TD).

Kelly v. Canadian Amateur Speed Skating Association (1995), 53 ACWS (3d) 750 (Ont. Ct. (Gen. Div.)).

Kligman, R.D., *Bias* (Markham, ON: Butterworths, 1998).

Kulesza v. Canadian Amateur Synchronized Swimming Association and Canadian Olympic Association, unreported decision of Ont. Ct. (Gen Div.) (Ottawa), Case no. 27763-0001, June 27, 1996.

Lakeside Colony of Hutterian Brethren v. Hofer, [1992] 3 SCR 165.

Lassen v. Yukon Weightlifting Association, unreported decision, Yukon SC (Whitehorse), May 19, 1995. *Lee v. Showmen's Guild of Great Britain,* [1952] 1 All ER 1175, [1952] QB 329 (CA).

McCaig v. Canadian Yachting Association et al., unreported decision, Man QB (Winnipeg), April 24, 1996.

McGarrigle v. Canadian Interuniversity Sport, [2003] OJ no. 1842 (QL) (SC).

Nicholson v. Haldimand Norfolk (Regional) Police Commissioners, [1979] 1 SCR 311.

Omaha v. British Columbia Broomball Society (1981), 13 ACWS (2d) 373 (BCSC).

Paterson v. Skate Canada (2004), Admin. LR (4th) 147, 2004 (Alta. QB).

Roberge v. Judo Canada and Morgan, arbitration award pursuant to article 5, Judo Canada National Team Handbook, June 26, 1996.

Trumbley v. Saskatchewan Amateur Hockey Association (SAHA) (1986), 49 Sask. R 296 (CA).

Doping in Sport

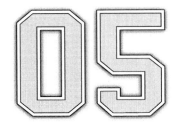

Introduction

"Doping" in the context of this chapter, refers to the use of a substance or a method banned by the World Anti-Doping Agency (WADA) or prohibited by an international sport governing body. Dick Pound, the current chief executive officer of WADA, and others believe drugs are one of the biggest threats facing sport today (Pound, 2006). Much has been written about the subject of drugs in sport from many perspectives including socio-historical, ethical, and physiological.

From a legal perspective, we can examine doping as a case study within the realm of administrative law and fairness in decision making, which was the subject matter of the preceding chapter. The use of banned substances and methods in sport is regulated through policies adopted by the sport organization. How that policy framework takes shape will be discussed in the first part of this chapter. The chapter continues with a discussion of the rationale behind anti-doping policies and a review of Canada's anti-doping policy.

Authority and Jurisdiction

In 1988 Canadian sprinter Ben Johnson set a world record of 9.79 seconds to win the 100-metre sprint at the Seoul Olympics, but soon thereafter was stripped of his gold medal and world record when he tested positive for the banned substance, steroid stanozolol. For Canada, this was a watershed event that catapulted it into the fore-front of the anti-doping movement.[1] The federal government launched a royal commission of inquiry into drug use in sport. Overseen by Justice Charles Dubin and referred to as the "Dubin Inquiry," the final report documented the frequent use and abuse of performance-enhancing substances among athletes in Canadian sport. The inquiry led directly to the development of the first Canadian Policy on Doping in Sport (as it was called at the time) and the establishment in 1991 of the Canadian Anti-Doping Organization—now known as the Canadian Centre for Ethics in Sport (CCES). This organization is responsible for the implementation of the Canadian anti-doping program including drug test administration and results management and interpretation.

CCES receives its mandate to manage the anti-doping program within the Canadian sport system from the Canadian Anti-Doping Policy itself. The policy, in turn, is adopted by sport governing bodies within the Canadian sport system. Not all sport organizations have adopted the policy; however, to be part of the Olympic movement and to receive federal government funding, individual sports must adopt the policy. Once adopted, it becomes part of the policy framework of the sport organization. As described in chapter 4, this policy framework constitutes the terms of the contract between the athlete and others within the sport organization and the organization itself and it is through this contract that athletes and others agree to be bound by anti-doping rules. This is reinforced through the "athlete agreement" that athletes sign with their sport governing body prior to participating in sanctioned events and through which athletes also consent to be bound to the policies of the sport organization, including its anti-doping policy (see *CCES et al. v. Adams et al.*).

An inherent part of this member–association contract is that decisions that affect an athlete or other individuals bound by the policy must be made fairly. As noted in the previous chapter, fairness is a flexible concept within the law. Nonetheless, there are certain principles that must be incorporated into the policy in order to meet the requirements of fairness. As elements of the policy are discussed later in this chapter, consider the elements of fairness that have been incorporated and in what ways.

In chapter 1 the hierarchical nature of sport both nationally and internationally was discussed. This hierarchical structure is also reflected in the area of doping

---

1   This was not the first time a Canadian was found to have been using a prohibited substance. Canada's first positive test result for a non-steroid infraction caused by the inadvertent use of a cold tablet containing a banned drug occurred at the 1975 Pan American Games. A bronze medal was withdrawn from the athlete.

control. In 1983 the International Olympic Committee (IOC) introduced its first list of banned substances and methods. This list governed Olympic and other major multisport competitions. At the time there was no common international anti-doping code that applied across both countries and sport disciplines. Although Canada has had a single code since 1991, many countries did not until recently have a national code and, although most international sport federations had some anti-doping measures because this was a requirement to participate in the Olympic Games, there has been very little consistency among them. Nonetheless, historically, most individual anti-doping codes did reflect, at a minimum, the IOC list of banned substances although occasionally there were discrepancies.[2]

By the mid to late 1990s, this lack of harmonization between and among anti-doping codes on the international stage was a huge problem. Existing anti-doping rules varied on such issues as when an infraction was declared (immediately on an adverse finding or after appeals had been exhausted, thus allowing the athlete to continue to compete until the conclusion of all appeals), who had the onus to prove an infraction (the athlete or the sport organization), and the nature of the penalty in the event of an infraction (which could vary on a first-time offence from a warning to a lifetime ban). The 1998 Tour de France doping scandal eventually galvanized international interests and resulted in the formation of the World Anti-Doping Agency (WADA) and a single anti-doping code. In the years since the formation of WADA, there has been steady progress in getting nations and international sport federations to sign on and agree to be bound by the harmonized code.[3]

The WADA Code is reflected in the Canadian Anti-Doping Code, although they are separate documents. Just as appeals from decisions under the Canadian Code go to the Sport Dispute Resolution Centre of Canada (SDRCC) (see chapter 10 for

---

2   Ross Rebagliati, a Canadian snowboarder, tested positive for marijuana at the 1998 winter Olympic Games in Nagano, Japan. The IOC doping code at the time deferred to the list of banned substances of each particular sport. The International Ski Federation (ISF) of which snowboarding was a disciple, allowed the individual disciplines to identify their own banned list of substances. Snowboarding was a young discipline and had not yet developed its own list and thus referred to the list of the Alpine Ski Federation (another discipline of ISF). Marijuana, although on the list of a number of the disciplines, was not on that of the Alpine Ski Federation and thus was not a banned substance for Rebagliati. Thus there was no doping infraction and Rebagliati retained his first place finish and gold medal.

3   Only those international sport federations that had adopted and implemented the Code could participate in the 2004 Olympic Games in Athens. It took much longer for national governments to adopt the Code; however, the 191 member states of UNESCO (United Nations Educational, Scientific and Cultural Organization) accepted the anti-doping policy in 2005 at its 33rd General Conference by adopting the UNESCO resolution entitled "International Convention Against Doping in Sport Resolution."

a discussion of this national mediation/arbitration forum), appeals from decisions under WADA's Code, which would be applicable at the Olympic Games or other major multisport events, would be to the International Court of Arbitration for Sport (CAS). As well, CAS may ultimately hear appeals from the SDRCC.

Rationale for an Anti-Doping Policy

The use of performance-enhancing substances or methods has not always been considered "cheating." Indeed, according to Beamish and Ritchie (2006: 107) use of performance-enhancing substances or methods can be traced back to ancient times where the Greeks and Romans used dietary supplements, stimulants, hallucinogens, and even testicular extracts to gain a competitive advantage. Beamish and Ritchie maintain that for at least the last 100 years the use of performance-enhancing substances and methods has been a critical part of the overriding objective of high-performance sport—that is, a drive toward competitive excellence. They write at page 5:

> The stark truth is that the widespread use of performance enhancing substances in the latter half of the nineteenth century and on into the present is the direct result of a particular set of social and political circumstances and decisions in which winning and the scientifically and technologically assisted pursuit of the linear record became the overriding objectives within several well-funded, extremely sophisticated, high performance sport systems.

Ironically, some of the practices that were once condoned have now been banned or are being discussed in that regard. For example, blood boosting—a performance-enhancing technique whereby an athlete's blood is withdrawn and then reinjected—was developed by researchers in response to concerns that the health of athletes participating in the 1960 Mexico City Olympic Games would be jeopardized because of such high altitudes. The procedure was openly condoned and used by athletes (including the gold-medal American cyclist in the 1984 Olympic Games in Los Angeles) right up to the time the IOC published its first list of banned substances and practices, which outlawed it.

It has only been in the last 50 to 60 years that the use of performance-enhancing substances or methods has been termed "cheating." This begs the question, "What is cheating as it relates to doping?" If there is not a reliable test for a substance or a way of monitoring certain practices, is the substance or pratice implicitly allowed despite its being dangerous, performance-enhancing, and contrary to the spirit of sport?

The anti-doping movement seems to rest on three basic rationales. The first rationale in favour of doping control relates to issues of health and harm to the athlete. The second rationale is that the use of performance-enhancing substances or methods unfairly "tilts" the playing field and that "true sportsmanship" rests on a level playing field. The third rationale is that the use of performance-enhancing substances or methods is against the "spirit of sport"—that is, it is a perversion of the very ideals that underlie sport.

Many authors argue that on close scrutiny, these rationales simply do not hold water. In sport there are many hazards that directly impact the health of the athlete—in fact, some sports by their very nature are hazardous and unhealthy. Furthermore, such a concern represents a paternalistic approach, one that we do not see directed at other sectors of society. The argument that the playing field is tilted by performance-enhancing substances or methods is often countered by pointing at the discrepancy in training aids, competitive opportunities, sport science support, nutrition, equipment, and facilities between and among countries and athletes.[4] In other words, the playing field is already tilted by factors other than performance-enhancing substances or methods. Finally, with regard to the third rationale that use of performance-enhancing substances or methods is a perversion of the very ideals underlying sport, some suggest such a view of sport is more myth than reality: "[A]ncient Games, the Modern Olympic Games and the world of contemporary high performance sport are socially, historically and politically shaped activity that are constituted by athletes, officials, politicians, spectators, and, in the case of the contemporary period, advertisers, manufactures, media and others" (Beamish and Ritchie, 2006: 114). Sport, it is suggested, is part of an "increasingly commercialized and professionalized, and often exploitative international system" (Beamish and Ritchie, 2006: 115).

On the other side of the argument are those who contend that the presence of other factors that impact the "level" playing field ought not dissuade those making efforts to correct doping matters. Furthermore, health risks should be a concern. The drive to win often blinds athletes to the risks they are taking, including the use of substances and methods with unknown effects. Although some athletes will consider the effect of substances and methods on their body in both the long and

---

4   Citing a concern for players' health and an advantage to high-altitude teams over visiting lowland rivals, FIFA, the international governing body for soccer, ruled that international soccer games would no longer be permitted at altitude venues above 8,200 feet. Latin American countries, many of which are at altitudes higher than the ban, viewed the ban as discriminatory and arbitrary insisting many factors affect the sport and create advantages and disadvantages for every team.

short term, others will fall prey to the seduction and possibilities of "winning at any cost." Perhaps, it is argued, these people need to be saved from themselves.

Understandably, there are proponents on both sides of the issues identified above and there is little consensus even within each side. Whether we should be engaged in anti-doping initiatives (which are now central to the Canadian sport system) and the underlying ethical and moral rationale for such engagement make for an interesting, controversial, and critical discussion. However, it is not the purpose of this chapter to explore this question—readers interested are encouraged to consult other writings, including those listed at the end of this chapter.

What is important to the remainder of this chapter, however, is looking at how the rationale for an anti-doping policy informs and is consistent with the framework of the policy—that is, do the various policy elements address the concerns underlying the rationale? Furthermore, why is this consistency important from a legal perspective? It is important because doping and anti-doping policies and regulations are, to one degree or another, an intrusion into an individual's human rights. As noted by Schneider (2006: 146): "For doping-free sport, which many want, including athletes, we need effective enforcement. But the steps required for effective enforcement can be very invasive of athletes' rights, particularly the personal right to privacy and confidentiality." In the Canadian workplace, for example, we permit mandatory drug testing only where there is a significant public interest or where public safety is at risk. Furthermore, in no sector of our society do we insist on an individual notifying officials of their whereabouts at all times (except in the limited situation of a designated long-term dangerous offender). Yet, this is a requirement of the Canadian anti-doping regime (as well as WADA's), considered necessary in order to conduct no-notice or minimal-notice, out-of-competition drug testing. Overall, effective anti-doping policy development requires a careful balance between unnecessary incursions into the rights of the individual and effective anti-doping tools that meet policy objectives. This is why policy measures must be consistent with and fulfill policy objectives, which themselves must be clear.

Table 5.1 identifies four key policy elements (each of which will be discussed later in the chapter) and the various options for policy content given policy objectives and considerations. The first column defines the extent to which fault on the athlete's part is an element of a doping offence or lack of fault is a defence. The second column defines the extent to which establishing a performance-enhancing effect is an element of a doping offence or alternatively, the extent to which the absence of a performance-enhancing effect is a defence. To the extent that fault and performance-enhancing effect are relevant, then the issue of who has the burden of proof (the athlete or the sport organization) must be addressed (as described in column 3). The fourth column defines possible penalty options based on considerations of intent

TABLE 5.1   Range of Possible Policy Options

Intent to cheat/fault	Performance-enhancing effect	Burden of proof	Penalty
Question of athlete's fault is not relevant. The offence occurs when a banned substance is detected in a valid test (strict liability rule).	The inclusion of a substance on a doping list and its general propensity to enhance cannot be challenged.	The athlete's lack of fault and absence of any performance-enhancing effect are not relevant so there is no issue as to proof.	Result and any record of it are cancelled and the athlete is suspended regardless of substance.
Proof of sabotage is a defence.	The fact that the banned substance would not have enhanced the athlete's performance in particular circumstances is not relevant.	If a banned substance is detected, the burden of proof is on the athlete to prove there was no fault on his or her part or that there was any performance-enhancing effect.	Result and any record of it are cancelled and the athlete is suspended, length of suspension dependent on nature of the banned substance (i.e., steroid versus amphetamine).
Proof of serious medical necessity is a defence.[1]	Proof of enhanced performance is an element of the offence.	The athlete must prove the absence of fault or performance-enhancing effect.	Result and any record of it are cancelled; however, the athlete may argue no negligence or fault or limited negligence or fault and have the suspension reduced in whole or in part.
Lack of negligence or fault on the part of the athlete or anyone associated with the athlete is a defence.		The burden of proof for all elements of the offence including proof of the athlete's negligence and the existence of any performance-enhancing effect is on the sport organization.	No performance-enhancement effect or proof of serious medical necessity results in no penalty.
No personal fault on the part of the athlete is a defence.			
Intent to enhance performance is a necessary element of the offence.			

[1] Therapeutic use exemptions (TUEs) must be identified and receive consent prior to training and competition.

Adapted from: R.R. Young, "Problems with the Definition of Doping: Does Lack of Fault or the Absence of Performance Enhancing Effect Matter?" paper presented at an international symposium on Doping in Sport and Its Legal and Social Control, University of Alabama, Birmingham, AL, August 8, 1996.

(fault) and performance-enhancing effect. It is important that policy content support and be consistent with policy objectives. For example, if it is believed that banned substances and methods provide an advantage to those using them and the policy objective is to eradicate such advantages, "intent" should not be part of the policy—the fact that the substance is in the body or the method used (no matter how it got there or why it is being used) creates the unfair advantage. Similarly, if a winning athlete's performance was enhanced by a banned substance, it would be unfair to the other competitors to let that athlete keep a gold medal, regardless of how the banned substance got into the athlete's system. However, a lack of any fault or negligence on the part of the athlete in ingesting the substance may justify no suspension. In the same vein, lack of fault may be relevant when considering sanctions for some substances such as ephedrine (a stimulant often found in decongestants) and not relevant for positive steroid tests where a sanction may be automatic. Maintaining consistency between the policy objectives and the policy content becomes increasingly difficult as the number of objectives the policy is intended to serve is increased.

Canadian Anti-Doping Policy

The broad strokes of the Canadian Anti-Doping Policy are fairly simple. An anti-doping infraction occurs in two ways: through the use of a prohibited substance or method or through a refusal (including non-availability) to take an anti-doping test. In general, the penalty for a first-time offence is a two-year suspension from involvement in sport in *any* capacity and for a second offence, a lifetime suspension. For those substances for which inadvertent use may be more likely (for example, the banned substance may be commonly found in cold remedies), a first infraction may result in a warning and reprimand up to a one-year suspension, a second offence in a two-year suspension, and a third offence is a lifetime suspension. An athlete's government financial assistance is permanently lost with a first-time infraction and, where the offence occurs *within a competition*, the athlete is disqualified from that competition and any result or record of it is erased.

Unless an individual waives his or her right to a hearing, the determination of a doping violation is heard by a sole arbitrator before the Doping Dispute Panel housed within the Sport Dispute Resolution Centre of Canada (SDRCC—discussed in chapter 10). Appeals of such decisions are heard by the Doping Appeal Panel also housed within the SDRCC. Both levels of decision are public and are posted on the SDRCC website.

The anti-doping policy covers more than the actions of athletes. Anyone associated with a sport organization or an event subject to anti-doping provisions is subject to the requirements of the policy. Coaches who possess or traffic in substances on the banned list or doctors who prescribe banned substances have run afoul of anti-doping initiatives in Canada.[5]

There are four elements of the Canadian Anti-Doping Policy that are particularly important to its overall scheme: (1) whether an intent to dope is necessary, (2) whether it is necessary to show that the substance or method had a performance-enhancing effect, (3) the onus of proof and standard of proof, and (4) "out-of-competition" testing. Each of these elements is discussed below (these elements are also laid out in table 5.1).

Intention

Must an athlete have an intention to commit a doping offence in order for there to be a doping infraction? What if he or she inadvertently consumes a mislabelled vitamin supplement, which contains a banned substance, such as what happened in the 1994 case of Jim Dan Corbett, a Canadian weightlifter at the 1994 Commonwealth Games?[6] Or, what if a positive test comes as a result of sabotage by a third party?

The WADA Code (as well as the Canadian anti-doping policies that preceded 2004 when the Canadian Code was modified to fall in line with the WADA Code) is based on the legal notion of "strict liability." As such, intention is irrelevant. If a prohibited substance is found in the system of an athlete through an adverse analytical finding, then a doping infraction is said to have occurred. As noted in chapter 3 on violence in sport, proving the mental element of intent can be very difficult. Furthermore, if the concern is over the effect the substance may have on athletic performance either directly or indirectly through enhanced training, the effect becomes real once the substance is in the system, regardless of intent. How the substance got into the athlete's system becomes a mitigating factor that is considered when determining the length of the sanction. Note that the notion of strict liability contrasts sharply to the elements of fairness discussed in chapter 4. Strict liability is not foreign to Canadian law but it is typically reserved for situations where the public may be at risk: for example, in drinking and driving laws where an impaired driving

---

5   Cecil Russell is a Canadian swimming coach who received a lifetime suspension under the Canadian Anti-Doping Policy for trafficking in steroids in 1997. Dr. Jamie Astaphan, personal physician to Canadian sprinter Ben Johnson at the time of Johnson's doping infraction at the 1998 Seoul Olympics, was found guilty of professional misconduct by the Ontario College of Physicians and Surgeons in 1991 and barred from medical practice for 18 months for prescribing steroids to athletes. The Canadian Anti-Doping Policy had not yet come into effect.

6   Corbett had shown the labelling of the substance to the Canadian Commonwealth Games doctor as well as to officials of CCES before its ingestion and both had told him that the product contained no banned substance.

charge will be laid when blood alcohol content exceeds a threshold, regardless of the driver's intent or how the alcohol may have been ingested. The strict liability of an anti-doping regime for sport has been up-held by the courts in Britain although it has not yet been challenged in Canada (see Houlihan, 2006).

There are two exceptions to the strict liability rule under the Canadian anti-doping rules. These exceptions do not eliminate the anti-doping violation per se, but they do allow the suspension to be reduced. In other words, the exceptions speak to the penalty, not to the declaration of the infraction itself (and thus, strictly speaking, may not be exceptions as much as a way to limit the effects of strict liability). The exceptions are very narrow and the athlete has the onus of convincing a doping tribunal that he or she is entitled to the benefit of the exception.

For the first exception to take effect under the Canadian policy, the athlete must demonstrate two things: first that there was an *absolute lack* of fault or carelessness on his or her part—that is, the athlete did not, and could not have known or suspected that he or she had used or been administered the prohibited substance. Second, the athlete must also show *how* the substance got into his or her body. It is not enough to simply claim inadvertent use or that the athlete has no knowledge of how the substance got into his or her body. This two-part test is very difficult to meet but, if successful, the result will be the entire elimination of the suspension. However, the finding of an infraction will remain and this becomes important in the event of a second infraction, which brings with it a lifetime suspension.

For the second exception to take effect under the Canadian policy, the athlete must establish that his or her own fault or negligence was not a *significant* factor in the violation. The request for an exception will not succeed if the athlete simply suggests how other circumstances may have contributed to the violation—the athlete must show that his or her own conduct was not a significant causal factor compared with other *specific* circumstances. This test is less difficult to meet, and if successful, the athlete's suspension may be reduced up to 50 percent.

Performance-Enhancing Effect

The extent to which a particular substance or method enhances performance varies depending on the sport activity, how much of the substance was used, when the substance was taken, the rate of dissipation of the substance from the body, the size of the athlete and his or her rate of metabolism, among other factors. It is virtually impossible to accurately measure the performance-enhancing effect of a substance given the number of variables that must be taken into account. As long as a substance is found on the prohibited list, its performance-enhancing effect, or lack thereof, is not relevant to a finding of a doping infraction.

Onus of Proof and Standard of Proof

The initial onus of proof under the Canadian policy rests with the doping control authorities to show that a positive test result is valid and accurate by demonstrating that proper sample collection procedures were followed, the chain of custody of the sample was not broken, and that the laboratory testing was done to the appropriate standard. It is then up to the athlete to show that there was a departure from the acceptable standard (a small deviation will not necessarily suffice; it must be shown that the deviation in fact caused the positive outcome) or some other error occurred that calls into question the validity or integrity of the positive test result.

Although the doping-control authorities have the onus to prove that a positive test result is valid and accurate, the onus shifts to the athlete to prove either a complete lack of fault or no significant fault, as discussed above.

In chapter 3 the notion of standard of proof was introduced and was discussed in terms of the civil standard (a balance of probabilities) and the criminal standard (beyond a reasonable doubt). Notwithstanding the foregoing, the standard used to prove a doping infraction is not a familiar one to Canadians, although it does exist in Europe. In the Canadian policy, the Doping Control Authority must prove to "a comfortable satisfaction" that a violation occurred.[7] The standard imposed on the athlete to prove a deviation from procedures or some error is still the civil standard of a "balance of probabilities."

"In-Competition" Testing Versus "Out-of-Competition" Testing

Any credible anti-doping program must use "out-of-competition" testing with little or no advance notice that a test will take place. Without such testing, athletes can easily manage their consumption of prohibited substances to assist in training without resulting in a positive test during competition. Certain substances such as anabolic steroids are known to clear the system within a specified period of time, and their consumption can be stopped before a test so as to not show up in a urine sample. Steroids achieve their intended effect in training by permitting the user to train more rigorously and recover more rapidly than would be possible without

---

7   The standard of a "comfortable satisfaction" is somewhere between the civil standard of a "balance of probabilities" and the criminal standard of "beyong a reasonable doubt." It comes from an Australian case (*Briginshaw v. Briginshaw*) and is also known as the "Briginshaw standard." This higher standard is used when a civil case raises allegations of moral wrongdoing that may have grave consequences for the defendant.

their use. Stopping their use can be timed quite specifically so that the user will not test positive during the course of the competition. Only an "out-of-competition" test with little or no notice to the athlete will determine use.

WADA's Prohibited List

The first list of prohibited substances was compiled by the International Olympic Committee in 1983. Over time the list became very cumbersome and inaccessible with little rationale for some substances on the list. After two years of intensive research and debate, in 2003 WADA announced a new comprehensive list of prohibited substances. Caffeine and pseudoephedrine were removed from the list. Marijuana, however, remained on the list, despite questions about its performance-enhancing effect in sport.

Changes to the list of banned substances and methods continue to take place. A method or substance may be included on the WADA's Prohibited List if it meets two of three criteria established by section 4.3 of the WADA Code:

- Will use of the substance or method enhance sport performance?

- Is there a health risk associated with use of the substance or method?

- Is use of the substance or method consistent with WADA's definition of "spirit of sport"?[8]

As an example, these three criteria were used in 2006 in a debate over whether hypoxic devices (that is, devices such as oxygen tents that affect the rate of transfer of oxygen to the blood) should be added to the IOC prohibited list. In applying the three criteria, the Ethical Issues Review Panel (EIRP) of CCES stated on the first criterion that the "active" use of such devices could enhance performance—that is, simply sleeping in a hypoxic chamber alone does not affect performance, but in *combination* with a certain optimal regime of physical training, performance could

---

8   WADA defines "spirit of sport" in the following way:

Anti-doping programs seek to preserve what is intrinsically valuable about sport. This intrinsic value is often referred to as "the spirit of sport"; it is the essence of Olympism; it is how we play true. The spirit of sport is the celebration of the human spirit, body and mind, and is characterized by the following values: ethics, fair play and honesty; health; excellence in performance; character and education; fun and joy; teamwork; dedication and commitment; respect for rules and laws; respect for self and other participants; courage; community and solidarity. Doping is fundamentally contrary to the spirit of sport. (WADA Code, 2003: 3)

be significantly enhanced. On the second criterion, the panel stated there were no reported injuries or known adverse health consequences attributed to the devices. Finally, on the third criterion, it was the view of the panel that "the argument suggesting these devices violate the 'spirit of sport' fails to withstand a logical test of consistency with other training regimes that are deemed to be acceptable [such as the treadmill or the shark skin swim suit]—both of which require active work to effect a result" (CCES, 2006). In the case of hypoxic training devices then, Canada's position to WADA was that such devices did not meet two out of three of the necessary criteria to be banned under WADA's Code of banned substances and thus should not be prohibited.

There is some controversy over the three criteria, particularly with regard to the somewhat vague definition of "spirit of sport" (see footnote 8 for a definition). Canada, through the CCES, has recommended to WADA that, in light of the three criteria, whether the substance or method enhances performance should be given greater weight over the other two criteria (CCES, March 29, 2007).

BOX 5.1   Banned Substances, Restricted Substances and Banned Methods

BANNED SUBSTANCES

Stimulants—a group of drugs that boost alertness and physical activity by increasing heart and breathing rates and brain function. By acting on the central nervous system, stimulants can stimulate the body both mentally and physically (amphetamines, for example, fit this description). Athletes may use stimulants to increase their ability to exercise at an optimal level, combat tiredness, or suppress appetite.

Narcotic analgesics—act on the brain and spinal cord to intercept pain stimuli. Athletes may use narcotic analgesics to help reduce or eliminate the pain from an injury, thus allowing them to train harder and for longer periods of time. Narcotic analgesics may also reduce anxiety, which may artificially enhance an athlete's performance.

Anabolic Androgenic Steroids—synthetic versions of the hormone testosterone. Natural testosterone provides "anabolic" (muscle building) and "androgenic" (masculinizing) effects. Athletes may use them to increase muscle size and strength, reduce the amount of time required to recover after exercise, and to train harder and for longer periods of time.

Diuretics—any drugs that increase the rate at which the body excretes urine. Diuretics are commonly used by athletes for two purposes: quick, temporary weight loss to meet weight categories within specific sports and to "flush out" other substances or drugs from the body in an attempt to avoid detection of their use (i.e., "masking" their use).

Peptide hormones, mimetics and analogues—Peptide hormones are substances that are produced by glands in the body that can affect organs and tissues to change bodily functions. Athletes use peptide hormones to stimulate the production of naturally occurring hormones, increase muscle growth and strength, and increase the production of red blood cells to improve the blood's ability to carry oxygen. Examples are erythropoietin (EPO), human growth hormones (HGH), and insulin. Mimetics are substances that imitate the action of other related drugs. Analogues are chemically produced drugs designed to have similar effects to naturally produced compounds in the body.

RESTRICTED SUBSTANCES

Local anesthetics—The topical use of local anesthetics, such as creams, ointments, lozenges, sprays, and drops are permitted but systemic injections are prohibited.

Glucocorticosteroids—powerful anti-inflammatory agents that are commonly used to treat asthma by relaxing the muscles that surround the airways and opening up the air passages, as well as other chronic inflammatory conditions such as arthritis, inflamed joints, and allergic reactions. They can provide the same advantages as a stimulant or, if administered into the bloodstream, have anabolic effects. Athletes may use them to increase their muscle size and reduce body fat.

Beta-blockers—used in the treatment of high blood pressure and some heart problems. Athletes may use beta-blockers to stop their hands and bodies from shaking while competing in a sport that requires accuracy or a steady hand or trigger finger.

Alcohol—a central nervous system depressant that slows down the actions of the brain and body. Combining alcohol with other drugs can magnify the effects of the alcohol or other drugs administered at the same time.

Cannabinoids—are psychoactive chemicals derived from the cannabis plant that cause a feeling of relaxation. Marijuana and hashish are forms of cannabis.

BANNED METHODS

Blood doping—the intravenous administration of red blood cells or other products (artificial oxygen carriers) to increase the blood's oxygen-carrying capacity and thereby enhance athletic performance. Blood doping may involve the use of the athlete's own blood that had been previously withdrawn.

Urine manipulation—examples of banned practices include catheterization, urine substitution, and urine tampering and the use of substances that modify kidney function.

Gene or cell doping—the non-therapeutic use of genes, genetic elements, or cells that have the capacity to enhance athletic performance (for example, a synthetic gene is transferred into human cells to manipulate or trigger a specific response within the body that will improve athletic performance).

Professional Sport and Drug Testing

A review of the varied anti-doping policies in professional sport is beyond the scope of this chapter. Such policies are enormously inconsistent and range from no drug testing to drug testing that conforms with WADA rules. For example, the Canadian Football League (CFL) has no anti-doping program but others, such as the Association of Professional Tennis Players (ATP) are aligned with the International Tennis Federation and, therefore, comply with the WADA Code (indeed, the ATP has the most comprehensive anti-doping policy of any professional sport). The key differences between anti-doping policies in the professional ranks of sport include: what substances are banned (usually only steroids), the use of out-of-competition testing with no or limited notice (rarely done), and the nature of the penalty imposed for an infraction. For example, the National Football League (NFL) imposes a four-game suspension for a first positive test, arguing that the playing season is short and the playing life of an athlete is, on average, four years. Any longer suspension, it is argued, would be unfairly onerous.

Before 2006, players in the National Hockey League (NHL) were required to be tested for performance-enhancing substances if they participated in the Olympic Games and world championships, the testing being done under the anti-doping policy of the International Ice Hockey Federation (IIHF). However, such testing would not commence until players had been selected or declared themselves available for international competition—usually only months before the competition (thus virtually eliminating out-of-competition testing). The current anti-doping policy of the NHL requires that every player be subject to up to two "no-notice" tests during the regular playing season and it follows the WADA list of banned substances (see NHL anti-doping policy).

Following the intervention of the United States Congress in 2005, Major League Baseball was forced to alter its minimal anti-doping policy by widening the scope of substances for which it tested from only anabolic steroids to include amphetamines (that is, stimulants). A first positive test for amphetamine use leads to counselling, while a second positive test leads to a 25-game suspension. A first positive test for steroids results in a 50-game suspension, a second positive test results in a further 50 games, and a third positive test results in a lifetime suspension with the opportunity to seek reinstatement after two years. Players are to be tested at least twice a year (once being during spring training camp) with a first positive test triggering six additional random tests over the next 12 months.

As cited earlier, the CFL does not currently have an anti-doping policy. However, in 2007 the NFL and its players' association reached agreement on a series of improvements to their policy including a 40 percent increase in the number of players randomly tested each week during the pre-season, regular season, and post-season from seven to ten per team. The number of random off-season tests was increased in 2006 from a maximum of two per player to six per player. The list of banned substances increasingly resembles the WADA list—erythropoietin (EPO) being added in 2007. Although the period of suspension remains at four games for a first offence, the new collective bargaining agreement provides for automatic forfeiture of a prorated portion of a player's signing bonus if he is suspended for violating the substance abuse policy.

At the time of the most recent (2005) collective agreement within the National Basketball Association (NBA), the use of social or recreational drugs has had a higher public relations priority than testing for performance-enhancing substances. Indeed, the NBA specifically excludes out-of-season testing. NBA players participating in the Olympic Games are, however, subject to the WADA Code through the international basketball federation (known by its French acronym FIBA—Fédération Internationale de Basketball). As with NHL players, only once a player in the NBA is selected to a national team does he become subject to testing under the WADA Code.

REFERENCES

Beamish, R. and I. Ritchie, *Fastest, Highest, Strongest: A Critique of High Performance Sport* (New York: Routledge, 2006), at 107.

Briginshaw v. Briginshaw (1938), 60 CLR 336 (Aust.).

CCES et al. v. Adams et al., No. SDRCC DT 06-0039, Doping Tribunal (Ordinary Division), June 11, 2007, where Adjudication R. MacLaren confirmed the contractual basis of doping policies and dismissed the proposition that the *Canadian Charter of Rights and Freedoms* applies to anti-doping matters in Canada.

CCES, Letter to WADA Re Canadian Sport Community Submission on Proposed New World Anti-Doping Code (v. 1.0), March 29, 2007.

CCES, Submission to WADA Concerning the Status of Hypoxic Devices, found at http://www.cces.ca/pdfs/CCES-PAPER-HypoxicDevices-e.pdf.

Dubin, C.L., *Commission of Inquiry into the Use of Drugs and Banned Practices Intended to Increase Athletic Performance* (Ottawa: Supply and Services, 1990).

Houlihan, B., "Civil Rights, Doping Control and the World Anti-Doping Code," in D. McArdle and R. Giulianotti (eds.), *Sport Civil Liberties and Human Rights* (London: Routledge, 2006).

NHL, Anti-Doping Policy, http://nhlpa.com/PerformanceEnhancing/index.asp.

Pound, D., *Inside Dope: How Drugs Are the Biggest Threat to Sports, Why You Should Care, and What Can Be Done About Them* (Toronto: John Wiley, 2006).

Schneider, A., "Privacy, Confidentiality and Human Rights in Sport," in D. McArdle and R. Giulianotti (eds.), *Sport, Civil Liberties and Human Rights* (London: Routledge, 2006), at 146-64.

World Anti-Doping Agency (WADA), *World Anti-Doping Code* (Montreal: WADA, 2003).

Discrimination in Sport

Introduction

To discriminate in the colloquial sense generally means to make a distinction. We know that some forms of discrimination are completely acceptable: distinguishing between students on the basis of their academic grades, or declining to sell alcohol or tobacco products to minors. Other forms of discrimination, depending on the context, *might be* legally unacceptable and yet others *are absolutely* unacceptable.

In Canada, the legal basis of discrimination comes from statute law, specifically, the *Canadian Charter of Rights and Freedoms* and federal and provincial/territorial human rights legislation. Both are considered to be "quasi-constitutional" documents. They are, in effect, a reflection of Canadian values on human rights and are given very broad and liberal interpretation. Discrimination is a central human rights issue but it is only one of many topics of discussion around the broader issue of human rights.[1] In this chapter we do not address the topic of human rights from this broad perspective but rather focus on discrimination. This chapter is about determining when a rule, policy, program, or act within a sport organization that discriminates in some form or fashion will be considered unacceptable discrimination and thus illegal.

---

1 Children's right to play, athletes' rights, gender equity issues, racism in sport, publicity rights, and privacy rights are all human rights issues.

Jurisdiction

Charter of Rights and Freedoms

Jurisdiction is an important issue in discrimination law, particularly because it applies to sport bodies. Sport, the activity, is offered by and through a number of different organizations—schools (both public and private); colleges and universities; municipal recreation departments; private clubs and facilities; teams and leagues; and provincial, national, and international sport governing bodies. The nature of the organization is very important in determining what, if any, legislation applies.

The *Canadian Charter of Rights and Freedoms* (the Charter) applies to matters of "government action." Corporate entities that arise from government statute clearly are a part of government action. From this perspective public school sport programs, and municipal sport and recreation programs, certainly come under the jurisdiction of the Charter. At the other extreme, private schools, private clubs, and other similar sorts of privately owned businesses are not a part of "government action" and thus are not subject to Charter provisions. This fact often comes as a surprise to the typical sport manager, sport participant, or lay person, because there is a widespread belief that the Charter affects all areas of our lives and that sport participation is a basic right or privilege that ought to be subject to the Charter. In fact, the Charter's direct influence on sport in Canada is minimal.

At one point in Canada university sport programs were considered to fall under the jurisdiction of the Charter (see *Beattie*); however, subsequent case law makes it clear that universities and colleges are not part of "government action" and are thus not subject to the jurisdiction of the Charter (see *McKinney*). Provincial and national sport organizations, as well, are not subject to the Charter. This was made clear in the case of *Blainey v. Ontario Minor Hockey Association.* Justine Blainey wanted to play hockey but there was no girls' hockey team. She was refused access to a boys' team. Blainey originally brought a complaint under the Ontario *Human Rights Code.* At the time, section 1 of the Code stated:

> Every person has a right to equal treatment with respect to services, goods and facilities, without discrimination because of race, ancestry, place of origin, colour, ethnic origin, citizenship, creed, sex, sexual orientation, age, marital status, family status or handicap.

A subsequent section specifically excluded sport or athletic activity from the anti-discrimination provision. Then section 19 read:

> The right under Section 1 to equal treatment with respect to services, goods and facilities is not infringed where membership in an athletic organization or participation in an athletic activity is restricted to persons of the same sex.

Her case was thus denied by the Ontario Human Rights Tribunal. Blainey then brought an action before the Ontario courts claiming that Ontario human rights legislation was a form of government action (because it was passed by the Ontario legislature) and that section 19 breached the anti-discrimination section of the Charter (section 15). The section was ultimately struck down and Justine Blainey was permitted to play on the boys' hockey team.

It may be that certain programs within a private organization could attract Charter application. For example, Canada's Athlete Assistant Program (AAP) is administered by each national sport governing body that "recommends" potential recipients to the government of Canada, which retains the ultimate decision-making status in the allocation of AAP funds. AAP is one of the few programs in which the government of Canada maintains an active role, not just in allocating funds, but in determining who should receive the program's funding. The federal government, therefore, has direct party status and this may bring the AAP program, or parts of it, under the jurisdiction of the Charter.

Human Rights Legislation

Human rights legislation exists at the federal level, as well as within each province and territory of Canada. The wording of the legislation itself stipulates to what and whom it applies. Across every province and territory, as well as federally, an organization offering services or access to programs and facilities to the "public" comes under the jurisdiction of the human rights laws of that jurisdiction. Determining what "public" means has been the subject matter of a number of cases. Before the Supreme Court of Canada decision in *Berg v. University of British Columbia*, provincial sport organizations were considered "private" organizations and beyond the jurisdiction of human rights legislation (see, for example, *Ontario Rural Softball* and *Cummings*). Similarly, a university athletic program was not subject to human rights jurisdiction and, undoubtedly, national sport governing bodies would have been viewed similarly. In the *Berg* case, a university attempted to limit the activities of a particular student on the basis of a prohibited ground. The court viewed the university's service as open to the public, even though there may be legitimate entrance requirements to be met. Once that "public" has been defined through entrance requirements, an organization may not discriminate against any member in any of its programming or operations. It is now well established that provincial and national sport organizations, as well as universities and colleges, are seen to offer membership and programs to the "public" even though there may be some entrance requirements or criteria to such membership (see *Sahyoun* and *Wood*). In other words, "public" does not necessarily mean the public at large and, as noted by the court in *Berg*, every organization has its own public as defined by its mandate and rules.

Some clubs offering sport or physical activity programs are, however, fully private clubs. They may limit their membership in ways that a "public" organization cannot under either the Charter or human rights legislation. A religiously based club, a women-only fitness club, and certain golf, tennis, and country clubs might be private and thus not subject to human rights legislation. Even a local soccer club might be interpreted as private: it differs from the provincial soccer association in that the latter has a province-wide mandate to govern the sport and offers its membership to the public at large (although only a subset of the public may choose to participate), while the former has no such mandate and may limit membership as it chooses.

Private clubs are not monolithic and may at times offer discrete services or programs to the public. For example, a private cultural centre may operate a retail store or feature a historical display open to the public. Such discrete services will be subject to the jurisdiction of human rights legislation. In *Gould v. Yukon Order of Pioneers*, the Yukon Order of Pioneers was a private club for a select group of people who could show a direct ancestral link to a Yukon pioneer. Part of the club's mandate was to preserve, as a public archive, the history of the Yukon. The court ruled in this case that although the archives were public, the club itself was private and its activities outside those related to its public mandate were not under the jurisdiction of human rights legislation. Access to the archives was, however, public and the club could not discriminate with regard to that service.

As can be seen from table 6.1, different sport organizations and activities fall within different spheres of jurisdiction as far as the topic of discrimination is concerned. There are also some additional jurisdictional "twists" unique to the sport world. The first is the situation where a national sport organization may be running an event, such as a national championship, in a particular province or territory. A participant wishes to challenge one of its rules. Under what human rights legislation should a claim be brought?

TABLE 6.1   Statutory Jurisdiction

	Charter	Human Rights
Schools	Yes	Yes
Municipal programs	Yes	Yes
Universities/colleges	No	Yes
National/provincial sport organization or club	No	Yes
Commercial business	No	No
Private-member club	No	Yes/No
Independent schools	No	No

In *Wood v. Canadian Soccer Association,* the national association argued that because it was incorporated federally, any claim should come under the jurisdiction of the *Canadian Human Rights Act.* The tribunal ruled that the association was not an interprovincial undertaking and could not be said to be involved in interprovincial or international trade or commerce and thus was not subject to the federal legislation. The tribunal found that the activities of the association fell under the jurisdiction of the human rights legislation in the province in which the event took place. Contrast that to the case of *Re Canadian Football league (CFL) and the Canadian Human Rights Commission,* a matter involving the CFL. In that case the tribunal found that the operation of an interprovincial or international professional sports league might constitute an interprovincial undertaking placing it under the jurisdiction of the federal Act. (But see *Sahyoun,* where the tribunal rejected the argument that the Canadian Colleges Athletic Association (CCAA), the governing body for college athletics in Canada, was involved in interprovincial trade or commerce.) Given that there are some differences in human rights legislation from province to province, variable outcomes to a claim could arise depending on where a claim is raised, and under what jurisdiction. Where a sport deals with interprovincial competition, this can present some interesting issues.

The second unique jurisdictional issue arises when international rules or national rules conflict with the applicable human rights legislation. Pardeep Singh Nagra, a Sikh boxer, was initially barred from competition in Canada because he refused to shave his beard for religious reasons. The "clean-shaven" rule came from the International Amateur Boxing Association (IABA), who maintained that it was a safety rule, citing incidents of corneal abrasions from loose beard hairs. The Canadian Amateur Boxing Association (CABA) faced sanctions from the IABA if they allowed Mr. Nagra to participate and further, Mr. Nagra would be barred from international competition by the IABA should he succeed in national competition and advance. Eventually, the IABA agreed not to impose sanctions if CABA was directed by way of a court order to allow Mr. Nagra to box. The latter concern was never resolved because Mr. Nagra did not progress to international competition.

Proving a Claim of Discrimination

The most common forum for an allegation of discrimination within sport is through a claim under the applicable human rights act. The legislative scheme is fairly similar from province to province although the prohibited grounds of discrimination, and exceptions that permit discrimination in certain circumstances, do vary. Essentially, the legislation features a provision similar to the following:

It is a discriminatory practice in the provisions of goods, services, facilities or accommodation customarily available to the general public:

(a) to deny, or deny access to, any goods, service, facility, or accommodation to any individual, or

(b) to differentiate adversely in relation to any individual, on a prohibited ground of discrimination.

By breaking down the provision, the elements of what needs to be proven for a successful discrimination complaint emerge. In order to succeed in a claim, the claimant must prove a *prima facie*[2] case by meeting four tests (see *Hill*):

- Is the impugned act or activity included under the Act?
- Is the impugned act or activity available to the public?
- Is there discrimination in the provision of the act or activity?
- Is the discriminatory act or activity based on a prohibited ground?

If a claim for discrimination is proven, in many cases (although not always[3]) there may be an opportunity for the respondent to argue a reasonable justification for the discrimination (also known as a bona fide qualification [BFQ]). The four tests are examined in more detail below.

Is the Impugned Act or Activity Included Under the Act?

The scope of federal, provincial, and territorial human rights legislation in Canada is broad and prohibits discrimination in a number of areas including employment, housing, and admission to professional and trade organizations, among others. In sport, the most common area in which claims are brought is in the "provision of services, facilities, and accommodation." Facilities are self-explanatory, as are accommodations (e.g., hotels, in-home billets, etc.). The definition of a "service" can be fairly broad as it applies to sport organizations and includes any sport program or event (see *Wood*) as well as eligibility and participation rules (see *Sahyoun*).

Is the Impugned Act or Activity Available to the Public?

The second test requires the claimant to prove that the act or activity is available to the public. This is essentially the test of jurisdiction as previously described. Where an

---

2 A *prima facie* case is one that addresses the allegations made, and that, if believed, justifies a verdict in the complainant's favour in the absence of a response from the respondent.

3 See section 5(2) of the New Brunswick *Human Rights Act*—no exception in the case of nationality, place of origin, etc.

activity is that of a national body being run through or managed by a provincial or territorial sport body (such as a national championship being managed by the provincial or territorial organization), both the national organization and the provincial/territorial organization will typically be named as respondents. Similarly, where national rules are incorporated into provincial or territorial activities, both bodies may be respondents (see *Sahyoun*). It is not possible for the provincial/territorial organization to seek exemption by arguing that the activity or rule is not actually theirs, or that they are required to implement the activity or rule on behalf of the national body.

Is There Discrimination in the Provision of the Act or Activity?

With one exception, provincial human rights statutes do not actually define discrimination.[4] In most cases, therefore, it is necessary to rely on the definition of discrimination that has evolved through the common law. The classic definition of discrimination comes from *Andrews v. Law Society of British Columbia*, a decision of the Supreme Court of Canada:

> Discrimination may be described as a distinction, whether intentional or not but based on grounds relating to personal characteristics of the individual or group, which has the effect of imposing burdens, obligations or disadvantages, on such individual or group not imposed upon others, or which withholds or limits access to opportunities, benefits and advantages available to other members of society. Distinctions based on personal characteristics attributed to an individual solely on the basis of association with a group will rarely escape the charge of discrimination, while those based on an individual's merits and capacities will rarely be so classed.

There are two main arms, or categories, of discrimination. The first is "direct" discrimination (also known as "overt" discrimination) and it refers to the direct and usually intentional differential treatment of another person, or group of persons, characterized by a prohibited ground. A prohibition such as "girls may not play on boys' teams" would be an example of direct discrimination. The second category of discrimination focuses on the "effect" of the discriminatory act on others, regardless of intent. A rule or practice that appears neutral may *unintentionally* single out particular people identified by a prohibited ground, therefore resulting in inequitable treatment. Such treatment is called "adverse effect" or "indirect"

---

4   Section 9(1) of the Manitoba *Human Rights Code* defines discrimination for the purposes of that Code.

discrimination and brings with it a duty to provide reasonable accommodation, short of undue hardship. An example of indirect discrimination might be rules of play that preclude a person with a particular disability.[5] A modification of the rules to accommodate the person treated differentially may be necessary.[6]

Very close to "adverse effect" discrimination, and often not well differentiated, is a third category of discrimination—"systemic discrimination." Where adverse discrimination relates to the operation of a particular rule or practice, systemic discrimination stems from the operation of a system of procedures, rules, and attitudes over time that, perhaps unintentionally, have the effect of disproportionately affecting a particular group.

An example of systemic discrimination can be seen in the case of *Morrison v. City of Coquitlam*. David Morrison was the father of two young female gymnasts. He also had a son who played minor hockey. He brought a complaint alleging that the allocation of resources, either as direct financial subsidy or tax relief, by the City of Coquitlam in British Columbia to sport and recreation facilities and organizations, disproportionately benefited male-dominated sports over female-dominated sports. Based on subsequent research, the City of Coquitlam was satisfied that girls were adversely affected by the subsidy policy of the city. The parties ultimately entered into a voluntary settlement without a tribunal hearing and an actual finding of discrimination on a prohibited ground.

Is the Discriminatory Act or Activity Based on a Prohibited Ground?

Each human rights act in Canada sets out a series of grounds on which discrimination is prohibited (see table 6.2). While across jurisdictions the grounds are basically the same, there are some subtle differences and there are also variations to the exceptions to the prohibitions that are permitted. For example, Ontario is one of the few jurisdictions to prohibit discrimination on the basis of citizenship, but at the same time section 7 of its Code allows an exemption for situations where citizenship is used as a criterion for participation in athletic or recreational activities. Section 19(2)

---

5 Some recent examples of this in Canada are the soccer or taekwondo rules that prevent wearing headgear that indirectly result in differential treatment of Muslim women or Sikh men, or the school football rule that requires chairs be over 5 metres from the sideline of the field, which results in differential treatment of an assistant football coach who is a paraplegic and requires the use of a wheelchair.

6 The case of *Casey Martin v. PGA* would be an example of this if it were to occur in Canada. The "no cart on the golf course" rule was modified to allow Martin to continue playing on the PGA Tour.

TABLE 6.2 Prohibited Grounds of Discrimination in the Provision of Services, Facilities, and Accommodation (Federal and Provincial/Territorial)

	Federal	British Columbia	Alberta	Manitoba	Saskatchewan	Ontario	Quebec	New Brunswick	Nova Scotia	Prince Edward Island	Newfoundland & Labrador	Northwest Territories	Yukon	Nunavut
Race	x	x	x	x	x	x	x	x	x	x	x	x	x	x
Colour	x	x	x	x	x	x	x	x	x	x	x	x	x	x
Religion	x	x	x	x	x		x	x	x	x	x	x	x	x
Creed				x	x	x				x	x	x	x	x
Ancestry		x	x	x	x	x		x				x	x	x
Place of origin		x	x	x	x	x		x				x	x	x
National origin	x			x	x		x	x	x	x	x	x	x	
Ethnic origin	x			x		x	x		x	x	x	x	x	x
Citizenship						x^2								x
Political belief				x			x	x	x	x	x	x	x	
Sex (including pregnancy)/gender	x	x^1	x	x	x	x	x		x	x	x	x	x	x
Sexual orientation	x	x		x	x	x	x	x	x	x	x	x	x	x
Gender identity				x								x		
Age	x			x	x	x	x	x	x	x	x	x	x	x
Disability	x	x^1	x	x	x	x	x	x	x	x	x	x	x	x
Social origin/condition							x					x	x	
Marital status	x	x	x	x	x	x	x	x	x	x	x	x	x	x
Family status	x	x	x	x	x	x			x	x	x	x	x	x
Dependence on alcohol														
Association									x			x	x	
Source of income			x	x	x				x	x			x	x
Pardoned conviction	x											x	x	x
Class of person										x				
Language							x						x	

1 Certain exceptions apply
2 Excluding sport

of the Ontario *Human Rights Code* also allows a recreational club to restrict or qualify access to its services or facilities on the basis of age, sex, marital status, or family status.

In sport, the most common grounds upon which claims of discrimination have been made are sex, age, disability, place of origin, and citizenship.

Sex

It has been settled law for some time that where there is no girls' team or comparable opportunity to participate, girls will be permitted to play on a boys' team, unless safety is an issue (see *Forbes* and *Comm. des droits de la personne*). The decision in *Casselman v. Ontario Soccer Association* suggests that regardless of the nature of the opportunity available, girls may choose to play in an integrated setting. In this case, two girls played on a mixed soccer team until they were banned at the quarter-finals stage of a competition. They were given the opportunity to play on an all-girls team, but the calibre of the team was not comparable. The Ontario Human Rights Tribunal found in favour of the girls and ordered that

> [the Ontario Soccer Association] be barred from enforcing, promulgating or monitoring any rule, regulation, directive, custom or usage which bars or restricts in any fashion whatsoever females from participating with males in soccer on an integrated basis.

In *Pasternak and Pasternak v. Manitoba High School Sports Association (MHSSA)*, some 17 years later, the Pasternak twins made a complaint to the Manitoba Human Rights Commission when the MHSSA would not let them play on their high school boys' ice hockey team. There did exist a girls' team at the school; however, the Pasternaks argued that this team did not play at a skill level that was appropriate for them. MHSSA argued that the high school girls' team was new and it needed the leadership and skill of the Pasternak twins to develop further. In other words, allowing the top players to play elsewhere essentially undermined the formative girls' team. The tribunal rejected these arguments, stating that the girls did not sign up to be leaders or pioneers, but to be players on a school team commensurate with their level of skill. This decision confirms that girls can play on boys' teams if they are at the same skill level. This decision is consistent with the earlier decisions in both *Blainey* and *Casselman*.

Finally, the definition of sex is broadly interpreted to include discrimination on the basis of pregnancy, as well as gender identification including transgender and transsexual identification. Sexual orientation is not included under this ground but nonetheless is a prohibited ground under both the Charter and human rights legislation throughout Canada.

BOX 6.1   IOC Statement on Sexual Harassment and Abuse

In February 2007, the Executive Board of the International Olympic Committee (IOC) adopted a *Consensus Statement on Sexual Harassment and Abuse in Sport*. The document defines the problem, identifies risk factors, and provides guidelines for prevention and resolution. The statement is one of several published by the Medical Commission of the IOC, whose mandate involves promoting the health of athletes. Existing policy frameworks within sport organizations in Canada already largely comply with the policy guidelines of the statement, but could be improved with the addition of references to *hazing* (defined by the IOC as "abusive initiation rituals that often have sexual components and in which newcomers are targeted") and *homophobia* (defined as "a form of prejudice and discrimination ranging from passive resentment to active victimization of lesbian, gay, bisexual and transgendered people"). The statement is a significant document that has the potential to advance human rights protections within the international sport community. Under Canadian law, discrimination on the basis of sex and sexual orientation is already prohibited, but this is not the case in most countries of the world.

As well, the *Consensus Statement on Sexual Harassment and Abuse in Sport* makes reference to the issue of gender. This has been a major controversy for the IOC over the years, since sex testing was first introduced in 1966 at the European Athletics Championships in response to allegations that some female competitors were actually male. Sex testing continued in the Olympics and other major international sporting events until 1999, and throughout that time was widely criticized as being intrusive and discriminatory. The targets for this testing were invariably women, who were required to undergo visual inspections as well as to provide bodily fluids for DNA testing. In May 2004, the IOC approved a policy (called the *Stockholm Consensus*) setting out the strict conditions under which individuals would be permitted to compete athletically as a sex different from their birth sex. Lacking awareness about gender transition issues, the global sport community has widely accepted this policy document as providing the best available guide for determining the eligibility of transitioned individuals to participate in sport. It is acknowledged, however, that there have been very few scientific studies of the impact of gender transition on athletic performance. It is also accepted that the *Stockholm Consensus* is discriminatory toward individuals who undergo sex reassignment. In Canada, transitioned female athletes (individuals born male who have become female through medical intervention) have recently been reinstated to eligibility in the sports of cycling and water ski/wakeboard (see Corbett, 2006).

Age

One of the traditional means of categorization in sport is by age. Many jurisdictions limit the application of human rights legislation to those who have reached the age of majority in that jurisdiction. In those jurisdictions it is thus acceptable to differentiate on the basis of age with regard to minors. Several jurisdictions also limit the upper age to which human rights legislation will apply.

The central issue in age discrimination cases is whether or not there is a reasonable justification for such discrimination. Clearly, human rights law does allow age discrimination such as when policies or rules prevent the sale of cigarettes to minors, or when schools organize physical activities by age. As is the case in providing a reasonable justification for exceptions on other prohibited grounds, once a *prima facie* case of discrimination on the basis of age has been proven by the claimant, the onus shifts to the respondent to prove a reasonable justification for the discrimination. In sport, two justifications are a concern for the physical safety of the participant.[7]

Often, although not always, age correlates with one's physiological developmental level and performance. As such, it is commonly used as an indicator of readiness and skill at a particular point in a person's life. However, when such a correlation is not accurate,[8] the justification of developmental readiness in order to discriminate on the basis of age may not be appropriate or acceptable, particularly when the appropriate level of skill to participate in a higher age bracket has been achieved.

It is important to consider that the argument for any justification must be supported by more than impressionistic evidence or anecdote; scientific expert evidence is often needed but may be difficult to obtain. For example, if a long-term practice is challenged as discriminatory on a prohibited ground, there may be some concern that removing or altering the discriminatory practice may cause untoward consequences. Simply stating one's concern over the possible consequences will not be sufficient. Some evidence that the concerns will, if fact, occur with their attendant consequences must be offered.

Disability

Disability or handicap under Canadian human rights legislation is defined very broadly (see Pentney). Nonetheless, the central question in most discrimination cases has been the "effect" the disability has as opposed to the cause of the disability. As with claims based on other prohibited grounds, once a *prima facie* case of discrimination on the prohibited ground of disability has been proven by a claimant, the onus moves to the respondent to prove a reasonable justification. The concept of "reasonable accommodation" is a fundamental element in issues of discrimination on the basis of disability. As Pentney notes at page 7A.4:

> This phrase describes a legal duty or responsibility to take positive action to accommodate the unique needs of the disabled in the workplace, and in the provision of services, facilities or dwelling places.

---

7   These two justifications are expressly set out in Saskatchewan's human rights legislation.

8   The long-term athlete development (LTAD) model is described in detail in the LTAD resource paper, *Canadian Sport for Life.*

In *Youth Bowling Council v. McLeod*, the claimant was an 11-year-old girl with cerebral palsy. She was excluded from a bowling competition because she used the assistance of a wooden ramp to deliver the bowling ball. The court found that the effect of the claimant's condition was to make bowling impossible without the use of the ramp. It found the ramp to be a reasonable accommodation under the circumstances. The court found that the council had a duty to accommodate the claimant to the point of undue hardship. In defining the threshold of undue hardship in this case the court wrote (at 458 OR):

> The point [of undue hardship] is reached ... when the proposed accommodation would impact significantly upon the way in which the other participants would be required to play or would give the accommodated person an actual advantage over others in such participation. The Code does not require that essential elements of a sport be altered for all participants in order in order to accommodate those who for whatever reason cannot perform those essential elements.

In 2006, Sport Canada published a policy paper, *Sport for Persons with a Disability*. The policy paper recognizes and embraces the move from a medical definition of disability to a social model of understanding the systemic barriers that prevent the full and active participation of persons with disabilities in sport. Among the barriers identified are financial cost (special transportation and specialized equipment, for example), environmental barriers (particularly climatic obstacles), lack of opportunities for infants and youth to learn fundamental movement skills, and the need for specialized facilities, equipment, and coaches. The policy paper calls for an action plan with specifically identified initiatives aimed at the full participation of persons with disabilities at every level of the sport hierarchy.

Citizenship and Place of Origin

Participation on national teams and Olympic teams in the international sport arena is based on citizenship, as is participation of young elite Canadian athletes in the Canada Games. Only Ontario and Nunavut explicitly *include* citizenship as a prohibited ground in their respective human rights statutes, although Ontario then exempts its application when it involves participation in athletic or recreational activity (section 16(2)). Nonetheless, citizenship has been found to be an analogous ground to place of origin within the context of the Charter. In *Sayhoun v. ACAA & CCAA*, Mr. Sayhoun attempted to draw the same connection between citizenship and place of origin using human rights legislation. Mr. Sayhoun was a full-time international student at the University of New Brunswick wishing to play varsity soccer. The Canadian College Athletic Association (CCAA) had a rule limiting the number of non-Canadian citizens on a soccer team to three (using a quota system of "one-in-six" players), which effectively precluded Mr. Sayhoun from the team (the Atlantic College Athletic Association [ACAA] incorporated the CCAA rule into its eligibility rules). Mr. Sayhoun challenged the rule under the New Brunswick *Human Rights Act* claiming discrimination on the basis of place of origin and nationality, as citizenship was not a prohibited ground under the New Brunswick Act. The claimant argued that a very broad interpretation must be given to the wording of the Act in order to give full effect to the intent of the legislation—in this case to ensure members of the university community are treated fairly with regard to opportunities to participate in the athletic program (particularly where over one-third of the student body at this particular university was made up of international students). In this case the adjudicator, although sympathetic, was of the view that such a broad interpretation amounted to a rewriting of the prohibited grounds and thus dismissed the claim.

Is There a Reasonable Justification for the Discrimination?

Human rights legislation does recognize that in certain circumstances discrimination on a prohibited ground may be necessary for reasons of public policy, decency, or safety (see the British Columbia and Saskatchewan human rights codes). Many of the human rights statutes build in a provision whereby a party may argue a reasonable justification for the discrimination (also known as a bona fide qualification, or BFQ). Where this is argued, a three-part test applies (see *British Columbia (Superintendent of Motor Vehicles)* also known as the *Grismer Estate* case). The party seeking a BFQ must demonstrate that

- the "rule" or practice was adopted for a purpose or goal that is rationally connected to the function being performed;
- the "rule" or practice was adopted in good faith, in the belief that it is necessary for the fulfillment of the purpose or goal; and
- the "rule" is reasonably necessary to accomplish its purpose or goal, in the sense that the respondent cannot accommodate persons with the characteristics of the claimant without incurring undue hardship (that is, it is the least restrictive alternative).

As noted previously, any justification must be supported by more than impressionistic evidence or anecdote; expert evidence is often needed. Thus, where a sport organization is in the position of arguing a BFQ, such arguments must be supported by substantial and bona fide evidence that such an exception is reasonable and necessary under the circumstances.

Affirmative Action Programs

Every jurisdiction in Canada makes provision for "special programs," also known as affirmative action programs, and their close ally, employment equity programs. These programs are intended to break historic or systemic patterns that have worked to disadvantage certain groups of people. In all cases, these special programs are explicitly not to be considered as a contravention of any anti-discrimination statute.

As noted by Pentney at page 4-147:

> Although the right to non-discrimination is essentially an individual right, in a country that recognizes that justice and equality of dignity involves recognition of rights which one has a member of a group, it should be no great extension of this principle that the rights of individuals who are members of a disadvantaged group might best be realized by programmes which are directed towards aiding those groups to reach the same "starting line" as the rest of the population.

In *Blainey v. Ontario Hockey Association (No. 1)*, the Ontario Women's Hockey Association (OWHA) was found to be operating a "special program" as defined in section 14(1) of the Ontario *Human Rights Code*. After reviewing the relative positions of the men's and women's hockey programs in Ontario, the tribunal accepted that the OWHA needed to exclude men from its program in order for it to survive. As noted in the decision:

> The evidence clearly establishes that as a group females in this province do not have the same opportunity to play organized competitive hockey. Female hockey must continually struggle for access to ice time. Because of these handicaps, the program offered by the OWHA does not have the same level of participation as does male hockey ... Although prepubescent girls can compete equally with prepubescent boys, to allow young boys to play on girls' teams would lead to serious difficulties for female hockey. Many parents are opposed to their daughters playing hockey, even on all-female teams. This opposition would likely intensify if males were permitted to play on female teams. Most females desire to play on all-female teams. To allow males to play female hockey would likely result in a large number of female players deciding to leave the sport.

The OWHA also had a rule preventing girls playing on boys' teams, which it maintained was a necessary part of building the girls' program. The OWHA argument was that the highly skilled players were necessary to help continue develop the girls' program. The essential argument of the respondents in *Blainey*, and in *Pasternak* as well as in other cases that have not gone to a hearing, has been that if each of the most skillful players on a girls' team was siphoned off to the boys' team, the girls' teams could never develop a level of skill beyond that point where the players left; in other words, they could never reach a level of excellence where the most skillful female players could compete. The tribunal in *Blainey* found no evidence to suggest boys' hockey needed to be protected from an influx of female players, but more pointedly found there was no evidence that any such influx of female players to boys' teams would occur as a result of striking down the rule barring the claimant from playing on the boys' team. In the result the tribunal recognized the girls' team as a "special program" under the Ontario Code but struck down the rule preventing girls playing on boys' teams as not necessary to the development of a "special program." In a second decision, *Blainey v. Ontario Hockey Association (No. 2)*, the tribunal declared that the Ontario Hockey Association must permit females to participate with males "on an integrated basis." The tribunal in *Pasternak* followed the decision in *Blainey*.

Sexual Harassment

Sexual harassment is viewed as a form of discrimination, at least in Canada. Sexual harassment is prohibited under human rights legislation. In *Janzen v. Platy Enterprises Ltd.*, the Supreme Court of Canada set out the definition of "sexual harassment" in a three-part test as follows:

- the impugned conduct is unwelcome;

- the impugned conduct is of a sexual nature; and

- the conduct detrimentally affects the work or service environment or leads to adverse job or service-related consequences for the victim of the harassment.

With regard to the first test, some conduct (such as a sexual assault) is so egregious it is inherently unwelcome. Other conduct is ambiguous and thus some external signal or message from the complainant, such as a comment or a gesture, is needed to indicate its unwelcome nature. The appropriate standard against which to measure the complainant's conduct is that of a reasonable person in the circumstances.

Not all affectionate conduct is necessarily sexual in nature. Greeting another person with a kiss to the cheek does not necessarily have sexual overtones. Thus, the second test requires that the complainant reasonably interpret the conduct as being sexual in nature; in other words, the test is a subjective one (what the complainant reasonably believes) as opposed to an objective one (what a reasonable person in like circumstances would believe).

In order for the conduct to meet the third test and have an adverse effect, it must be of a sufficiently serious nature or sufficiently repetitive. The less serious the conduct, the greater is the need to demonstrate its persistence in order to demonstrate its adverse effect.

In *Madsen v. Torry & Canadian Tenpin Federation Inc.*, the defendant Torry was a director of the Canadian Tenpin Federation (CTF). While alone in a hotel room with the complainant, Torry made an advance toward her and brushed her cheek with a kiss. The complainant withdrew and Torry made no further advances. The tribunal found Torry's act to be sexual in nature but not of a degree of persistence or repetitiveness to amount to sexual harassment.

REFERENCES

Andrews v. Law Society of British Columbia, [1989] 1 SCR 143.

Beattie v. Acadia University (1976), 72 DLR (3d) 718 (NSCA).

Berg v. University of British Columbia (1993), 18 CHRR D/310 (SCC).

Blainey v. Ontario Hockey Association (1986), 54 OR (2d) 513, 26 DLR (4th) 728 (CA); rev'g. (1985), 52 OR (2d) 225, 21 DLR (4th) 599 (HCJ).

Blainey v. Ontario Hockey Association (No. 1) (1987), 9 CHRR D/4549 (Ont. Bd. Inq.).

Blainey v. Ontario Hockey Association (No. 2) (1988), 9 CHRR D/4972 (Ont. Bd. Inq.).

British Columbia (Superintendent of Motor Vehicles) v. British Columbia (Council of Human Rights), [1999] 3 SCR 868.

Canadian Anti-Doping Policy (version 5.0) (Ottawa: Canadian Centre for Ethics in Sport, 2007).

Canadian Charter of Rights and Freedoms, part 1 of the *Constitution Act, 1982*, schedule B of the *Canada Act, 1982* (UK), 1982, c. 11.

Canadian Football League (CFL), Re and the Canadian Human Rights Commission, [1980] 2 FC 329, 109 DLR (3d) 397, 1 CHRR D/45.

Canadian Human Rights Act, RSC 1985, c. H-6.

Casey Martin v. PGA, 532 US 661 (2001).

Casselman v. Ontario Soccer Association (1993), 23 CHRR D/397.

Comm. des droits de la personne v. Fédération québécoise de hockey sur glace inc., unreported decision of the Quebec Superior Court, file no. 500-05-024964-775, December 20, 1977.

Corbett, R., *Transgendered and Transitioned Athletes in the Sport System*, brief prepared for the Gay and Lesbian International Sport Association, 2006.

Cummings v. Ontario Minor Hockey Association (1979), 26 OR (2d) 7 (CA), where the team's facilities were also considered private.

Forbes v. Yarmouth Minor Hockey Association, unreported decision of the Nova Scotia Board of Inquiry, October 27, 1978.

Gould v. Yukon Order of Pioneers (1996), 133 DLR (4th) 449 (SCC).

Hill v. Air Canada, 2003 CHTR 9, at 36.

Human Rights Act (New Brunswick), SNB 1973, c. H-11.

Human Rights Act (Ontario), RSO 1990, c. H.19.

Human Rights Code (BC), RSBC 1996, c. 210.

Human Rights Code (Manitoba), CCSM c. H175.

Janzen v. Platy Enterprises Ltd., [1989] 1 SCR 1252, at para. 20.

LTAD, Canadian Sport for Life, resource paper found at http://www.cd.gov.ab.ca/building_communities/sport_recreation/resources_links/sport_resources/pdf/LTAD_english_booklet_Oct%207.pdf

Madsen v. Torry and Canadian Tenpin Federation Inc., 2005 BCHRT 144.

McKinney v. University of Guelph, [1990] 3 SCR 229, 13 CHRR D/171.

Nagra v. Canadian Amateur Boxing Association, unreported decision of the Ontario Superior Court of Justice, January 12, 2002, file no. 99-CV-180990.

Ontario Rural Softball Association v. Bannerman (1979), 26 OR (2d) 134 (CA).

Pasternak and Pasternak v. Manitoba High School Sport Association, Inc., unreported decision of the Manitoba Human Rights Commission, September 22, 2006.

Pentney, W., *Discrimination and the Law* (Scarborough, ON: Thomson Carswell, looseleaf), at 7A-8.2.

Sahyoun v. Atlantic Colleges Athletic Association (ACAA) and Canadian Colleges Athletic Association (CCAA), unreported decision of the New Brunswick Labour and Employment Board of Inquiry, July 20, 2004.

Saskatchewan Human Rights Code, SS 1979, c. S-24.1

Sport Canada, *Sport for Persons with a Disability,* June 2006 policy paper found at http://www.pch.gc.ca/progs/sc/pol/pwad/pwad_e.pdf.

Sykes, J.B. (ed.), *The Concise Oxford Dictionary* (Oxford: Clarendon, 1976), at 294.

Wood v. Canadian Soccer Association (1984), 5 CHRR D/2024 (Can. Trib.).

Youth Bowling Council v. McLeod (1990), 75 OR (2d) 451, 74 DLR (4th) 625 (Div. Ct.).

Working Relationships

Introduction

Managers of sport organizations are on the "front lines" when it comes to working relationships. They must identify and hire appropriate staff, motivate volunteers, supervise workers located both in and out of the office, complete performance appraisals, and, on occasion, oversee the termination of employees or contractors. There is an extensive body of published material, statutes, and legal decisions covering every facet of what is known generally as "labour and employment" law. It is not important for a sport manager to know everything about this highly specialized field. However, some issues cannot be ignored when seeking to avoid the pitfalls that commonly arise in working relationships.

Our goal in this chapter is to simplify and present a few of the issues associated with the working relationship. This material is not intended to be an exhaustive survey of the law or of every employment-related issue or problem that may arise. Instead, we have selected only the practical information that a sport manager must know, and which has a legal component. We have structured the chapter into two main parts: *creating the relationship* and *terminating the relationship*. This is consistent with what a manager actually does and it reflects that part of a manager's duties that have significant legal implications. In addition, we also identify a few important issues to consider when *managing* both employees and contractors during their employment relationship.

Creating the Relationship

In any situation where new workers are being hired there are inevitably legal, technical, and personal issues to be addressed. The proposed staff member must have the skills, aptitude, and training to do the tasks or duties identified. The successful candidate will also need to have the interpersonal and communication skills to fit into the office environment and be an effective member of the team. These technical and personal issues, although important in a hiring decision, are beyond the scope of this chapter.

Instead, our focus here is on the four legal issues that must be considered each and every time a manager initiates a new working relationship. These four issues are: the proper use of screening, the option to hire an "employee" or an "independent contractor," deciding on the term or length of the relationship, and ensuring there is consideration present to support the employment contract. The section closes with some essential clauses to include in a written contract.

This chapter focuses on employees and independent contractors—but what about volunteers? Volunteers are the lifeblood of sport organizations, and sport as a segment of the non-profit sector in Canada involves more volunteers than any other segment. How are volunteers characterized in law? A volunteer is not an employee even if the work performed is similar to that done by an employee. This differentiation exists because there is no salary paid to a volunteer and the benefits and protections typically afforded to employees are not universally applicable. However, despite the clear distinction between employees and volunteers, the law is clear that there is an overriding legal obligation on the part of the employer to treat volunteers fairly. Chapter 4 addresses the issue of sport organizations as tribunals and their procedural fairness obligations.

Screening

The "screening" of employees or volunteers means different things to different people. At its most basic, screening is about trying to control the risk—which is always present to a greater or lesser degree—that an employee, volunteer, or contractor may cause harm to a person the employer is responsible for protecting and keeping safe. This is of paramount concern to sport managers, because the majority of sport organizations provide services to children and youth. Although screening is certainly applicable to employees, volunteers, and contractors, for convenience, only the term "employee" will be used throughout this section.

Essentially, screening can be defined as the employer performing, with the consent of the potential employee, a suitable degree of research to be sure the employee is personally appropriate for the job or task he or she is going to be asked to perform. There are a great many elements, or tools, that can be included in a full screening process. The actual challenge presented to the sport manager is to select and use only the most effective and efficient screening tools for each position and for each potential employee. When it comes to screening, quite often "less is more."

The first step is to begin by looking at the job itself—not the employee to be hired. Employers should first evaluate the job or task for its underlying risk potential. In this analysis, risk potential can be defined as the likelihood or chance that a person engaged to perform that particular job or task might, as a result of the way the job is designed or defined, be in a position to negatively affect a participant's safety or well-being. Remember, this evaluation is of the job or the position—regardless of the person to be hired. The higher the risk that may be associated with the position, the more complete the screening process should become for the potential employee who will fill the position.

For positions with little or no direct contact between the employee and participant, the risk potential is probably very low. There will certainly be a higher element of risk potential if the job involves direct contact with participants, especially if they are children and youth. However, risk potential is probably mitigated for any position if the employee is never left alone with youth participants and all activities to be performed are supervised by a more senior staff member. High-risk positions involve the employee having extensive direct contact with young athletes, including multiday travel to competitions, with no supervision and, perhaps, a significant degree of power or authority over the participants. This power and authority can be manifested by the employee selecting teams, granting scholarships or awards, and recommending advancement. An awareness of the increasing potential for risk between different positions within the organization is essential so that screening resources and tools can be used effectively.

The actual elements that can be used to screen the potential employee are many and varied. They include, but are not limited to, preparing an accurate *job description* with strict limits on the scope of work to be performed, and an *application form* that solicits the information and consents the employer requires to learn more about the candidate and to perform further screening steps. *Interviews* must be carefully designed and conducted and all *references* that are provided by the candidate for levels of education, health status, previous employment, and security issues (to name a few) should be followed up. Once hired, the employee needs to be *trained* properly, *supervised* or mentored while in training, and *evaluated regularly*. Effective screening is not a discrete step or a single tool—it should be considered a process that lasts for the duration of the term of employment.

It is important to understand that not every candidate for every position needs to be screened using every available screening tool or technique. Although there will be some degree of screening involved for all employees that are to be hired (for example, an interview), not every position demands a full screening. Rather, the manager needs to find a balance between the rights of the employee and the need for screening, based on the risk inherent in the position. For example, a male coach who is largely unsupervised and will be coaching young boys for extended periods away from home may be screened, in addition to all other appropriate elements, with a Police Records Check (PRC) searching for criminal convictions for sexual misconduct, assault, or child pornography. A receptionist will, in most cases, be only minimally screened through perhaps an interview and a check of his or her references. A volunteer offering to help out with the technology systems and corporate communications will certainly be screened—but with a focus on previous employment or volunteer experience, specific training taken, references, and perhaps security. This volunteer need not consent to a PRC. Our point is that there must be a rational link between a position's underlying risk potential and the degree of screening.

To carry out screening steps, it is necessary to obtain the employee's consent. This is most easily done through the application form. Such consent should cover the right of the employer to obtain the desired information, the extent of the use to be made of the information uncovered by the employer during screening, and what will happen to the information after the employer uses it for the agreed screening purposes. When obtaining consent to obtain a PRC, the employer should advise the employee how the information will be safeguarded and when and how it will be destroyed after it is used.

Obtaining consents to screen for a position sends a strong message to potential employees that an employer is serious about its obligations to provide a safe environment. A potential employee's refusal to give consent for a reasonable request relating to screening is a warning sign, and the employer might want to consider hiring another candidate, or at the very least find an alternative method to obtain the information the employer is seeking.

When screening, it is important to be both prudent and thorough. But being too aggressive with screening procedures can sometimes backfire. Not many employment positions demand medical, education, fraud, credit, or security checks. Not every employee or volunteer needs to be screened using police records. Interview questions should not venture into areas that are prohibited by human rights legislation such as age, religion, marital status, or sexual orientation. In summary, the employer should seek out what is reasonably needed to evaluate a candidate for a specific position, but go no further.

Police Records Checks (PRCs)

One component of screening that has received much attention recently is the Police Records Check, or PRC. Many people think that screening equates to searching police databases for criminal convictions and nothing more. This is far from the case—a PRC is but one of many tools used in employee and volunteer screening, and like other screening tools, it has both benefits and weaknesses. The primary benefit of a PRC is that it allows an employer to screen out those persons who have previous convictions for designated offences that render them unsuitable to be placed in positions of trust and authority over children. A PRC's limitations include the following:

- A PRC offers only a single "snapshot" of a person's status. A new PRC requires a fresh consent. A fee is required for each PRC so it is not economical to obtain a regular PRC for each employee.

- PRC results vary greatly from one police jurisdiction to the next.

- A PRC will not pick up a criminal conviction for which a pardon has been granted. As well, certain sexual offences are "red flagged" but details are not provided.

- Offenders who have not yet been caught will not have convictions registered.

Human rights legislation throughout Canada specifically prohibits discrimination on the basis of a person's "record of convictions." Accordingly, it is not advisable to take the position that only a candidate with no convictions will be hired. Discrimination based on a record of convictions may be allowed if the employer can demonstrate a *bona fide occupational requirement* (BFOR). A BFOR is a good faith and reasonable requirement that a conviction for a certain offence is fundamentally incompatible with the specific position of employment. Whether or not a BFOR exists for an employment or volunteer position will depend on the nature and circumstances of the position.

Because PRCs give rise to human rights and privacy concerns, it is advisable to design a PRC policy in advance of any screening, so as to have the benefit of a well-thought-out framework within which to operate. This will also be helpful if a disgruntled candidate who was not hired on the basis of a PRC claims the employer treated him or her in an unfair fashion. Pointing to the pre-existing policy will strengthen the employer's argument that all candidates for that position were treated equitably. The added benefit is that a PRC policy is an incentive for "self-screening"—individuals who know they will not pass a PRC will not apply, or may quietly leave the organization.

BOX 7.1   PRC Policy

A PRC policy needs to address five key issues:

1. *Who should be screened with a PRC?* This question entails deciding what positions in the organization pose the requisite degree of risk to vulnerable members. All positions that place staff or volunteers in positions of trust and authority that involve unsupervised contact with minors require this level of screening.

2. *What level of information is sought?* A standard police check provides a search result from the Canadian Police Information Centre (CPIC) database. A basic CPIC search will reveal only criminal convictions. A detailed search using a variety of local and regional databases will reveal a mountain of information: probation orders, judicial orders, charges, discharge records, civil litigation judgments, suspect data where a person was under suspicion, and information when a person was a witness or complainant. Decide what information is actually needed and do not overreach.

3. *What information generated in a PRC will constitute a BFOR?* In other words, what information, including a record of a conviction, is incompatible with the position of trust and authority being screened for? This goes to the root of what the screening is all about—trying to identify what conduct poses a risk to vulnerable participants. In each case, the employer needs to make a rational link between the conviction and the position to be filled. Each conviction will be associated with different risks (fraud, drug use, sexual offences) and so the information that may be generated in a PRC should be debated, in advance, in order that conclusions may be drawn as to what convictions are incompatible with what positions.

4. *Who reviews the PRC results?* Due to privacy concerns and the highly sensitive nature of the information disclosed through a PRC, the internal circulation needs to be very limited.

5. *How to keep this information secure and confidential?* The information will have to be treated as confidential and protected to the extent agreed on in the specific consent that allowed its collection. It is a good idea to insert in the PRC policy either a duty to return all copies of the information to the candidate who supplied them, or to destroy the data after a set period of time.

Employee or Contractor?

This section discusses the differences between two approaches to employment—the worker as an employee or the worker as an independent contractor. Properly structuring this relationship is important for both legal and financial reasons, not only to the worker but also to the employer. An employee performs general duties for regular pay, with income taxes, employment insurance premiums, and government pension plan contributions withheld by the employer and remitted to the government in regular installments. An employee may participate in the employer's benefits and private pension program. In contrast, an independent contractor provides his or her services to an employer for an agreed fee. The terms and conditions of the relationship between the independent contractor and the employer are set out in a written agreement. The employer pays the independent contractor the full amount of the contract according to the agreed payment schedule and does not withhold taxes or other payments. The independent contractor is in business for himself and is responsible for making tax and other payments to the government directly.

There are advantages and disadvantages associated with each approach to employment. Often it will be clear from the nature of work that the position is intended to be filled with one or the other. In some situations, a worker may be both at the same time—an employee for an organization fulfilling her full-time employment duties during the day but an independent contractor perhaps one night a week or on the weekends when she is hired, on her own account, by other parties to perform bookkeeping tasks or teach a single athlete certain skills. Approaches to employees and contractors differ in three main areas: personal liability; taxes, benefits, and pensions; and dismissal. Each of these will be discussed in turn.

The issue of *personal liability* is primarily a legal one. Typically, an employer is responsible (or "liable") for the wrongful acts of employees acting within the scope of their employment duties. This is known as vicarious liability and was discussed in chapter 2. The underlying rationale for this legal principle is that the employer and employee are considered associated parties in the ongoing business of the employer's organization. The employer is held responsible for damages caused to others by the employee while performing the work of the organization. Most employers have the resources (usually insurance) to cover such damages, whereas the individual employee typically does not.

The liability situation for the independent contractor is quite different. The independent contractor is his or her own employer and is thus responsible for his or her own negligent acts. Instead of having the protection of the employer's liability insurance policy, the independent contractor may be personally liable for damages flowing from his or her own actions. He or she may also be responsible for any legal costs that might be incurred to defend a lawsuit from other parties, whether or not the lawsuit is successful. The independent contractor clearly has legal obligations that the employee does not have. The prudent independent contractor may wish to purchase liability insurance.

The issue of *taxes, benefits, and pensions* is primarily a financial one. An employer is responsible for withholding certain payroll deductions on behalf of an employee, including income tax, employment insurance premiums, old age pension, and, in some provinces, health care premiums. Employers also pay workers' compensation premiums for their employees. Employers are required by provincial and territorial employment laws to pay overtime wages or to provide time off in lieu of extra time worked. They are also required to pay wages on statutory holidays when the employee does not work, and to provide the employee with a minimum number of paid holidays per year. Some employers may also contribute to additional benefits for employees, such as extended health care insurance programs and retirement savings plans.

An independent contractor, on the other hand, has none of these benefits provided. The independent contractor does not get paid for overtime or holidays. The independent contractor is not covered by workers' compensation and in many cases must pay his or her own health care insurance. The independent contractor is also responsible for funding his or her own benefits and pension programs.

Tax advantages may be a factor to consider for an independent contractor. With careful tax planning, it is possible to achieve, with the same pay, higher earnings when self-employed than when employed, particularly if the self-employed individual has an incorporated company. This tax advantage occurs for two reasons: first, many ongoing expenses can be legitimately linked to the pursuit of business and can be used to offset income before taxes, and second, except at very low personal income levels, the corporate income tax rate is lower than that for individuals. Note, however, that corporate income is taxed twice, once when it goes into the company (as revenue) and a second time when it is removed from the company and goes to the worker to spend as salary or a dividend. Determining the actual effective tax rate will usually require professional advice.

The third issue, *dismissal*, relates to job security. Under provincial law, an employer must have "cause" to dismiss an employee without notice. Lacking "cause," as defined by the law, an employer can terminate an employee at any time but only if the employer provides proper notice of termination as set out in the employment standards legislation or in the employment contract. Provincial employment standards law provides much protection for employees. The relationship between the independent contractor and the employer, on the other hand, is governed primarily by the terms of the contract the parties negotiate, and becomes, in general, a matter of contract law. Any dispute about the termination of employment is typically dealt with as a standard breach of contract.

An employee's employment is ongoing, the employee is paid regularly by the employer, taxes and other deductions are withheld, benefits are provided, the employee is paid for holidays, and a T4 income tax slip is issued at the end of the year. A contractor is a party to a fixed-term contract to perform specific tasks; receives an honorarium, stipend, or other lump sum; and his or her employer does not withhold taxes and other payments such as EI or CPP. Not clearly establishing the worker's legal status can create serious problems for both the worker and the employer, as described in the cases below:

Jannine Puri and Rae Anne Hesketh were figure skating coaches with the Campbell River Skating Club. They both taught skating to child and youth members of the club one or two hours a day, in addition to teaching many private lessons. Although the club provided the skating facility through a rental arrangement with the municipality, the coaches provided their own music and stopwatches and also coordinated their coaching schedules from home offices. Both earned the majority of their incomes by teaching private lessons that had nothing to do with the club. In fact, their working arrangement was very common in figure skating circles across Canada. Nonetheless, the court found that they were employees of the club, not independent contractors, and the club was ordered to pay remittances to employment insurance and the Canada Pension Plan for the two years covered by the period of tax assessment (see *Puri v. Minister of National Revenue*).

This decision followed closely on the court's decision in the case of *Whistler Mountain Ski Club v. Minister of National Revenue*, which found that individuals retained to teach lessons in alpine ski racing to members of a non-profit ski club were employees, not contractors, even though they were not supervised during their teaching, they provided lessons to others, and they supplied their own equipment for the job. This was the same conclusion in the case of the *Moose Jaw Kinsmen Flying Fins*, described in chapter 2, where the court found that a swim coach who had been with a small club earning a modest honorarium for some 12 years was an employee and not a contractor. In this case, the unpaid remittances, interest, penalties, and legal costs caused the club to go into bankruptcy, with the result that individual directors were personally responsible for these payments.

There are four tests, or factors, typically used to determine whether an individual is an employee or an independent contractor, but no single factor is definitive. Instead, the factors are used in combination and are applied to the circumstances of each individual case. These four tests were articulated by the Federal Court of Appeal in *Weibe Door Services Ltd. v. Minister of National Revenue*. The four tests are control, integration, financial risk, and specific tasks.

Control

The greater the degree of control and independence the worker has in the workplace, the more likely that person will be considered an independent contractor. Several factors, such as the authority to make decisions, hire assistants, define the scope of the work, set one's own schedule, or terminate the working relationship will influence the degree of control that the individual has.

Integration

This factor examines whether the tasks performed by an individual form an essential part of the organization's day-to-day business. If the tasks are "integral" to the business, it is likely that an employee relationship exists. In the cases about figure skating and alpine ski coaches described above, the courts found that both these activities were integral to the core activities of the respective skating and ski clubs.

On the other hand, if the tasks are not integral to the regular daily operation of the business, this is a strong argument that an independent contractor relationship exists. This test is also influenced by whether the worker provides the same or similar services to other employers at the same time. If the worker does provide similar services to others, this is evidence that the contractor is truly independent.

Financial Risk

This factor deals with the possibility of financial risk. It has several facets including (1) control, (2) ownership of tools or equipment, and (3) chance of profit and risk of loss. The matter of control was discussed above. The second facet is particularly important: does the worker supply his or her own equipment and supplies or is the worker entirely reliant on the employer to supply him or her with all of the equipment and supplies necessary to complete the task to be performed? A self-employed person would likely pay for his or her own equipment and supplies (and claim them as an expense against taxable income), whereas an employee would have these supplied by the employer. Similarly, a self-employed worker would likely include within the contract a certain amount for administrative expenses (including out-of-pocket expenses such as meals, travel, and accommodation). An employee, on the other hand, would be reimbursed by the employer for out-of-pocket expenses.

Self-employment creates, by necessity, the opportunity of profit and the risk of loss that is normally absent from the consideration of employees. For example, if the contractor performs competently he or she will be rewarded financially under the terms of the contract, and conversely, if the contractor's work does not satisfy the terms of the contract, contract payments may be withheld. Likewise, an independent contractor would not get paid if he or she were unable to complete the work due to illness, adverse weather conditions, or other factors beyond the contractor's control.

Specific Tasks

This final factor relates to whether the work is project-specific or ongoing. An employee relationship generally exists where an individual provides services to an employer, over a longer period of time, without any reference to a specified result or task. Contractors are typically hired for a shorter time period, to achieve a specific result, or to do a specific task.

Canadian courts have validated these four tests as proper factors to consider but often phrase the test more simply. The central inquiry should be whether or not the person hired to perform the services is performing them as a person in business on his or her own account. If the anser is "no," the person is an employee. If the answer is "yes," the person is a contractor.

The consequences of making a mistake with regard to the correct interpretation of a worker's status can be quite serious for both the purported contractor and for the employer. For instance, the employer may have to pay all outstanding employment insurance and Canada Pension Plan contributions, perhaps with a fine. The employee will have many, if not all, of the previously submitted expense deductions challenged and may have to pay additional amounts to the government as penalties and fines. Importantly, most employment standards legislation specifies that the benefits and protections under the law accrue to every employee, and thus contractors who are deemed to be employees after the fact are entitled to this protection.

Set out below are some practical suggestions to assist the employer who wants to be sure the creation of an independent contractor relationship will withstand serious scrutiny:

- Ensure that no statutory deductions are made and provide no benefits whatsoever such as health, dental, overtime, lieu days, or paid vacations, etc.

- Hours of work should not be monitored and tracked.

- Be careful how the reporting/supervisory structure is designed. True contractors receive little direct supervision as they go about performing their tasks (they are the experts—which is the reason they were hired), although they typically do report to some official of the organization that hired them.

- Avoid exclusivity clauses if at all possible. True contractors perform work for multiple parties concurrently.

- Structure the pay arrangement so there is some chance of profit (build in a commission or bonus scheme) and, conversely, some risk of a loss (perhaps tied to poor results or failure to finish a task on time).

- Have all termination rights mutual between the parties with no additional notice payable to the contractor if the contract is terminated before the term expires.

- Where possible, have the contractor work away from the employer's place of business. Alternatively, structure some "rental" of the premises used by the contractor.

- Avoid stating general "duties" the contractor should perform. Instead, list all the specific tasks the contractor is responsible to get done and the time frame in which he or she is to do them.

- Avoid job titles within the organization. Contractors should not serve as a volunteer or director of the employer and must avoid business cards indicating any association with the employing organization—all these factors have been considered evidence of an employment relationship.

- To the extent the contractor is using the employer's equipment or supplies, arrange a "rental" or some service fee paid back to the employer.

- Keep the term of the contract as short as possible to perform the required tasks. The longer the term, the more it begins to look like an employment relationship.

- There should be no reimbursement for the contractor's normal business expenses. Such expenses should be built into the fee paid to the contractor. The contractor should submit an invoice each month for payment. The payment of wages without an invoice is a clear indication of an employee relationship. GST, if applicable, should be charged to the employer.

- Contractors should arrange all their own insurance at their own expense.

- A contractor can incorporate a business and have the contractor's corporation contract with the employer for the provision of the required services.

In conclusion, all of the considerations listed above are used to determine whether an individual is actually an employee or a contractor. The focus of the inquiry is to try to determine the true nature of the relationship, regardless of what it might be called on paper or what the parties believe the relationship to be.

Length of the Contract Term

When engaging staff to perform work or provide services, a fundamental question must be addressed: Is the contract with the worker to be open-ended or is it for a fixed term? Both types of contract are possible but there are significant implications flowing from the length of term that is selected. Fixed-term contracts indicate on their face the starting date and the date the contract will terminate. In contrast, open-ended contracts indicate the start date but provide no termination date. Open-ended contracts should clearly provide a mechanism to calculate the appropriate notice period required on termination—whenever that date of termination arrives.

In the case of independent contractors, the choice is easy—contractors are always hired for a term that matches the time to perform the task they were hired to complete. Rarely is a contractor's term longer than one year. Contractors should never be hired for open-ended terms because this is considered a very strong indication that the worker is in fact an employee.

It was once typical for sport organizations to hire employees for a fixed term. Coaches were routinely hired for the four-year quadrennial planning and performance cycle based around the Olympic Games. Other staff was hired on rather short, fixed terms that were open to renewal. In all cases, the commencement date was when the contract was signed and the termination date was clearly specified. At the end of the term, the intention was that the respective obligations of the parties were at an end—unless their contracts were renewed. These annual contracts were renewed constantly.

A fixed-term contract may be renewed on mutual consent. When this occurs, the term starts over and the employee commences a new period of employment. Fixed-term contracts (most often 6 months or 12 months) generally specify the exact termination date, subject to the potential for earlier termination pursuant to the terms contained in the contract. Employers use fixed-term contracts to increase staffing flexibility. The theory is that the term of employment an employer must commit to is short but, if desired, the term can be extended by renewing it regularly. The belief is that the employer reduces his or her risk of paying significant notice when, or if, a decision is made to eventually terminate the employee. This is a tempting strategy for employers, but it is far from foolproof.

First, care must be taken not to run afoul of provincial employment standards legislation that deems a fixed-term contract to be potentially open-ended for the purpose of calculating the notice required on termination. For example, Ontario's *Employment Standards Act, 2000*, Regulation 288/01 contains the general provision that workers hired for a fixed term are not entitled to notice on termination. However, section 2(2) is clear that this rule does not apply in many situations—if the work is completed sooner than the fixed term; if the term is greater than 12 months or the work is not completed more than 12 months after the term commences; or if employment continues for more than 3 months after the expiry of the term or the completion of the task.

The legislative presumption in Ontario, and in other provinces, is that lengthy ongoing work pursuant to a purportedly fixed-term contract is, in fact, open-ended employment. Notice periods on termination (or payment instead of notice) must be calculated accordingly.

The case of *Ceccol v. Ontario Gymnastic Federation* is instructive with regard to how fixed-term contracts do not always limit notice periods, as intended. Ms. Ceccol worked for the federation as the administration director. Starting in 1986, she annually signed a standard form of employment contract for a one-year term. Among other things, this contract specified that the Ontario *Employment Standards Act* would apply with regard to the termination of her employment. This would provide a minimum period of notice. At the expiry of one annual term, Ms. Ceccol was advised that her contract would not be renewed. Because the federation viewed her as a "contract worker," employed for a fixed term, it gave her no formal advance notice of termination. Ms. Ceccol sued for wrongful dismissal and sought reasonable notice of termination.

The judge hearing the case decided that notwithstanding the one-year fixed-term contract and the specific reference to the *Employment Standards Act*, reasonable notice of termination was required. Ms. Ceccol's notice was initially calculated at 16 months but was reduced to 12 months due to her failure to mitigate her damages and seek new work. The court found that the federation's behaviour toward Ms. Ceccol over 16 years, and the reasonable expectations that such behaviour created, overrode the actual words in the contract it signed with her. Ms. Ceccol was referred to by management as a "full-time" employee. Her performance reviews referred to her as a "full-time" employee. She was offered the option of joining the full-time employees' group pension plan. The federation invested in multiyear education and training programs for her and she was given significant responsibilities, the scope of which extended far beyond a one-year-term contract.

Most importantly, the court found that the federation could have easily drawn Ms. Ceccol's attention to the termination clause on each annual renewal if it was intended to apply to her. This was not done. Accordingly, as a result of the federation's conduct, Ms. Ceccol formed the reasonable opinion that she was a full-time permanent employee and that her fixed-term contract, signed annually when it came up for renewal, was for the federation's administrative convenience only.

If employers wish to use renewable, fixed-term contracts to enable them to limit the provision of notice payable on termination, it is possible to do so; but, a much more explicit agreement between the parties is required to rebut the legal presumption that reasonable notice must be provided to terminated employees. The additional risk facing employers with employees subject to fixed-term contracts is the danger that without a clearly drafted "escape clause" in the contract, on any termination during the fixed term, the unexpired portion of the balance of the term may have to be paid out to the employee.

On balance, it is generally preferable to enter into well-drafted open-ended contracts for most positions to be filled by employees. Exceptions to this suggested rule include very short-term positions (for a few weeks or months) and relationships with employees whose employment with the employer will not realistically be renewed more than once, if at all.

Consideration

The existence of consideration to support a contract is absolutely critical. Unfortunately, this factor is often ignored in employment contracts. To create a valid and legally enforceable contract there must be mutual promises made supported by some benefit or "consideration" flowing between the parties. At law, contracts are valid only if all parties to the bargain mutually promise to perform some act or to undertake to perform some obligation for the other's benefit. In an employment situation, the classic "bargain" consists of an employee's promise to accept the position and do the work expected in return for the employer's promise to pay the wages and provide the benefits that have been agreed to.

The tricky part, and the part that consistently causes problems, is the legal rule that *consideration must be present*. This means that it must be present and flow between the parties at the time the contract is formed—not afterward. Unilateral or mutual promises that are made after the essential bargain has been struck are "past consideration" and will not support a valid contract. In other words, if an individual gives up something without receiving anything in return (no matter how minimal), there is no consideration present and the contract may be held invalid.

How is this relevant? Courts have held that a contract of employment signed when an individual is already employed, and at work, lacks consideration. In *Francis v. Canadian Imperial Bank of Commerce*, an offer of employment was made and was accepted, conditional only upon the receipt of a letter of reference. The reference was duly provided and the employee began work. On his first day on the job the employee was presented with various documents to sign, one of which was an employment contract. The employee signed the contract. This contract contained a termination clause that specified that the employee could be dismissed, without cause, on three months notice. After eight years of employment, the employee was dismissed and given three months notice. He subsequently commenced an action for wrongful dismissal. The court concluded that the employment contract he signed, which specified a maximum of three months notice, was unenforceable. It held that the terms of his employment were those terms contained in the original letter offering employment to the employee, which the employee had accepted. Because the employee had started work on the strength of the terms contained in the letter, and that letter made no mention of notice on termination or an obligation to sign an employment contract, the contract containing the three-month notice period was not supported by consideration and was invalid. Significantly longer notice had to be given to this employee. This same reasoning was upheld by the Ontario Court of Appeal in the 2004 case of *Hobbs v. TDI Canada Ltd.*

In summary, the obvious dangers for employers relating to a lack of consideration are (1) having the employment contract signed after the employment relationship has been created (whether verbally or by way of a letter containing an offer that is accepted) and the employee has started work, (2) during the employment relationship, attempting to amend a pre-existing employment contract, (3) during the employment relationship, whether or not there is a pre-existing contract, insisting that an employee sign a new contract with terms different from those governing the existing relationship, and (4) at the end of the relationship, on termination of employment, if a release is signed by an employee but the employee received no payment or benefit in excess of the required statutory minimum entitlements. In all these situations, even if the employee signs the contract or the release, the employee may subsequently claim that the contract or release is invalid for lack of consideration.

How can an employer overcome a lack of consideration? Although some courts have held that a lengthy continuation of employment following a unilateral amendment to a contract, or the execution of a contract after work has commenced, can constitute adequate consideration for the changes to the employment relationship, prudent employers should be wary (see *Watson v. Moore Corp.*). The employer should ensure that consideration is present to support any contract or release signed or any amendment to the current employment relationship.

It is certainly possible to generate fresh consideration to support a contract amendment during the employment term. For example, a "benefit" is received when the employee is granted a promotion, or is given an increase in responsibilities, a bonus, a stock option or an increase in pay. The employer needs to directly link this "benefit" to the new "promise" or obligation the employer intends the employee to be bound by. The new or additional benefit granted and the fresh obligation assumed must be offered and accepted together. In this fashion, an additional payment or benefit given to the employee, however small, can create the new consideration to save the contract, release, or a contract amendment from attack at a later date.

Unique Contract Terms for Employees

Due to the typically unequal bargaining position of the parties, contracts of employment are carefully scrutinized by the courts more often than other commercial arrangements. Because the employer is often in the more powerful negotiating position, the employer needs to act reasonably and fairly at all times. Ambiguous terms and conditions in an employee's contract will generally be interpreted against the employer. We deal with general contract formation and typical contract terms in chapter 9, but the following issues are unique to employment relationships. These issues must be addressed in every employment contract:

- Nothing in the contract must infringe applicable provincial employment standards legislation. This includes provisions governing termination notice, overtime pay, hours of work, or entitlement to vacations. If terms in the contract, either express or implied, infringe provincial employment standards legislation, they will be struck down. This is because the parties by their private agreement cannot mutually agree to avoid the minimum standards set out in the law.

- It is not necessary for the parties to express in precise detail exactly what an employee will be doing day by day. This is often unknown. Far better to describe, in general terms, the types of work to be performed and responsibilities assumed. If required, a schedule can be attached that lists the general duties that the employee will be expected to perform. Although there is no need to include a long, detailed list of the precise duties and responsibilities, it is critical to insert a clause that empowers the employer to make reasonable changes to the employee's duties and responsibilities from time to time during the ongoing term of the contract. The employer needs the flexibility to reasonably amend the scope of work expected from an employee as the business changes over time. As we will see later in this chapter when we discuss constructive dismissal, this flexibility is essential for the employer, but it must be exercised with care.

- The parties' respective rights on the termination of the relationship must be specified in detail. Notice period calculations in the event of termination without "cause" must be inserted. If there are no provisions regarding termination inserted in a contract, the presumption in favour of providing "reasonable notice" to an employee on termination will prevail. The concept of "reasonable notice" will be discussed later in this chapter.

- It is typical to include some reference to reporting and evaluation. Specify who the employee reports to and detail who reviews the employee, how often this takes place, and against which criteria the job performance will be evaluated.

- Salary and benefits payable to the employee need to be crystal clear and easily calculated. The salary an employee receives is often the most critical factor in accepting a job. Most employees assume that their salaries will go up over time. Must the employee's salary be increased if there is low inflation and only mediocre performance evaluations? If an employee's pay will be reviewed after the contract has commenced, all parties should specify in advance the basis on which such an adjustment can take place.

- Clarity is especially important when some element of commission or incentive pay is being offered in addition to a base salary. The four most common problems with calculating commissions, royalties, or incentive pay are the following: (1) the contract does not accurately specify what revenue streams attract the additional payment to the employee (only deals the employee closed herself, excluding certain product lines; on revenues over a certain sum, subject to a cap); (2) not clearly listing which deductions are allowed to be offset from "gross" revenue to get to a "net" figure on which the calculations are most often based (typical deductions from "gross" are a list of regular expenses, taxes, and the value of returns); (3) not specifying when the obligation to pay commission or royalties is at an end (is this when the employment relationship ends or will the obligation to pay sums of money to the employee survive the termination of the employment relationship?); and (4) how will "value in kind" or "contra" be valued by the employer for purposes of additional compensation to the employee (should the "widget" being supplied be valued on a cost-to-manufacture price, notional retail price, a wholesale price, or some other method of valuation, or should it be excluded from the calculation of commission or incentive pay totally?).

Unique Contract Terms for Contractors

As we saw above, whether a contractor is actually an independent contractor in business for himself or herself depends on many factors. It is important not to include in a contract with an independent contractor any terms and conditions that undercut the intended employment status. Common mistakes are including clauses that provide employee benefits, contemplate termination for "just cause," reference salary and tax deductions, and outline reporting or supervision functions. It is important to avoid any language in the contract that comes across as "employee" language.

The following terms should be included, at a minimum, in every contractor's employment contract :

- Both parties need to confirm in the contract that the relationship is not that of employer and employee. Despite the fact that the wording inserted in the contract is not determinative of a worker's status, such a clause will provide evidence that at the commencement of the relationship the parties intended to avoid an employee–employer relationship.

- Instead of the general duties or the list of responsibilities typically set out in an employee's contract, the independent contractor will need to have inserted in the contract the very specific tasks he or she is responsible for completing and the time within which to finish the work. Independent contractors are hired to perform certain specific tasks over a set time because of their expertise in a particular area. Always insert in the contract with an independent contractor a discrete list of tasks to perform, the time allowed in which to complete the set tasks, and the fee to be paid when the tasks are completed.

- The right to terminate a contractor's contract before the tasks are completed will largely be a function of how the parties negotiated the contract and what early termination provisions were inserted. No unique benefits or protections typically afforded employees should be inserted. It is usual to provide that the contract may be terminated if the contractor refuses or fails to perform the tasks he or she agreed to perform in a timely fashion or if the quality of the work is not acceptable. There is often inserted a relatively short period of time to allow the contractor to cure any defaults or deficiencies brought to his or her attention. Once this "cure" period has expired, with the defaults or deficiencies remaining outstanding, the employer may then terminate the contract. Because in the situation described above the contract will end with not all the contemplated work completed or tasks performed, it is prudent to insert in the contract what happens after an early termination and specify each party's rights and obligations on termination.

- It is advisable to confirm in the contract that the independent contractor is free to work for others during the term of the contract. Even if the contractor will in all likelihood only perform work for the one employer during the term of the contract, establishing that the contractor has the flexibility to seek other work with other employers will be a strong indicator that this worker is a contractor and not an employee.

Terminating the Relationship

Bringing a working relationship to a close can be a difficult and painful experience for all involved. The employment relationship is often fundamental to an individual's sense of personal worth. Managers who have the responsibility to terminate an employment relationship need to be sensitive to the human and social implications of losing a job. They also need to be knowledgeable about the employer's legal obligations.

There are three ways that the employment of an employee can be brought intentionally to an end: *resignation, termination for "just cause,"* and *termination without cause.* Because the consequences of a "constructive dismissal" are rarely intended, we will discuss this separately. For independent contractors, their rights on termination depend on what has been bargained for in the contract. We will review each method of termination in turn.

Resignation of an Employee

An employee may decide to end the employment relationship at any time. In some cases, the contract of employment requires a period of notice be provided by an employee in advance of quitting or resigning from a job. This is rarely longer than two weeks. In practice, this requirement is not often enforced by the employer if it is not respected by the employee. If the employee's resignation is tendered freely, without the existence of any threats or pressure on the part of the employer, there is no further obligation on the part of the employer beyond the regular statutory payments owing, such as accrued vacation pay or overtime. No notice or severance needs to be paid on a resignation. Note that an employee's resignation letter or notice of resignation must be formally accepted by the employer before it can be effective. Employers should accept all tendered resignations in writing. The employee may withdraw an offer to resign at any time before it is formally accepted, so employers are encouraged to accept quickly any offers of resignation tendered by employees they no longer wish to employ.

Termination of an Employee for Just Cause

If an employee engages in conduct that represents a fundamental breach of the employment relationship, or in conduct that is incompatible with the duties the employee must perform in fulfilling the employment relationship, the employer may claim that the employee's conduct represents "just cause" for termination. If there is just cause the employer can terminate the employment relationship without providing any notice of the termination. This is an important exception to the usual situation where the employer must provide the terminated employee with reasonable notice of termination, or pay in lieu of such notice.

When an employee seriously misbehaves, the employer is faced with the issue of determining what conduct on the part of the employee is sufficiently egregious so that just cause can be alleged and, if need be, proven. It is often very hard for the employer to accept (in the heat of the moment) that the conduct of an employee is not sufficiently *bad* to justify an immediate termination for cause. In short, every employer is forced to evaluate and analyze whether or not the misconduct on the part of an employee constitutes just cause. The answer in every situation is: "It all depends." It depends largely on the factors set out in more detail below.

Progressive Discipline

Most, although not all, employee misconduct is ongoing in nature. It is quite rare to see a single, isolated incident of misconduct reach the level of just cause. It is, therefore, much easier to justify a dismissal for cause in the case of ongoing misconduct, if there is a complete record specifying in detail the previous transgressions of the employee. The record will show that the discipline imposed on the employee has also been progressive and that the ongoing misconduct eventually led to the termination for cause. Progressive discipline should, at a minimum, encompass the following:

- The conduct complained of must be clearly and unambiguously drawn to the attention of the employee. Policies or rules prohibiting the conduct must be drawn to the employee's attention and explained.

- A written note should be placed in the employee's employment file specifying the misconduct, confirming that the employee was spoken to about the problem, and outlining the discipline or sanction imposed. The discipline or sanction can be increased in severity with each occurrence.

- When the employee's conduct reaches a critical stage, the employee must be told in clear terms that if the inappropriate conduct continues, the employer will consider such conduct "cause" for dismissal and the employee will be dismissed immediately, with no notice.

It is very important to stress that progressive discipline is not required in every situation. There are examples of an employee's misconduct happening only a single time, which will be enough to justify a termination for cause, particularly where this conduct adversely affects other employees. This is discussed below. Each situation where misconduct occurs must be analyzed and evaluated on its own merits—no two situations are the same.

If the employee's conduct in a particular instance is not enough to justify termination for cause, or if a decision is made not to terminate the employee even in the face of conduct that may have been cause for dismissal, it is still essential to document the incident in detail. Ignoring or doing nothing about employee misconduct is never recommended. This can lead to an argument being made, perhaps at a later wrongful dismissal trial, that the employer has condoned similar behaviour in the past. The employee will inevitably claim that he or she did not know that the conduct that led to the termination was, in fact, unacceptable.

Near Cause

This concept once served to operate as a somewhat flexible middle ground between the extremes of a finding of cause (with no notice required) and the requirement to give reasonable notice (which can be quite lengthy) when there was no cause for the dismissal. The concept of near cause arose as a result of the difficulties of accurately categorizing the conduct of employees into tight compartments with greatly different results. The courts in Canada have now rejected the concept of near cause. On the question of the proper notice period, the Supreme Court of Canada stated in *Dowling v. Halifax (City)*: "We do not accept any argument relating to near cause." In the result, employers must be able to make out a case for cause or be prepared to provide the usual measure of reasonable notice to terminated employees. Getting close to cause is just not good enough.

Conduct

Have the rules setting out the standards of conduct and behaviour that the employer expects the employee to follow been made perfectly clear? The employer cannot expect employees to follow a certain standard of conduct if behaviour that is prohibited is never articulated. Often a company has policies and rules governing conduct in place but they are never published or circulated. Worse, the policies may be well known but are never enforced. If there is a zero-tolerance policy for harassment, has this been explained to the employees? Have the implications of a failure to comply with a code of conduct been outlined? Employers should educate and inform their employees about conduct that is unacceptable. All rules and policies should be made clear and should be enforced consistently. If this is done, the employee will be unable to claim that the conduct that is complained of is acceptable.

Potential Claims by Other Employees

Employers should always consider the implications of an employee's misconduct on the other employees. Specifically, they should question whether the conduct of a misbehaving employee raises the possibility that other staff will launch a human rights complaint or a civil action against the employer. This is possible in sexual harassment situations and is a major reason that employers are starting to treat these complaints so seriously. Misconduct that amounts to cause in the relationship between the employer and the employee (insubordination, theft, absenteeism) may also directly affect other employees. These employees also have legal rights, and their rights must be respected by the employer.

Two Ontario Court of Appeal decisions (*Gonsalves* and *Bannister*) confirm that in the face of harassment caused by employees in positions of authority, and with supervisory functions, the employer was justified in terminating the employees for cause. The protection of the remaining employees and maintaining a workplace free from harassment was a central theme in both decisions. However, the potential liability of the employer from other employees' claims should never serve to elevate an employee's misconduct to the threshold of cause if it were not otherwise justified.

Length of Service

As a general rule, the longer the employee has been on the job, the tougher it will be for the employer to show that the conduct complained of amounts to cause. There are two reasons for this. First, the courts tend to recognize that the employer owes a higher duty to be scrupulously fair to long-service employees. When these employees misbehave, there should always be proper progressive discipline, clear indications of what conduct is allowed and what is prohibited, and express warnings that further misconduct will result in termination for cause. If the misconduct is a single occurrence, it should be very obvious that the behaviour amounts to cause or the employer should not allege it. Second, the courts tend to view the conduct of more senior employees in the context of the person's behaviour throughout the entire length of service. A single incident by an employee with an otherwise unblemished record will probably not be sufficient to justify termination for cause.

Conduct That Is Cause for Termination

Some contracts of employment list examples of misconduct that will be deemed to be cause, thereby justifying dismissal without notice. This is a potentially dangerous practice. Care must be taken to ensure that the list of misconduct specified in the contract is not exhaustive. If it is, the employee may try to show that the acts complained of were not expressly prohibited and, accordingly, are not acts for which the employer can terminate without reasonable notice. If a descriptive list of misconduct amounting to cause is included in the contract, the prefatory words "including, but not limited to" should always be included.

In most situations, single instances of significant employee fraud, theft, harassment, and dishonesty will be considered cause and will justify termination without notice. There is a growing trend in the workplace for zero-tolerance policies on sexual harassment, especially if the conduct is by a person in a position of authority over the victim. However, employers are advised to be very prudent when alleging cause. The fact that an employee "screwed up" or did not perform his or her job well is rarely, if ever, enough. In situations where the misconduct is ongoing, the most common example of behaviour that justifies termination for cause is consistent insubordination and a consistent failure to follow directions and/or company policy.

It is important to note that instances of employee misconduct amounting to cause that took place during the period of employment and that were discovered only after the termination of the employee can be relied on at a trial to mount a defence in a wrongful dismissal action. The determination of whether there is sufficient improper conduct to immediately terminate for cause is one of the most difficult decisions in employment law. This is especially true for long-term staff with an otherwise good employment record. In light of the Supreme Court of Canada decision in *Wallace v. United Grain Growers Limited*, a case that addresses the employer's duty to act in good faith during the termination process, there is now a significant risk that employers who make allegations of cause that are malicious, improper, or that cannot be substantiated may face, as a penalty, the imposition of a much longer notice period. Thus, the cost of getting the decision to terminate for cause wrong can be high. Accordingly, any decision to allege cause must be a rational decision, made only after all the facts, relevant circumstances, and risks to the employer are carefully assessed.

Termination of an Employee Without Cause

For all contracts of indefinite employment, the employer may terminate an employee at any time provided the employer provides appropriate notice of the termination of employment to the employee. There is a legal presumption that employees will be provided with reasonable notice of their termination from employment. This presumption in favour of the employee is likely to be rebutted only by the clear and unambiguous words contained in an employment contract. Accordingly, many contracts of employment try to rebut the presumption of reasonable notice by expressly specifying the precise notice that is required to be given on termination (inevitably lower than reasonable notice) and the method of calculating this mutually agreed notice period. This type of notice calculation should be inserted in every open-ended employment contract.

The notice of termination may actually be given to the employee in advance or there may be a "payment in lieu of notice." Notice actually provided to an employee in advance, perhaps many months ahead of the termination date, is called "working notice." The employee knows on receiving the notice of termination that the actual termination will be effective at some fixed date in the future. The employee continues to work for the employer during this notice period, all the while looking for new employment. Alternatively, no advance notice need be given to the employee of the termination of employment. In this case, the employee is notified of the termination, to take effect immediately, and a sum of money representing the salary for the notice period, plus certain benefits but less various deductions, is paid to the employee in a lump sum once the termination takes effect. This is known as "pay in lieu of notice." It is usually a business decision whether an employer wishes to have a terminated employee remain in the workplace for the length of the notice period because this period may be lengthy and the employee may be unproductive, disruptive, or worse during this time. The contract of employment should allow for both options on termination and expressly state that the specified notice of termination may be given or "pay in lieu thereof."

What notice of termination should be provided? What is fair? What is reasonable? If the employer and employee are negotiating this clause in the employment contract, both parties can propose what notice of termination seems fair and reasonable to them. In this scenario, agreement must be reached or the employee will not sign the contract and commence work. This is an area where strong negotiation skills and motivation on the part of the employee can have a significant payback many years later. In every case, the notice mutually agreed to be provided on termination must be greater than the statutory minimums imposed in the jurisdiction governing the employment relationship. If the notice specified in the contract is less than the statutory minimum, that provision in the contract will not be valid. It is, of course, far more challenging to mutually agree on the length of reasonable notice in the face of a termination decision when the contract is silent on this issue. In this situation, the employer must calculate and propose a reasonable notice period in the face of an employee who is not happy at being terminated and who will be seeking the longest notice period (and greatest compensation) possible.

In determining the reasonable notice to be provided on termination in any given case, it is common to consider the following factors: the employee's age, education, position held, level of responsibility, years of service, salary, and likelihood of finding

---

BOX 7.2 Severance or Notice?

These terms are often used interchangeably but their technical meaning is quite different. "Notice" is the advance warning that must be given to every employee with an indefinite term of employment that his or her employment will terminate. If the duration of the notice is not specified in the contract it must be reasonable. Instead of receiving the notice, a monetary payment can be provided "in lieu." "Severance," on the other hand, is payable only in limited situations typically tied to major employment layoffs and the sudden discontinuance of a significant part of a large business. Pursuant to applicable employment standards legislation, which varies from province to province, severance pay is typically required only if (1) employment has been continuous for a number of years, (2) there have been significant and recent staff reductions or downsizing, and (3) the employer has a relatively large payroll. Importantly, severance, if it is applicable, is usually payable in addition to any other payment required to be made to the employee, including notice, as a result of the termination of employment.

alternative employment. Canadian courts have also considered such factors as the promise of job security for many years when hiring the now terminated employee, or the employer providing the employee with an inducement to leave previous secure employment to take the job with the employer. Both of these final two factors tend to increase otherwise applicable notice periods. It is a very good idea to retain experienced legal assistance to calculate any offer of reasonable notice in a contested termination battle. Experienced counsel will quickly and accurately be able to access the relevant factors applicable in the situation and they will be aware of what courts have granted similar employees—if the alleged wrongful dismissal claim ends up in a trial. What the employee might eventually win at trial, and the time and cost of conducting a trial, does inform the strategic calculation of what might be reasonable notice and is the context within which many offers are made.

In all termination decisions, the employer must act fairly and demonstrate good faith toward the departing employee. It is now the law in Canada that the manner of dismissal, in essence how the employer behaved, can significantly increase the notice required to be paid to the departing employee. The Supreme Court of Canada in *Wallace v. United Grain Growers Limited* held that bad faith conduct on the part of the employer in connection with termination may be compensated for by increasing the otherwise reasonable notice period. In *Wallace*, the 59-year-old employee was a top salesman who had been with the employer for over 14 years but he was discharged suddenly, without explanation. In addition, he had been promised that he could remain in his job until retirement. When Wallace sued the employer for wrongful dismissal the employer claimed Wallace had been fired for cause because he was insubordinate and had failed to perform his job adequately—both claims had no merit and were abandoned at the initial trial. Wallace was devastated by the employer's conduct and was unable to locate new employment.

The court could not have been clearer when it stated: "employers ought to be candid, reasonable, forthright with their employees and should refrain from engaging in conduct that is unfair or is in bad faith by being, for example, untruthful, misleading or unduly insensitive." In short, playing "hard ball" with an employee on termination is not a good idea. Tactics such as alleging the existence of cause when it is not warranted, refusing a reference letter, or being insensitive regarding the timing of the dismissal or the manner of providing notification to the employee will all potentially serve to increase the notice period.

Constructive Dismissal

Any unilateral action on the part of the employer, if it represents a fundamental breach of a major term of the employment relationship, may allow an employee to claim that a "constructive dismissal" has occurred. The Supreme Court of Canada in *Farber v. Royal Trust Corporation* stated as follows:

> Where an employer decides unilaterally to make substantial changes to the essential terms of an employee's contract of employment and the employee does not agree to the changes and leaves his or her job, the employee has not resigned, but has been dismissed. Since the employer has not formally dismissed the employee this is referred to as "constructive dismissal." By unilaterally seeking to make substantial changes to the essential terms of the employment contract, the employer is ceasing to meet its obligation and is therefore terminating the contract.

It is an implied term in all employment contracts that substantial changes to the duties and status of the employee cannot be made unilaterally by the employer. However, an employer can make amendments to the employment relationship if such changes are contemplated by the employment contract as a component of the employer's ongoing discretion as a manager. The extent of the employer's discretion to amend the contract of employment will depend, in large measure, on the nature of the agreement between the parties and what the employment contract allows with regard to changing duties and responsibilities. The employer has the right to reasonably restructure its organization from time to time, and not every change in position will constitute constructive dismissal. The question is whether the terms and conditions of employment newly imposed by the employer can no longer be said to be the ones under which the employee initially agreed to work. The following are examples of the types of changes that have traditionally led to a finding that constructive dismissal has occurred.

Demanding an employee's resignation has generally been considered an act of constructive dismissal. The onus of proving that a resignation is voluntary lies with the employer. The court will be seeking to discover whether the "forced" resignation resulted from some overt pressure by the employer.

A significant or an unjustified demotion can constitute constructive dismissal. In the case of *Canadian Bechtel Ltd. v. Mollenkopf* the court stated: "[a]n employer must have some latitude to make changes in the disposition of ... forces as ... business needs change. That an employee does not like a proposed new assignment does not turn the proposal into a constructive dismissal." Most demotions, certainly those with a change of salary, prestige, and responsibilities, will be considered constructive dismissal.

A significant reduction in pay almost always constitutes constructive dismissal. However, if the salary reduction is not significant, is partly or fully offset by other increases or benefits, and if the change was the result of the company's legitimate business requirements, it may not be constructive dismissal. It is important to note that even with no change in salary, a change in benefits that results in a significant amendment to the employee's overall remuneration can also result in a constructive dismissal. Any change in the employment terms that reduces the employee's ability to earn income can constitute constructive dismissal.

A change in corporate reporting procedures, by itself, may not constitute constructive dismissal. The issue will be how fundamental the employee's reporting structure is to the employee's overall employment and whether the change in reporting structure is, in fact, a form of demotion. Many employees experience the problem of having to report to a former subordinate. However, the fact that a previous

---

BOX 7.3 Termination Interviews

The termination interview poses practical, legal, and emotional challenges. Here are some tips:

- The employer should provide the employee with a short termination letter. It should unequivocally confirm the effective date of termination, briefly state the reason for the dismissal, and propose a settlement offer. It should confirm that "cause" is not alleged, if this is the case.

- The employee's direct manager should conduct the interview. The location should be private and discreet. It is advisable to have a second person present during the interview as a witness.

- The manager should not attempt to justify the termination decision—the goal of the interview is simply to communicate the decision that was made to the employee. The manager should review the termination letter with the employee but there is no need to negotiate the offer or debate its terms.

- The employer should select the time and date of the termination interview with care. Major holidays or a day with known personal importance to the employee should be avoided. The employer should select a time of day that will be the least conspicuous so that when the employee returns company property or removes personal belongings from an office the other staff will not be aware of the situation.

- The employee should be allowed a reasonable amount of time to reflect on the termination letter and should be encouraged to obtain legal advice before accepting the settlement offer or signing a release.

Every possible effort should be made to treat the employee with sensitivity and discretion. In no event should the employee be embarrassed or humiliated. A truthful reference letter should be provided in all terminations without cause. The manager can quickly inform the remaining staff of the termination decision and can explain the implications of the termination, if any, on the remaining employees.

subordinate has been appointed to supervise an employee does not give rise, by it-self, to constructive dismissal. Usually, it is rare that only the reporting functions have changed. If, as a result of the restructuring, the employee's roles and respon-sibilities have also been altered, this may affect the eventual decision of whether constructive dismissal has occurred.

Whether a geographical transfer amounts to constructive dismissal depends on the employment relationship in existence and the employee's working conditions. If it is clear that the organization frequently transfers it employees, and the employee is aware of this, the employee may be under an obligation to accept the transfer. As a general rule, the employer has the right to transfer its employees. At issue will be the reasonable expectation of the employee that he or she may be requested to transfer to a new location in the course of employment.

In general, to establish constructive dismissal, the conduct of the employer must be so significant as to amount to a repudiation of the employment relationship. If an employee is harassed, insulted, or treated in a manner that violates human rights legislation, the employee can claim constructive dismissal.

The employer should always include a term in the employment contract specify-ing that it has the authority to change the employee's salary, position, responsibilities, and duties from time to time as the employer sees fit. The employer will then be in a position to argue that it retained the authority and discretion to make reasonable changes to the employment relationship.

As well, the employer can always make a change to the employment contract, whether fundamental or not, by providing the employee with reasonable notice of the proposed change. Even if the change is fundamental—that is, it goes to the root of the employment relationship—the employee can be given reasonable notice of that change. It will then be up to the employee to consider the change during the notice period that has been provided and either accept the change or seek another position of employment during the notice period.

Termination of a Contractor

Contractors are treated very differently than employees with regard to terminating a contract of employment. The biggest difference is that most of the common law and statutory protection designed to protect employees on a termination of their employment is not applicable to contractors. Because most contractors are hired on a fixed-term basis, the employment will end when the term expires—which is often when the negotiated tasks are completed. No advance notice of termination is required because the contract contemplated such a termination when it was ex-ecuted. However, the situation changes when an employer intends to terminate a contract before the conclusion of its stated term. As will be seen below, the rights and responsibilities of the employer and contractor on termination are largely driven by the contract they negotiated. It is far better to have considered, negotiated, and agreed on contentious issues in advance—when a degree of goodwill was present in the relationship.

The starting point for any analysis of a proposed mid-term termination of a contractor is always the contract pursuant to which the contractor was engaged. Does it allow for early termination of the contract if certain "events of default" are committed? Are these events clearly described and do they relate to the quality of the work performed as well as the timing of deliveries? Can the contract be unilaterally terminated for any reason at all on a certain period of notice being given? Is there a requirement to provide notice of a "default" and to give the contractor some time to "cure" the default? If early termination is possible, will the contractor be paid for all work done up to the date of termination? What work product will be transferred and assigned to the employer, and what happens to the project that is half completed? What is possible regarding an early termination, and the intermediate steps that need to be taken to reach the desired result, should be clearly defined in the contract. If the contract is silent on these issues, the employer should make every effort to treat the contractor fairly. The challenge will be to negotiate in good faith an end to the relationship, within the framework of the existing contract, when one party to it is not satisfied with the other party's performance.

Managing Employees

Once the employment relationship has been created and the employee begins to work, relatively few purely legal issues arise in the course of employment. There are two critical exceptions: adherence to employment standards legislation and an awareness of changes in employee duties that may be construed as constructive dismissal.

First, managers must realize that all the employee benefits and protections contained in provincial employment standards legislation must be respected. It is not possible for the employer and the employee to agree to ignore or to expressly "contract out" of these provincial laws. The provisions in provincial laws that typically cause problems for sport managers during the term of employment include annual vacations, overtime pay, and weekly hours of work. These problems arise from the inherent nature of employment in a sport organization—the seasonal training and competition schedule, the periodic major games in far-flung locations, sporadic bursts of travel, and long hours on weekends with volunteers at meetings and conferences.

A strategy that managers often employ to compensate employees for all this excess work is the use of "lieu days" to compensate staff for the inevitable extra days or extra hours worked. Compensating with lieu days is acceptable; but the devil is in the details—what is considered extra time; how much time is granted in lieu; when these lieu days must be used; how to carry the lieu days (all or only some) and vacations forward into a new year. These issues demand a coherent policy, consistent enforcement, and clear communication with staff. The point is this—managers must always recall that the underlying minimum legal employment standards must be respected. However, with imagination and flexibility, managers have some latitude to design practical solutions to the problem of extra work while staying at all times inside the parameters imposed by the law.

Second, any intended revision or amendment to an employee's duties, pay, responsibilities, or location of work during the employment term must be critically evaluated against a possible claim that the employee has been "constructively dismissed," a situation discussed above. At a minimum, be sensitive when any changes to the status quo are contemplated. The employment contract should give the employer the authority to adjust an employee's duties and responsibilities during its term. Where possible, the employer should seek mutual agreement for any minor adjustments to the employment relationship or provide "reasonable notice" to the employee of more significant changes.

Managing Contractors

Once contractors sign a contract and begin to work for the employer there is a tendency on the part of many employers (in an understandable effort to be equitable and fair) to start to treat contractors like all the other staff—who are typically employees. Employers should resist this temptation. The critical distinction between employees and contractors must be maintained throughout the term of the contractor's employment. "Benefit creep" can occur when contractors (especially long-term ones) become inadvertently too closely integrated into the governance or operations of an organization. Good contractors are perceived, over time, as valuable contributors of the organization and as such are to be "rewarded." For example, they receive corporate business cards, sit on committees that make decisions for the employer, neglect to submit monthly invoices but are paid anyway, are reimbursed for certain expenses on the same scale as employees, join a company benefits program or contribute to a company-supported pension plan. Of course, all these factors are indications of a true employee relationship that is not at all consistent with the role of a contractor.

In addition, the employer may begin to actively supervise, control, or direct the activities and performance of the contractor, as it does with its employees. It is far better for the employer to be content to manage and merely oversee the work of the contractor, who is, after all, the expert, as the contractor gets on with the job of completing the agreed tasks, to the quality standards and on the schedule negotiated in the contract.

Despite the warning not to "supervise" and to be content with "managing," there is a practical concern that sport managers should keep in mind when overseeing the work performed by contractors. The two most common problems encountered are that the inevitable changes or adjustments to the relationship are not documented and that performance failures go unchallenged. Although the "expert," the contractor must still perform the contract he or she has signed. As shown above, the actual contract document the contractor has negotiated and signed governs in large measure the professional relationship the contractor has with the employer. The contract will set out standards of performance and quality, approval mechanisms, and delivery times. "Overseeing" a contractor should mean constantly staying on top of the work actually being done, watching critical timelines, reviewing work quality and, most importantly, ensuring the contractor stays within the parameters defined in the contract for the successful performance of the various tasks.

If at any time the performance of the contract seems to be going off the rails, employers should not be reticent—they should demand answers of the contractor. Although precisely how the contractor does the work pursuant to the contract is properly inside his or her sphere of expertise, all issues over quality control and timing should be addressed by the employer.

What if the tasks to be performed by the contractor are varied, a fee is increased, the quality of a product changed or a deliverable timeline extended? These adjustments are rather common in contractor agreements with a term of many months. To begin, employers should strictly follow the procedures contained in the contract to create evidence of any "change orders" and other amendments or revisions to the contract such as pricing and deliverable dates. Employers should sign and attach amending agreements (with supporting consideration) to the initial contract. It is important to document carefully how the new arrangement has been altered, on mutual consent, from the contract pursuant to which the contractor began the work. Because the contract will be the primary governing document of the relationship, it should accurately reflect the current basis of the mutual agreement. When changes are made, the underlying contract should reflect the revisions.

Appendix 7.1: Contract Clauses Relating to Working Relationships

Employees

Employee Duties

You shall perform diligently and conscientiously those duties as are customarily rendered by and required of an [*insert*] and as the employer may reasonably require from time to time. The scope and nature of your employment duties will change during the course of your employment as the needs of the employer change over time. You agree to perform the duties prescribed, whatever they may be, to the best of your ability and to the satisfaction of the employer. Without restricting the generality of the foregoing, you shall be responsible for the performance of the duties set out in Schedule "A" attached hereto.

Employee Termination Clause

a. The employment of the Employee may be terminated only in the following manner and only in the following circumstances:

   i. At any time, ABC may notify the Employee of her/his immediate dismissal, for cause. No notice of termination or severance pay is required to be given.

   ii. At any time, ABC may terminate the employment of the Employee, without cause, by giving to the Employee the following working notice of termination or pay in lieu of notice:
   [*insert agreed-upon notice provisions—must be greater than employment standard legislated minimums*]

   At the discretion of ABC, in lieu of the working notice of termination specified above, the employer may pay to the Employee, by lump sum or at its choice, regular salary continuation payments equivalent to the salary the Employee would have been entitled to receive during the applicable period of notice specified above. All benefits accruing to the Employee as a result of his/her employment with ABC shall, if possible, and subject to the terms of any insured benefit plans, continue through the statutory notice period required by the *Employment Standards Act*.

b. Notwithstanding paragraph 5(a) above, this Agreement shall be terminated immediately, without notice, upon the death of the Employee or if the Employee is incapable, as a result of total mental or physical incapacity, confirmed in writing by the Employee's medical doctor, of returning to work to perform the duties of the Employee.

c. If the Employee resigns his/her employment with ABC, ABC shall be given three (3) weeks prior notice of the effective date of the resignation. ABC may waive the resignation notice period in whole or in part by providing regular salary for the period so waived.

d. Upon termination of employment pursuant to paragraphs (a) or (b) above, the Employee shall have no claim against ABC for any loss or damage for notice, or further pay in lieu thereof, except as described in paragraphs (a) and (b) regardless of the length of time the Employee was employed by ABC pursuant to this Agreement.

By initialling in the adjoining box the Employee acknowledges having read and understood paragraphs (a), (b), (c), and (d) above.

Employee Commission Clause

It is anticipated that you will be spending approximately 70 percent of your time on business development. Commissions are paid out on sales in excess of your Minimum Quarterly Base Target of $75,000.00 for sales generated by you alone. If you achieve your Minimum Quarterly Base Target, your sales commissions will be based on the dollar value of signed new business contracts, which you alone negotiate and close quarterly, and will be paid at the rate of 5.0 percent of gross sales less charges. Your commission will be payable in the month following the quarter end (April, July, October, January). No commission shall be payable to you after the quarter end in which the effective date of your termination of employment may fall. "Charges" are costs directly related to reasonably required outsourced services. Today, the outsourced services are for online media, studio work, and talent; however, this can change from time to time depending on the business proposal in consideration.

Sample "Net" Clause

Throughout the Term, ABC shall pay to the Employee royalties, based on Net Sales of Licensed Product, at the rate of eight percent (8%) of Net Sales. "Net Sales" shall mean the gross wholesale revenue received by ABC from the sale of all Licensed Products, less taxes, cash, trade, sales, and other program discounts, adjusted for legitimate merchandise returns which are credited to ABC's customers. Except as specified herein, no other deductions or set-offs from gross wholesale revenue shall be permitted in calculating Net Sales. Net Sales shall be as computed by ABC's accounting system, guidance for which is established by generally accepted accounting principles.

Contractors

Contractor Termination

This Agreement shall be terminated immediately upon the death of the Contractor. In addition, this Agreement shall be terminated immediately if the Contractor is incapable, as a result of mental or physical incapacity, of performing the services, duties, and specific tasks set out herein for a period of two (2) consecutive months.

Either party may terminate this Agreement, upon the occurrence of any of the following events, such termination to be effective immediately upon receipt by the other party of written notice to the effect that:

a. A party is materially in default of any of the provisions, terms, or conditions contained herein and if such party shall have failed to remedy such default within thirty (30) days after written notice of such default has been delivered by the other party;

b. A party becomes bankrupt or insolvent or makes an assignment for the benefit of such parties' creditors, has a petition of bankruptcy filed against him, or attempts to avail himself of any protection arising out of an applicable statute relating to insolvent debtors.

This Agreement may be terminated by either party at any time by giving to the other party advance written notice of such termination ("the notice"). The notice must be given to the other party not less than thirty (30) days in advance of the termination date. In the event the notice is given by one party to the other, the terms and conditions contained in this agreement shall continue in full force and effect until the termination date.

The Contractor's right to receive payment from the employer for all work performed prior to the termination of this Agreement shall survive the expiry or termination of this Agreement. On termination the Contractor must immediately cease work on the project and return all materials and property of the employer.

REFERENCES

Bannister v. General Motors (1998), 164 DLR (4th) 325, [1998] OJ no. 3402 (QL) (Ont. CA).

Canadian Bechtel Ltd. v. Mollenkopf (1978), 1 CCEL 95 (Ont. CA).

Ceccol v. Ontario Gymnastic Federation, [1999] OJ no. 304 (QL) (Ont. Ct. (Gen. Div.)).

Dowling v. Halifax (City), [1998] 1 SCR 22.

Employment Standards Act, 2000, SO 2000, c. 41, O. Reg. 288/01.

Farber v. Royal Trust Corporation, [1997] 1 SCR 846.

Francis v. Canadian Imperial Bank of Commerce (1997), 7 CCEL (2d) 1 (Ont. CA).

Gonsalves v. Catholic Church Extension Society (1998), 164 DLR (4th) 339, 39 CCCEL (2d) 104 (Ont. CA).

Hobbs v. TDI Canada Ltd. (2004), 246 DLR (4th) 43, [2004] OJ no. 4876 (QL) (Ont. CA).

Moose Jaw Kinsmen Flying Fins Inc. v. Minister of National Revenue (1988), 88 DTC 6099 (FCA).

Puri v. Minister of National Revenue, 1998 CanLII 473 (TCC).

Wallace v. United Grain Growers Limited, [1997] 3 SCR 701.

Watson v. Moore Corp. (1994), 20 CCEL (2d) 17 (BCSC).

Weibe Door Services Ltd. v. Minister of National Revenue, [1986] 3 FC 553 (FCA).

Whistler Mountain Ski Club v. Minister of National Revenue, unreported, 95-1723 (UI), August 2, 1996, Tax Court of Canada.

Intellectual Property and Licensing Agreements

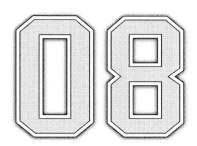

Introduction

In past decades, most not-for-profit sport organizations received the majority of their annual funding from federal and provincial governments. It is a far different story today. Although it is encouraging that since the end of the 1990s total government investment in elite and recreational sport continues to grow, partly in response to the growing awareness of the health benefits of an active lifestyle, fiscal restraint and debt reduction continue to be political realities. As a result, sport organizations at every level are being asked to do the same, or more, with less.

The cost to identify, develop, and train world-class athletes is rising. This leaves sport organizations with two options: lower their performance expectations and live within reduced means or aggressively seek out new sources of funding. Most sport and recreation organizations have chosen the latter route and inevitably they have turned to the private sector—to Canadian, US, and international corporations for funds and for commercial partnerships.

Private businesses around the world are hoping to ride the growing wave of interest in amateur sport and recreation activities. This interest is reflected in the worldwide multibillion dollar annual sponsorship market where large corporations are entering into highly visible contractual relationships with sport organizations, events, and athletes. It is well known, for example, that Tiger Woods is associated with Nike, Lance Armstrong rode his bike for the US Postal Service, and the Royal Bank has supported Canadian Olympic teams for decades. Championship games have title sponsors such as Tim Horton's, Bell Canada, and other major corporations. Some viewers think the half-time advertising extravaganza at the Super Bowl is a better show than the football game. Even distinct sports and teams have long-term sponsors clearly associated with their activities: examples are European football (soccer) teams who sport a corporate logo on their jersey instead of a team name. All of these corporations want to acquire, in association with their marketing and sales initiatives, the right to use property that is owned and controlled by the sport organizations, the events, and the athletes.

This chapter introduces one type of property owned by sport organizations and athletes—those assets that make up an organization's "intellectual property." Traditionally, property has been described as either "real" or "personal." Real property is land, buildings, and the structures that are permanently sitting on the land. Personal property is everything else. Personal property is further subdivided into either "tangible" property or "intangible" property. Tangible personal property includes those assets that a person owns that can be seen or touched such as a car, clothing, or sports equipment. Intangible personal property is far more nebulous because it cannot be seen or touched. For example, think of the difference between this book, which describes various rights and interests that a person can acquire, and the actual rights themselves. The book is tangible personal property. The various legal rights that a person may acquire are important, and real, but they exist only as concepts—they are intangible property. One type of intangible personal property is called "intellectual property" and it includes copyrights, trade-marks, patents, trade secrets, and personality rights, among other things.

Historically, the main sources of wealth in our society were based on the ownership of land, manufacturing facilities, and natural resources. These assets are real property. In our knowledge-based economy, wealth is now more closely associated with intellectual property. Our goal in this chapter is to introduce the most common types of intellectual property and to explain in a general fashion how rights in these valuable assets can be acquired, protected, and used. For each type of intellectual property presented in this chapter we will explain what it is, how it can be created, how best to protect it, and how it can be used. The final section introduces the concept of licensing, which is how many of these intellectual property rights are commercially "exploited"—that is, transferred to third parties who are allowed to use them in return for the payment of money, which eventually flows into the budgets of sport organizations.

Throughout the chapter, the term "organization" includes the many sport and recreation associations, not-for-profit as well as for-profit corporations, municipal recreation departments, educational institutions, and private clubs that own intellectual property and that daily enter into transactions to acquire the rights described in this chapter. It also includes not-for-profit organizations in the arts, education, human services, and health sectors.

Copyright

Of all the types of intellectual property a sport manager may encounter, copyright is by far the most prevalent and the most conceptually difficult to understand. Copyright can protect artistic, utilitarian, and even highly practical works. As such, copyright can exist in such varied things as a poem, a novel, a song or tune, an instruction manual, a database, or a computer software program. Copyright protects works of "authorship" in the expression of an original idea. The word authorship, when used in this sense, denotes the act of creating the end product produced by the actual writer or creator of the work. However, to acquire copyright in the work the author or creator must have set down in a tangible form an original expression of one or more ideas. Regardless of its popularity, utility, or commercial value, copyright protects most original work created by an author if the work is preserved in a tangible form such as a painting, photograph, manuscript, musical score, or computer source code. In Canada, copyright law is primarily governed by a federal statute, the *Copyright Act*. There are also various international treaties and conventions that affect how the rights of copyright owners in Canada may be protected.

Copyright does not protect every aspect of a creative work—it protects only the unique and original *expression of an idea*, but not the idea itself. This means that the various ideas and concepts that underlie a creative work are not protected and can be used by other authors to create similar works based on the same ideas and concepts. Independent creation of an original work is always permitted. For example, think how many novels or movies rely on the underlying concepts of love, betrayal, and ultimate redemption. Those ideas, standing alone, are not protected by copyright. There are literally thousands of ways to create an original work based on those three ideas. Only the particular author's unique and creative expression of those ideas is protected by copyright.

Copyright protection arises automatically on the creation of an original work and the copyright flows initially to the author of the work unless there is an agreement in place specifying otherwise. Such an agreement might allow a graphic artist to transfer his or her copyright in an original creative work to a purchaser of the art, or a songwriter to assign his or her copyright interest in a song to a publisher. There is no requirement for the initial author or creator of the original work to register or file anything to acquire a copyright. The familiar copyright notice of © is not required to obtain the rights of a copyright owner in Canada, but it is commonly used to provide public notice of copyright ownership, and the date it first arose. The copyright notice is usually inserted on the title page of the written work followed by the year of publication and the name of the copyright owner. Registration of copyright with the Canadian Intellectual Property Office (CIPO), the federal organization with responsibility to manage intellectual property in Canada, is voluntary but registration may assist the owner of the copyright in an infringement dispute and the act of registration creates a permanent record of the author, the owner, and the date of creation. Copyright registration is inexpensive and easy to do online by following the links located on the CIPO website (www.cipo.gc.ca).

Copyright may be easily transferred by the original author to another party, in whole or in part, and the transfer must be in writing to be effective. This transfer is usually described as an "assignment" because the rights held by one party are being assigned or moved to a new owner. It is well known that songwriters and novelists often assign copyright in a tune, verse, or book to a publisher to allow it to be published. In return for the assignment, the author commonly receives payment in the form of royalties based on the quantity of sales. A "royalty" is just a technical term used to describe a method of calculating a payment. For example, a royalty calculation may state that the author gets paid by the publisher a fee representing 5 percent of the first $50,000 in book sales. If more than one person created the work, there will be more than one author and each will have to assign his or her copyright to the new owner.

An important exception to the general rule that the author is the first copyright owner is if the author of an original creative work is an employee, acting within the

BOX 8.1
Examples of Copyright

Copyright materials that are common to sport organizations include databases, logos and designs, computer software, website graphics, all website content, training and leadership manuals, the content of coaches' certification courses, newsletters, internal publications, and other promotional and marketing materials.

scope of his or her employment. In this case, the owner of the copyright is the employer. There is deemed to be an automatic assignment of the copyright from the employee/author to the employer. However, be wary of two issues in the exception. For the exception to operate the author must be an "employee." An author who is an independent contractor or a volunteer remains the owner of all creative work unless and until it is assigned to others. The distinction between an employee and an independent contractor can be problematic (see chapter 7 for a full discussion). In addition, the employee must have created the work "in the course of his or her employment." Work created by volunteers or by employees in a capacity unconnected to their normal employment duties may not trigger the automatic assignment to the employer.

The duration of most copyright protection is the life of the author plus 50 years. This is a very long period of protection. Copyright does not just prohibit copying. During the protected period the owner of the copyright has the exclusive right to reproduce, perform, translate, or publish the work that is subject to copyright. The *Copyright Act* prohibits others from copying or publishing the original work without the consent of the copyright owner.

To be protected by copyright, the work must be "original." "Originality" means that the work must have been created by the author's labour and skill (not copied or restated) and it must be an expression of the author's own thoughts. The author's unique thoughts represent the required element of creativity. However, the threshold test for originality is quite low. Even a slight modification or an alteration to an existing work that is protected by copyright can give rise to an independent copyright if the modification of the existing work is original and shows a degree of skill and creativity on the part of the author.

In Canada, an author of a creative work has, in addition to copyright, what are termed "moral rights" in the work. Moral rights are independent from copyright and the holder of moral rights in a work may or may not be the copyright owner of that work. This will depend on whether the copyright has been assigned by the initial author because an assignment of copyright does not automatically waive or affect the underlying moral rights. Unlike copyright, moral rights cannot be assigned to others because they are specific to and remain with the initial author, although they can be waived, in writing, by the author. Only the author may elect to waive some or all of the moral rights associated with the work.

Moral rights give the author the right, where reasonable, to be associated with the work by name and allow the author to limit the use of the work and to prevent any modification or distortion of the work, if such distortion, modification, or unauthorized use would harm the reputation of the author. Moral rights give to the author the right to prevent others, including the copyright owner, from using the work in ways the author deems incompatible with the retained moral rights. The noted Canadian architect Douglas Cardinal once used his moral rights to prevent subsequent modifications to a church he had designed on the basis that the alterations were a distortion of the work and would harm his reputation. In another situation, a Canadian artist relied on his moral rights to prevent a shopping centre from tying Christmas bows around the necks of the geese he had sculpted. The bows were a distortion of the sculpture and would harm the artist's reputation. As a result, if an organization wishes to maintain complete control over copyrighted material that it owns it must also obtain from every author or creator a written waiver of all their moral rights. Appendix 8.4, at the end of this chapter, contains an example of a waiver of moral rights.

Trade-marks

A trade-mark can be a word, phrase, shape, or design, or a combination of these, that distinguishes the wares or services provided by one organization from the wares or services provided by another. A strong trade-mark creates a direct link in the public's mind between a product, service, or event bearing the trade-mark and the organization that owns the trade-mark. The Nike swoosh, or the International Olympic Committee's five interlocking rings, are examples of very strong trade-marks. Good trade-marks can become the public's "image" of an organization. In contrast to copyright, which protects all original creative work, the scope of protection afforded by a trade-mark is more limited. Trade-marks are used when protection is sought for a word, a logo, or a short phrase. In some cases the trade-mark will also be covered by copyright. For example, an independent designer may create a logo, and the designer will assign it to a sport organization which will then apply for a trade-mark that incorporates the logo.

Trade-marks are used to identify the source and/or the quality of a *ware* or a *service*. Wares are actual products such as shirts, shoes, cars, or boats that will be associated with the trade-mark. Services may be coaching, facility management, or translation that will be provided in association with the trade-mark. A trade-mark allows the public to identify the wares and the services that carry it with either a specific manufacturer or source of supply or a certain level of quality, or both. For example, the trade-mark TOYOTA indicates to the public that the vehicles bearing this mark come from Japan, or from TOYOTA factories around the world, and are of consistently high quality. No one else may use that trade-mark in association with the wares of cars and trucks. It is these features that make trade-marks so important in branding campaigns undertaken by organizations.

Typically, a trade-mark is associated with a rather limited range of wares and services. In the application form for registration of a trade-mark with the CIPO, the wares and services with which the trade-mark will be associated must be set out in detail. Wares might be described as follows: clothing—namely, shirts, golf shirts, and team uniforms; video games; computer games; vending machines; and sporting articles—namely, basketballs and golf balls. Services might be described as: arranging exhibitions of amateur sporting events and other events; organizing the promotional events of others; promoting the goods and services of others by arranging for sponsors to affiliate their goods and services with amateur sport and the national teams. Readers are encouraged to look at the list of wares and services associated with various marks by visiting the CIPO website.

Once the trade-mark is granted, the protection afforded to a trade-mark owner by reason of the registration will extend only to the listed wares and services. As a result, the trade-mark APPLE is legitimately used by different companies for wares as diverse as computers, record labels, fruit juice, and auto glass. Trade-marks can also cover a large variety of wares and services produced by one company provided the trade-mark application is sufficiently broad. For example, the trade-mark YAMAHA is properly associated with musical instruments; skis; motorcycles; outboard motors; and tennis, squash, and badminton racquets.

An important task for someone wishing to register a trade-mark is creating the appropriate list of wares and services and describing each in ordinary commercial terms. A list that is too wide and all-inclusive is not a good idea for two reasons. First, it will perhaps encroach on a third party's prior use of the trade-mark with some of the many listed wares or services. Second, if there is no reasonable likelihood of any future use of the trade-mark associated with a particular ware or service, there is no sense listing it in the application because the sworn "declaration of use," the last step in the registration process, will exclude any ware or service that has not been actually used. In contrast, a list that is too narrow may leave out important wares

---

BOX 8.2

Examples of Trade-marks

Common trade-marks registered by sport organizations include words alone and design elements, or both combined: the name of the organization, its logo alone and/or with the team name and other designs associated with a team, a team name, and an event name. The selection of the precise trade-mark will be a factor of how the mark is actually used—words alone, logo alone, or some combination of both.

or services that the organization actually wishes to associate with the proposed trade-mark, either now or in the future. There is no trade-mark protection associated with wares or services that are not specifically listed on the application form.

In Canada, trade-marks can be registered with CIPO, a branch of Industry Canada, pursuant to the *Trade-marks Act*, the federal statute that governs trade-marks in Canada. However, a word or logo does not have to be registered with CIPO to be valid as a trade-mark and to have certain limited rights associated with its use. Common law rights to a trade-mark can be acquired, without registration, if the trade-mark is used and is well known and recognized in a *local* area, but the common law rights will be effective only in that local area. Registration of the same word or logo as a trade-mark will ensure protection of the trade-mark across Canada, even in areas where it has never been used and is not at all known. It is important to note that registration of a trade-mark in Canada will create rights to the trade-mark only within Canada. To acquire protection in other jurisdictions, it is necessary to register in each foreign state.

The Registration Process

Generally, registration is available to the individual or organization that proposes to use, or has in fact first used, the trade-mark in Canada. The first step is to ensure the proposed trade-mark has been searched in the CIPO database to see if it might infringe any existing registered trade-marks (which is not uncommon). Additional searches are often made to review Canadian corporation names and the names of sole proprietors. This is required because any non-registered prior use of the proposed trade-mark in Canada may result in certain priorities arising in favour of the prior user. It is always a good idea to know who has been using the proposed trade-mark prior to the attempt at registration in order to avoid obvious conflicts.

If the searches indicate no obvious similar names or registrations, the application and the fees are submitted to CIPO. CIPO then reviews the application on its merits. Once the application is accepted it is published in the *Trade-marks Journal* so that the general public is given notice of the proposed trade-mark. Interested parties may file an objection to the proposed trade-mark within a set period of time claiming that it infringes an existing trade-mark or that it should not be registered for technical reasons such as "lack of distinctiveness" (where the trade-mark does not adequately distinguish the wares of a particular owner from another supplier of similar wares) or that it is "clearly descriptive" (where the words comprising the trade-mark are descriptive of the product, such as COLD BEER or FAST). An objection triggers what is known as an opposition proceeding where the rights of the parties are adjudicated. This opposition proceeding often takes a significant amount of time and money and many trade-mark applications are abandoned at this stage in the process. If the trade-mark application is allowed to be registered by CIPO, the applicant must, as a final step, swear a "declaration of use" that confirms that the trade-mark is in fact being used with all the listed wares and services contained in the application. The registration is granted for a period of 15 years and may be renewed for additional periods of 15 years.

The power of a registered trade-mark is that its owner can prevent competitors from across the country from using the same or a confusingly similar trade-mark. The trade-mark ensures that competitors cannot use it and thus confuse the public into thinking that their wares or services originated from the actual trade-mark owner or are of a certain quality. The extent of the actual protection obtained by the owner of a registered trade-mark depends on many factors beyond the scope of this chapter. Factors that are often relevant to the extent of the protection obtained include the inherent distinctiveness of the trade-mark (is it a coined or invented term, like XEROX or MAZDA, or a word in common usage?), the uniqueness of the wares and services associated with the trade-mark, and the prior history of its use because the person that can prove "first use" of the mark receives important rights in common law.

It is interesting to note a certain paradox: a descriptive mark is stronger from a marketing perspective but weaker from a legal perspective, in which uniqueness is favoured.

For sport organizations, the name of the organization, the name of an event, logos, flags, team names, and championships are all distinctive of a single source—the sport organization—and can be registered as a trade-mark. However, the organization must ensure in every instance prior to seeking a trade-mark registration that it obtains all rights, including copyright where appropriate, in the logo, design, words, or phrase sought to be protected by the trade-mark registration. Unfortunately, it is not uncommon for an organization to successfully register a specifically designed logo or unique phrase as a trade-mark only to discover that the owner of the copyright in the logo or phrase, or the holder of certain moral rights, remains the initial creator or designer—who may object to the eventual use of the trade-mark intended by the organization.

Official Marks

Section 9 of the *Trade-marks Act* states that any "badge, crest, emblem or mark" adopted and used by any "public authority," once notice of its adoption and use has been publicized, will be an official mark. Historically, official marks were used by governments to protect government emblems, regimental seals, and official coats of arms. As seen below, it is becoming more difficult for sport organizations to obtain the benefits of official marks.

Official marks are similar to trade-marks in that they are intending to be distinctive of a single source and standard of quality. Many sport organizations have found it possible to fit within the definition of a "public authority" as required by section 9 of the Act, and thus qualify to obtain official marks.

The Canadian Olympic Committee (COC) was an early sport organization to successfully claim that it was a "public authority" in the case *Registrar of Trademarks v. Canadian Olympic Association.* This case paved the way for the COC and numerous other non-profit sport organizations to obtain protection for their names and logos as official marks. It was common for the same term or logo to be registered both as a trade-mark and as an official mark to maximize the scope of potential protection.

There are several unique benefits associated with official marks:

- Only the organization that obtains an official mark may use it, and this organization can exclude others from using the mark. Unlike a trade-mark, it is not possible to have two organizations using a single official mark (for example, APPLE, which is used for both music and computers) for different wares or services.

- Unlike a trade-mark, there is no need to specify the exact wares or services with which the official mark is associated; the term may be descriptive, and there are no opposition procedures to enable third parties to challenge the official mark. This flexibility and the wide scope of protection is useful for many organizations that do not know precisely what use will be made, now or in the future, of the name or logo they are protecting.

- Finally, official marks are somewhat cheaper to obtain than trade-marks and the registration process is quicker.

To register an official mark, an applicant historically had to demonstrate that it is a "public authority" by showing that it performs public duties, that these duties are performed for public benefit and not private profit, and that the government exercises a significant degree of control over the organization. Courts generally placed greater emphasis on the criteria of public benefit and governmental control than on the requirement that the organization perform a public duty.

Because of the popularity of official marks there has been much litigation regarding who is properly considered a "public authority" and thus able to receive the benefits of an official mark registration. The case of *Ontario Assn. of Architects v. Architectural Technologists of Ontario* now makes it apparent, together with the practice notices issued from CIPO, that for an applicant to be considered a "public authority" the relevant government must exercise a significant degree of control over the activities of the organization and the organization's activities must benefit the public. The test of "government control" seems to have two related branches—demonstration of a degree of *ongoing influence* in the organization's governance and decision making as well as demonstration that there is *ongoing supervision* of the activities of the organization. The fact that an organization is a federally registered charity is not enough to automatically make it a "public authority." The threshold test is now clearly much higher than it was in the recent past. As a result, many Canadian sport organizations will be challenged to demonstrate to the registrar that there has been a sufficient degree of government control over the organization to enable it to be deemed a "public authority" and receive the benefit of official mark registration. Accordingly, far fewer sport organizations are likely to receive official marks.

Patents

A patent is a statutory monopoly granted by the government that gives the patent owner the exclusive right to make, use, and sell his or her invention to others. In return for disclosing the invention to the public, the government allows the inventor to benefit exclusively from the invention for a set period of time, after which the invention enters the public domain. The rationale for granting a patent monopoly is found in public policy—it encourages full disclosure of useful inventions so that they may be more quickly converted into commercial products. In Canada, the federal legislation controlling patents is the *Patent Act*.

In Canada, not every invention can be patented. For example, pure mathematical formulas or techniques that largely depend on personal skill and ideas cannot be patented. It is important to note that the range of items that may be patented is rapidly expanding, especially in the United States. In Canada, patents may be granted for "inventions," which are defined in the *Patent Act* as "a new and useful art, process, machine, manufacture or composition of matter," plus any improvements to these items. To qualify for patent protection an invention must be

- *novel*—an invention may fail the novelty test if it has already been publicly disclosed or if someone else has already applied for a patent for the same invention;
- *inventive/non-obvious*—there must be a creative and an inventive step taking the new invention beyond anything now in existence and known to the public (the invention must be original) and the inventive step must not be immediately obvious; and
- *useful*—an invention must work and provide utility to the public.

BOX 8.3   Examples of Patents

Many of the following inventions have been successfully patented and are commercially viable because they have enhanced athletic performance:

- the waffle sole on running shoes,
- the hinged speed skate (also called the Klapp skate),
- the shaped Alpine ski and breakaway slalom gates,
- drag pockets on swimsuits,
- various golf club innovations and golf ball dimple designs,
- the invention of breathable, water-repellent fabrics such as Gore-Tex,
- air-cushioning systems in athletic shoes,
- innovations in hockey sticks and blades of hockey skates,
- various sport drinks and nutritional supplements,
- oversize tennis racquets, and
- innovations in the design of exercise machines and fitness equipment.

A Canadian patent is valid for 20 years from the date on which the application is submitted to the Patent Branch of CIPO. In Canada, and in almost every country other than the United States, a patent is granted to the first person to file the application for a patent. In the United States a patent is granted to the first person to invent. This difference can result in evidentiary problems regarding who actually invented what—and when. It is important to note that public disclosure or use of the invention anywhere in the world prior to filing a patent application will, in most countries, prevent an inventor from obtaining patent protection. Only Canada and the United States allow a brief grace period of one year following public disclosure during which time an application for patent protection may be filed. Any new invention should be kept secret—premature public disclosure may preclude an invention from being patented. Inventors must be careful to have strict non-disclosure agreements associated with any dealings with the invention. Exposure in the public domain, such as in trade journals, must be avoided.

Historically, not many sport organizations, coaches, and athletes have filed patents, but this may change. The world of sport has witnessed many technological changes and often the impetus for such change comes directly from coaches, athletes, and other participants directly involved in the sport. Sport organizations are perfectly positioned to play a lead role in patenting new and useful inventions.

Trade Secrets

A trade secret is information that gives an organization some form of competitive advantage over other organizations. If the owner of the trade secret has sole access to this valuable information, it is possible to exclude others from using the information for their own benefit. A trade secret is valuable because it is secret and because it can be kept secret. Unlike a patent, there is no limit on the length of protection—simply as long as the secret can be kept secret.

The most famous trade secret in the world is probably the formula for the soft drink COCA-COLA. For a non-profit or sport organization, examples of trade secrets might include lists of members, databases of marketing contacts or donors, event-specific technical information, and various inventions that may not be patentable. There are no restrictions on the subject matter of trade secrets and there is no statutory basis for trade secret protection. As well, a trade secret is the only form of intellectual property that protects pure ideas.

Generally, trade secrets are the least expensive form of intellectual property to maintain and protect but the discipline to keep the secret protected consistently must come from within the organization. Trade secrets are protected by making certain that they remain confidential. This means establishing procedures to control the flow of information, such as

- marking documents containing trade secrets "strictly confidential";

- restricting the circulation of such documents to only those who truly "need to know" their contents;

- physically segregating these documents from others that are not confidential;

- executing non-disclosure agreements with staff, interns, volunteers, and any others who come into contact with confidential information and enforcing these agreements (see chapter 7 for more on this subject); and

- controlling or limiting access to both paper and electronic files containing trade secrets—this can be as simple as locking file drawers or putting password protection on certain computer files.

Personality Rights

Canadian courts have confirmed the existence of a common law tort (or "wrongdoing") of misappropriation of personality. Also known as the "right of publicity" in the United States, this tort is based on the legal principle that an individual has the exclusive right to market his or her image or likeness for personal gain.

A misappropriation of personality occurs in Canada where there has been some element of commercial use of a person's personality, the person is clearly identifiable in the medium used, the person does not consent to this use, and damages are proven. However, as shown below, recent decisions suggest that the Canadian courts will recognize in some provinces an individual's right to privacy even when there are no damages proven. There is further discussion below regarding the important distinction between the personal nature of privacy rights and the property interest reflected in a claim there has been a misappropriation of personality. These two rights reflect very different areas of the law and provide different forms of protection and, most importantly, different remedies if the rights are infringed.

An important case in Canada dealing with the tort of misappropriation of personality is *Gould Estate v. Stoddart Publishing Company* where the judge attempted to strike a balance between the competing rights of freedom of expression and an individual's right to market his own image. The estate of pianist Glenn Gould tried to prevent the publication of a book about Gould that included photographs of him and accompanying text.

The court saw the existence of some degree of commercial exploitation as being the key to the balance that was required to be struck, and Mr. Justice Lederman stated the following:

> It seems that the Courts have drawn a "sales vs. subject" distinction. Sales constitute commercial exploitation and invoke the tort of appropriation of personality. The identity of a celebrity is merely being used in some fashion. The activity cannot be said to be about the celebrity. This is in contrast to situations in which the celebrity is the actual subject of the work or enterprise, with biographies perhaps being the clearest example. These activities would not be within the ambit of the tort. To take a more concrete example, in endorsement situations, posters and board games, the essence of the activity is not the celebrity. It is the use of some attributes of the celebrity for another purpose. Biographies, other books, plays, and satirical skits are by their nature different. The subject of the activity is the celebrity and the work is an attempt to provide some insights about the celebrity.

The court held in *Gould Estate* that due to the overriding public interest in knowing more about the man, there was no misappropriation of Glenn Gould's personality when a book on the pianist was published. The personality and life of Glenn Gould was what the book was all about. In other situations involving films, books, or images of a person, if the "work or enterprise" is primarily about the person, it will be difficult to prove there was a misappropriation of personality.

The reasoning in *Gould Estate*, based on underlying commercial exploitation, was followed in the Ontario decision of *Delores Rose Horton v. Tim Donut Limited and Ronald V. Joyce* where the wife of deceased NHL star, Tim Horton, claimed there was a misappropriation of Tim Horton's personality when a portrait of Tim Horton was commissioned that would be displayed prominently in the chain's stores. The picture was intended for sale to the public and all proceeds would go to support a charitable foundation. The court concluded there was no misappropriation of the personality of Tim Horton because the main purpose of the portrait was charitable and commemorative rather than commercial.

Despite earlier cases that insisted on the need to have some degree of endorsement present in the use of an image before the tort could be invoked, in *Athans v. Canadian Adventure Camps Limited et al.* this "endorsement" requirement was eliminated. The plaintiff, Mr. Athans, was a well-known athlete and a successful competitor who had for many years used a black and white photograph of himself in action to promote and commercially endorse water ski products and training camps. The defendant, Canadian Adventure Camps Limited, used a stylized version of this image of Mr. Athans in a promotional brochure for the defendant's summer camp. Despite Mr. Athans's great notoriety in the relatively small Canadian water skiing community, the court found that the majority of the public who viewed the defendant's material containing the stylized version of Mr. Athans's personal trademark, would not associate it with Mr. Athans. Accordingly, the offending image could not reasonably be interpreted as an express endorsement by Mr. Athans of the defendant's summer camp. The concern was that the public might think that Mr. Athans was in fact endorsing the summer camp. Despite the lack of any express endorsement by Mr. Athans, the court allowed the action in favour of Mr. Athans on the following grounds:

> Commercial use of the plaintiff's representational image by the defendants without his consent constituted an invasion and … an impairment of his exclusive right to market his personality.

It appears that following the *Athans* decision, so long as there is an unauthorized "taking" of one or more indicia of a plaintiff's personality to the commercial benefit of a defendant, without the plaintiff's consent, and if damages are proven, it will be possible to invoke the tort of misappropriation of personality. There need not be an express endorsement associated with the use of a plaintiff's personality.

Personality is manifested in many ways. A person's "likeness" can be identified and exploited by using more than just an image. In *Krouse v. Chrysler Canada Limited et al.* the court stated:

> There may well be circumstances in which the Courts would be justified in holding a defendant liable … for appropriation of a plaintiff's personality, amounting to an invasion of his right to exploit his personality, by the use of his image, voice *or otherwise* with damage to the plaintiff. [Emphasis added.]

Likewise, in *Joseph v. Daniels*, the court decided that

> [f]rom my view of the authorities, I have concluded that it is the unauthorized use of a name or likeness of a person as a symbol of his identity that constitutes that essential element of the cause of action. The cause of action is proprietary in nature and the interest protected is that of the individual in the exclusive use of his own identity insofar as it is represented by his name, reputation, likeness, or other value. For the defendant to be found liable, he must be taking advantage of the name, reputation, likeness, or some other components of the plaintiff's individuality or personality which the viewer associates or identifies with the plaintiff.

The likeness of an athlete in a picture need not be an exact reproduction so long as the public can identify the athlete in the picture. The Olympic double gold medallist, Myriam Bédard, was able to force a major corporation to withdraw an advertisement it had published that used a photograph of her without her knowledge or consent. The photograph of Ms. Bédard had been altered very slightly for the advertisement (see figure 8.1). However, because the actual image of Ms. Bédard sprinting to the finish of an Olympic event had been previously published and was widely seen, the image in the photograph was well known and was publicly associated with her. Without her consent, a confusingly similar image could not be used for commercial purposes.

In the United States, at least for a well-known professional singer, "a voice is as distinctive as a face" (see *Bette Midler v. Ford Motor Co.*). Even the catchphrase "Here's Johnny!" was widely identifiable by the public with the entertainer Johnny

FIGURE 8.1

Myriam Bédard: Misappropriation of Personality

Source: CP (Frank Gunn)/Myriam Bédard. Reproduced by permission.

Carson and could not be used without his consent (see *Carson v. Here's Johnny Portable Toilets*). Canadian courts would likely have reached the same conclusions.

There is an important distinction to be made between Canada and the United States regarding how the rights associated with personality have been characterized. In the United States what is described as the "right to publicity" is a personal right, akin to libel. The rights to publicity are given broad protection; but in a number of states in the United States, the rights apply only to living persons. On the death of the person, the publicity rights expire. In contrast, in Canada the tort of misappropriation of personality has been consistently described as a proprietary right rather than a personal right. This distinction is important because property or proprietary rights do not end on a person's death. In *Gould Estate* the court agreed that the rights that were protected by the tort of misappropriation of personality were a form of intangible property and that those property rights can, on death, be passed along through a will to a person's heirs, and those rights can be enforced by the person's heirs. This reasoning has been consistently followed in Canada.

For sport organizations, the image and public persona of team members are important and valuable assets to market to sponsors. However, athletes at all levels in sport are increasingly aware that their images and personalities have commercial value and that the athlete has the right to exploit his or her own personality for profit. There have been numerous conflicts between the legitimate marketing and promotional needs of sport organizations and event organizers, and the rights of athletes and coaches to market their personalities for their own gain. These conflicts most often arise when athletes are required to sign agreements with their sport governing body and with major games organizers such as the Canadian Olympic Committee or Commonwealth Games Canada. Without exception, these agreements restrict the ability of the athlete to freely market his or her personality, as the athlete's personality rights are either assigned outright to the sport organization or restrictions are placed on the extent of the use that can be made of the athlete's personality without obtaining the prior consent of the sport organization.

Conflicts over personality rights are on the rise because of the increasing value of sponsorship contracts to the sport organization and because individual athletes realize their potential to enter lucrative personal endorsement contracts, all of which is consistent with the general commercialization of sport. In all likelihood, tension between protecting athletes' rights to market their personality and protecting an organization's financial bottom line will increase. Athlete agreements that routinely indicate that an organization's sponsors "trump" all athletes' sponsors or commercial activities will increasingly be challenged.

Who prevails in these conflicts will depend on many factors, not the least of which will be commitment and negotiating leverage. The most prominent athletes will probably have an advantage over other less-known athletes in these negotiations. Sport organizations and sponsors will want to be associated with a "famous" player even if there are pre-existing contracts or arrangements in place affecting that player that may compete with the services or products that the sport and its sponsors have attempted to protect. There tends to be more flexibility demonstrated when a sport "icon" comes to the table to discuss the terms for his or her potential participation on a national team. A star athlete, who has committed to do so, has the potential to insist on special treatment.

Protection similar to that afforded by the tort of misappropriation of personality exists in various provincial and federal statutes relating to privacy rights and human rights. The federal government and many provinces (but not all) have enacted statutes protecting privacy and personal information. A common theme in this privacy legislation is a prohibition against showing a person in an advertisement without that person's consent. This requirement mirrors the "commercial use" requirement of misappropriation of personality. Quebec has gone farther than other provinces in its *Civil Code* and the Quebec *Charter of Human Rights and Freedoms*. The *Civil Code* provides protection against the unauthorized use of a person's name, image, likeness, or voice. Section 5 of the Quebec Charter states: "Every person has the right to respect for his private life."

It is apparent that there is robust protection for privacy and personal autonomy in Quebec. Other provinces may follow suit. Courts in Quebec have awarded damages based on privacy considerations where a magazine article that exposed damaging personal and health information was published that allowed readers to identify a teacher even though no names were published. The court held that the publisher was primarily motivated by commercial considerations (see *Valiquette v. Gazette*). In the case below (see box 8.4), which was based strictly on personal privacy rights, there was clear recognition of the young woman's right to protect her image—even in the absence of actual damages. This type of reasoning regarding the proof of actual harm may flow from these privacy cases into the analysis of cases dealing with property rights.

The Intellectual Property Licence

Owners of property, including intellectual property, are not always able to maximally use and exploit the full range of rights that they control. For many organizations, some component of the assets that they own can be more effectively and profitably used by another entity. For example, it may be more profitable and draw broader exposure for a sport team to have its logo used in conjunction with the product of a particular sponsor. Or, it may be a more efficient business practice to have team products manufactured by a third party that specializes in the manufacturing process. Through licensing, it is possible for an owner to maintain ownership of his valuable asset, while allowing others to use it for a discrete period of time and pay the owner for the privilege of doing so.

A licence agreement is a form of contract that allows a licensee (the party using the asset) to do something that would otherwise be an infringement of the licensor's rights (where the licensor is the party who owns the asset). For example, a sport organization may not use an athlete's image and a sponsor may not use a logo of the sport organization without obtaining express permission to do so. The licensee acquires no underlying rights or property interests in an asset, but acquires a contractual right or a permission to use the licensed subject matter for a specific purpose and under strict conditions and limitations. An annotated licence agreement showing typical methods of dealing with intellectual property is reproduced in appendix 8.3.

Because a licence is an ongoing contract, it is essential that the licensing agreement be in writing. The end result of a licence is that people are using assets that they do not own. Organizations must take care to ensure that the licensee (the person who purchases the licence) is using the licensed material only as permitted in the written contract. The contract should clearly identify the licensed material, state the ways it may used, for what time period, and in what geographic territory.

Organizations that allow other parties to use their trade-marks should always do so by means of a written licence agreement. Licence agreements will usually insist

---

BOX 8.4   Case Study—Aubry v. Éditions Vice-Versa Inc.

Aubry v. Éditions Vice-Versa Inc. was decided by the Supreme Court of Canada pursuant to the unique provisions of Quebec's civil law and the Quebec Charter. These statutes expressly recognize a person's right to privacy in Quebec. In this case, a photo was taken of a young woman sitting in a busy public place and the photo was subsequently published in a newspaper. The Supreme Court ruled that damages could be awarded if an identifiable picture is published without permission. It also decided, to the surprise of many, that the right to privacy includes the ability to control the use of one's image even if the photo is flattering and not damaging to a person's reputation. The court balanced two sets of competing rights and found that the woman's right to protect her image (even when no real damages were proven) was more important than the paper's right to publish the photo without her permission. With the extension of privacy protection across Canada, such a result may be more common and will be based on both the existing tort of appropriation of personality and privacy legislation adopted in other provinces.

⬚⬚⬚ 8.5 Licensing Arrangements

The following are examples of licensing arrangements:

- Merchandising arrangements are licences whereby Sue is allowed to manufacture and sell products bearing Tom's trade-marks. The nature of the use, the range of products that may be manufactured, product specifications, and quality control are clearly identified in the licence agreement.
- Sport organizations often license to their sponsors the right to use, for certain purposes, the trade-marks, names, and logos of their organization, team, event, or championships.

---

that the owner of the trade-mark be publicly identified and indicate to the public that the user of the mark is permitted to do so under a licence from the owner (the licensor). Distinctiveness is an essential characteristic of a trade-mark because trade-marks should indicate to the public that products bearing a certain mark designate the wares of the owner of the mark and indicate that they are not from another supplier of similar wares. If a trade-mark is used by multiple parties the public will likely become confused about who is the actual owner. Certainly, unauthorized use of a trade-mark will detract from its distinctiveness and reduce its value and perhaps even its validity.

In Canada, the *Trade-marks Act* was amended in 1993 to introduce a scheme of controlled licensing by trade-mark owners. Section 50 of the *Trade-marks Act* requires that use of a trade-mark by a third party must be pursuant to a licence agreement from the owner, which gives the trade-mark owner control over the "character or quality of the wares or services" with which the trade-mark is used. This provision is required so that the quality of the products associated with the trade-mark can be kept consistently high by the owner—regardless of who is using the trade-mark and/or manufacturing products that bear it. If an owner of a trade-mark fails to comply with this section, he or she jeopardizes losing their registered trade-mark.

Licences can be granted to multiple parties. An organization should consider whether to grant exclusive or non-exclusive licences. Exclusive licences permit only the licensee to use the asset. An example would be the grant of a title sponsorship to an event. Non-exclusive licences mean that the owner can allow several parties to use the same asset. An example would be the typical grant to all sponsors of the organization the right to use a logo or team name. Some exclusive licences permit the owner to continue to use the asset as well, together with the exclusive licensee. These are often called "sole" licences because only the licensee may use the asset in

---

▦▧▨ 8.6   Important Considerations

Here are some important issues to consider when managing intellectual property:

1. Acquiring or registering intellectual property rights is an essential starting point—but it is never the end of the matter. All owners of intellectual property must take full responsibility for enforcing the various rights that they have acquired. No one will do this for an owner, and many people are happy to steal outright or chip away at an organization's intellectual property protection. It is the owner's task to take action against all potential infringers, copiers, poor-quality manufacturers and unauthorized users.

2. Intellectual property is presented here in six discrete pieces (copyright, trade-marks, official marks, patents, trade secrets, and personality rights). These assets are rarely identified or licensed in such separate packages. The sport manager most often encounters "bundles" of intellectual property that might include trade-marks (some registered and some not), copyright material, trade secrets, personality rights, designations, etc. The first task is to sort through the bundle to identify the relevant pieces, to determine to what extent they are protected, how protection can be bolstered (for example, by registration), and to decide how they might best be exploited, whether inside or outside the organization.

3. The same intellectual property owned by sport A is often used by many different organizations or sponsors. We previously saw that non-exclusive licences permit this. The risk is that items caught inside an exclusive grant not be licensed to third parties. In addition, sublicensing allows A to grant rights to B who will then pass certain of these rights along to C. This is why intellectual property is often managed by a licence agreement that permits rights to be granted to various parties. The sport manager must be constantly vigilant regarding the "flow-through" nature of these rights. What we mean by flow-through is this—the sport manager must not grant to a third party what the organization does not own, control, or have the right to use and license onward.

    Two scenarios are always problematic. First, when some but not all personality rights flow to sport A from its athletes who of course are the owners of these rights. Sport A must be very careful that it does not grant to a sponsor rights or privileges that it has not fully acquired from its respective athletes. Second, in event-hosting situations, it is common for event owners to appoint event hosts, who in turn hire and enter contracts with event managers, who in turn may enter contracts with event sponsors. All parties will wish to use, to a greater or lesser extent, some or all of each others' assets, names, and other intellectual property. It is critical to be sure that "rights received" mesh perfectly with "rights being granted" in this multiparty contractual chain.

addition to the owner. Thus, a variety of options are possible and the choice of option is essentially a business decision. Decisions about which form of licence to grant, and for what term, can have a huge impact on the stream of income earned by the licensor. Because payments to the owner in the licence agreement are often either a fixed sum for each licensee or royalties calculated on the amount of use of the licensed asset, having more licensees in place will often result in greater total payments to the owner. As well, shorter licence terms will benefit the owner if the value of the asset is rising, because a renegotiation will likely generate a higher total payment.

It is critical to consider how licence payments will be structured. Because a licensee is paying for use of an asset over a period of time, payments may also be made over time. The licence may provide for periodic payments during the term of the agreement; or alternatively, payments may be up front, based on royalties set at a fixed or varying percentage of sales, tied to profit, fixed for certain dates, or floating. Whatever the method selected, it is critical to describe the payment method clearly and in detail.

Appendix 8.1: Problems and Solutions

Described below are six common scenarios that often arise. These problems are illustrated through actual, practical examples that have had real-life consequences and, in many cases, significant financial implications for the sport organization.

The Case of the Offending Trade-mark

A local organization used an elaborate design incorporating symbols and words in its logo. The logo was well known in the community. A large company wished to use the distinctive logo as part of a national promotional campaign. A deal was signed.

The Problem

The logo had never been registered as a trade-mark. The sponsorship deal now gave significant national exposure to the logo. This exposure attracted the attention of another trade-mark owner who had registered a trade-mark in a design that he felt was substantially similar to the logo. The registered owner started an infringement action against the organization and the sponsor who was using the logo. The sponsorship arrangement fell apart and in addition, the organization was forced to stop using its logo entirely.

The Solution

If an organization is using a unique logo or a specific name in connection with its business, it should consider having the name and/or the logo registered as a trade-mark or an official mark. This will protect the logo across Canada regardless of where the logo was previously used or how extensively it was used. Although unregistered trade-marks are recognized under common law, the extent of such recognition is quite limited. Names and logos are an increasingly important component of an organization's assets and they should be fully protected—every sport and recreation organization should invest the money to obtain proper registration of all proprietary marks and designs.

The Case of the Stubborn Graphic Designer

An organization hired a freelance creative designer to develop a very striking logo. The organization decided to have the logo registered as a trade-mark, and this was successfully done.

The Problem

A few months later, the organization attempted to expand the use of the trade-mark by placing it on some clothing and equipment items that it decided to market, and was shocked to learn that a corporation objected to this use. In addition, the designer of the logo informed the organization that she was not happy with the use of the trade-mark on these new products and, as she remained the owner of the copyright in the logo, she refused to consent to this use. The organization couldn't understand how this happened because they believed they were the owner of a registered trade-mark.

The Solution

In this scenario, the organization is the owner of a registered trade-mark but many trade-marks provide only limited protection. When preparing a trade-mark application, it is critically important to claim all of the current and future "wares and services" with which the trade-mark is to be associated. If, at some point in the future, the trade-mark is used or associated with wares or services that were not initially identified in the application, a third party can object and a new trade-mark application may be required to gain (if available) the extended protection.

Be aware that there is always a danger when a trade-mark is assigned or licensed to a sponsor that the sponsor's use of the trade-mark might fall outside the areas of use claimed in the application. At the extreme, the sponsor might find itself the target of an infringement action.

The second problem in this scenario relates to copyright in the logo. Copyright belongs to the author or creator of an original work—in this case the graphic designer. The organization should have obtained a written assignment of copyright and a waiver of all moral rights from the designer when it paid for the designer's services.

The Case of the Overlooked Copyright and Moral Rights

An organization decided that it would sell instruction manuals to its members in an effort to raise funds. These manuals were written in part by the organization's coaches, officials, and professional staff. A company was hired to write a specific section of the manual relating to risk management and safety. An independent contractor was hired to write another small section. The manuals sold very well.

The Problem

After a year of brisk sales, the organization decided to seek out a sponsor for the production of the manual and successfully negotiated a deal with a pharmaceutical manufacturer. The independent contractor and one of the employees who contributed to the manual do not want their material used in this fashion. The employee admits that he is not the owner of the copyright but he nonetheless retains moral rights in the work. The independent contractor asserts that she is the owner of copyright in a small section of the material and that she also has moral rights in this work. The risk-management expert who worked for the contracting company cannot be found.

The Solution

Every organization should ensure that its employees and independent contractors sign written assignments of copyright and waivers of moral rights prior to creating or contributing to any new work on the organization's behalf. Organizations need to be particularly careful when contracting out creative work to corporations. In addition to the corporation providing an assignment of its copyright to the organization (moral rights accrue only to individuals), it is prudent to require that each of the corporation's employees and contractors that works on the project provide the same assignment and waiver. Remember, it is these individuals who will be the actual creators of the work and, depending on their employment status, may have acquired copyright and moral rights.

The Case of the Misappropriated Personality

A large company interested in launching a national advertising campaign approached a sport organization. It intended to use members of the national team because the athletes were all well known. The organization was in favour of this proposal and a sponsorship deal was signed.

The Problem

When the first billboard went up in Vancouver one of the national team athletes complained to the organization, and to the sponsor, that his image was being used without his consent. He claimed the sponsor had no right to commercially exploit his personality or likeness. The billboard had to be taken down and the entire advertising campaign was put on hold.

The Solution

Organizations walk a fine line when balancing their right to promote the sport or a specific event with the right of individual athletes or coaches to exploit their own personalities. If there is a commercial component to the use of an individual's likeness and the individual is readily identifiable to the public in the medium in which the likeness appears, it is wise to obtain the individual's consent to this use prior to selling or licensing the image. Such consent should be in writing, should refer specifically to the image being used, and should specify how the image is to be used and for how long the image may be used.

Although sport organizations may find these limitations inconvenient, Canadian courts are increasingly prepared to recognize the exclusive rights of individuals to market their personality and image. Attempts by organizations to usurp these rights can lead to legal challenges and awards for monetary damages, in addition to strained and awkward relationships between members and sponsors and between the organization and its athletes and coaches.

The Case of the Stolen Computer Code

An organization hired a firm to develop an interactive website. Once designed and built, the website files would be transferred to the organization for ongoing maintenance and future expansion. The organization made a pitch to its sponsors to advertise on specific sections of the website. The sponsors agreed.

The Problem

The firm that was contracted to design and build the website had agreed that the organization would be the absolute owner of the finished product and that all of the firm's rights in the product would be assigned to the organization when the work was delivered.

Unfortunately, the firm did not do the actual work—instead, an independent contractor hired by the firm prepared the software for the website and incorporated into it, without permission, significant amounts of source code and other material that was owned by a previous client of the contractor. The contractor refused to redo the work and remove the offending code. The owner of the code adamantly refused to allow the organization to make use of its code, which was now completely integrated into the finished product, without paying an exorbitant licence fee. On top of all these problems, the organization also learned that the catchy domain name that it had selected infringed a registered trade-mark.

The Solution

Although cyberspace is new frontier, it is apparent that most of the accepted principles of intellectual property ownership are in effect on the World Wide Web. Taking material from a website will infringe copyright. Likewise, a domain name can infringe a competitor's trade-mark. Most importantly, a company can assign or transfer only what it owns—in this scenario, the firm was unable to deliver a final product that would be 100 percent owned by the organization because of a third party's prior rights. If the organization had gone ahead and launched the website, it would have run the risk that the owner of the code would insist that all use of the source code cease.

When hiring a company or an individual to produce and deliver a creative work or a specific product, it is important to obtain a warranty to the effect that the company or individual owns all of the components to be incorporated into the work or product. This warranty should survive the termination of the supply contract. In some cases, an organization might wish to obtain financial security to back up such a warranty.

The Case of the Leaked Invention

A team of athletes, the coach, and the executive director of an organization, working together, designed an invention that clearly increased athletic performance. The invention had the potential to generate a significant amount of money for the organization. While in Europe one of the athletes disclosed to a journalist the details of the invention and the journalist published this information in a trade newspaper.

The Problem

Thirteen months later, the members of the team, the coach, and the sport organization formed a new company to exploit the invention and attempted to patent it in Canada, the United States, and the European Union. The patent examiner refused to issue a patent on the basis that the invention was already in the public domain.

The Solution

In most situations, a patent will be refused if there has been any public disclosure prior to filing the patent application. If the invention must be disclosed—for example, to potential investors in the new company—then it should be disclosed only to those individuals who have signed a detailed non-disclosure agreement. With such an agreement in place, disclosure will not be considered "public" and a patent can still be obtained.

Appendix 8.2: Problem-Solving Situation—Otto Wooten

Otto Wooten is the most successful bobsled driver in Canadian history. He is the current world champion and a ten-year veteran of the national team. With an engaging personality, Otto is well known to the Canadian public as a result of TV commercials, race site interviews, and event coverage at exotic locations around the globe. Otto is a good-looking fellow with long, jet-black hair that flutters out from under his distinctive racing helmet. He has painted his popular nickname on the red and white Canada One sled. It reads "WOOTS—I am Canadian."

Otto is an engineer and has recently designed a new steering mechanism that will help control the sled on tight turns. He is convinced that this idea will soon be standard on every competitive sled and will make him a very rich man. Otto has told no one about the invention except Mr. Smith, a personal friend and the executive director of the Canadian Sled Federation (CSF). Otto wants to show his concept drawings to BMW but he is worried that a large company from a nation with whom he competes will steal his ideas.

During the past summer, Otto worked for a month or so at the CSF head office filing papers and updating membership lists. He also took some time from his work at the CSF to write an instruction manual (in conjunction with his brakeman and using pictures drawn by his ex-girlfriend) in which he explained his theories on high-speed cornering techniques.

Mr. Smith decided that he would raise much-needed funds for the CSF by getting a trade-mark and an official mark on a design that his wife drew that incorporates Otto's helmet and flying hair to be meshed with the existing CSF logo. This trade-mark could be used for corporate fund raising if it is licensed to a major sponsor. In particular, BMW has expressed interest in a sponsorship and licensing deal with CSF and also wants to talk to Mr. Smith about Otto's steering mechanism. BMW is also willing to pay to publish the instruction manual that Otto wrote, which the CSF can then sell to its members for a small profit. This all seems like a good plan to Mr. Smith.

What problems might arise?

Appendix 8.3: Annotated ABC Sponsorship Agreement

(Note to reader: This agreement has had significant portions removed. The parts that remain are intended to illustrate how certain intellectual property rights may be granted in a typical sponsorship agreement.)

This Agreement is made and entered into by and between ABC ("ABC"), having its principal office at [*insert*] and XYZ Canada ("Sponsor"), having its principal office at [*insert*].

WHEREAS, ABC is the owner of the ABC trade-marks and official marks set out in Schedule A attached hereto (the "Licensed Marks"); [*Always specify precisely what names, marks, or designations are being granted in the agreement. It is common to attach a schedule to list and show them.*]

The parties agree as follows:

1. DEFINITIONS

For the purposes of this Agreement all terms with initial capital letters not defined elsewhere in this Agreement shall have the following meanings: [*Typically, additional terms are defined as well.*]

a. "XYZ Industry" means the business of packaging, marketing, selling, and/or distributing Products. [*Always be clear regarding the scope of the grant of rights. There are two overriding concerns; (1) the extent of the permitted uses and (2) ensuring there is no overlap in product categories.*]

b. "ABC Promotion" shall mean a consumer-directed or trade-directed promotion for Products conducted by Sponsor that uses the Licensed Marks or is otherwise identified or associated with ABC. [*These are events or promotions where sponsor can link its products with ABC or with an ABC team and use the trade-marks of ABC.*]

c. "Licensed Footage" shall mean video or film footage that contains a Licensed Mark that is obtained from ABC or an ABC-approved source.

d. "Licensed Photo" shall mean a photograph that contains a Licensed Mark that is obtained from ABC or an ABC-approved source.

e. "Official ABC Licensed Products" shall mean all products licensed by ABC for manufacture or sale by XYZ. [*These products will inevitably contain the trade-marks of the sponsor and the Licensed Marks.*]

f. "Player" shall mean a [sport] player who is a member of the then-current ABC Men's National Team or Women's National Team (as the case may be). [*Typically, these players will have signed an ABC Athlete Agreement where certain rights that the player controls, such as his personality rights, are granted to ABC and this permits ABC to pass on these rights to an ABC sponsor.*]

g. "Player Attributes" shall mean the name, nickname, photographs, portraits, likeness, and/or other identifiable features of an ABC Player preserved in any format or medium. [*This describes the extent of the player's "personality" obtained by ABC from the player and thus what ABC can grant to XYZ.*]

h. "Premium" shall mean any product or merchandise bearing, embodying, or implying an association with one or more Licensed Marks and given free of charge or offered for sale at substantially less than its regular selling price for the purpose of increasing the sale of, or publicizing, any Product and promoting the association of the Sponsor with ABC. [*Premiums and other small items that are given away often contain both the trade-marks of ABC and XYZ.*]

i. "Products" shall mean [*insert*]. [*This is where ABC will define the various product categories it intends to have associated with XYZ. If there is a grant of exclusivity to XYZ there can be no overlap between this list of products and the product categories to be associated with any other sponsor. Great care is required to divide product categories and industries in a sensible fashion to allow the maximum number of sponsors to be associated with ABC.*]

j. "Net Sales" shall mean the gross wholesale revenue received by XYZ from the sale of all Licensed Products, less cash, trade, sales, and other program discounts, adjusted for legitimate merchandise returns, which are credited to XYZ's customers. Except as specified herein, no other deductions or set-offs from gross wholesale revenue shall be permitted in calculating Net Sales. [*Net sales is a calculation that will define the royalty payments so it must be precisely set out. The trick is to minimize the number of allowable deductions from gross revenue.*]

3. TERRITORY

Unless otherwise specified, the rights granted by ABC to the Sponsor under this Agreement shall be exercisable throughout Canada only (the "Territory"). [*Typically, the intellectual property owned by ABC, such as a trade-mark, will have been registered and trademark protection is valid only in Canada.*]

4. SPONSORSHIP RIGHTS AND OBLIGATIONS

a. During the term of this Agreement, Sponsor shall be provided with exclusivity in the XYZ Industry and in the following Product categories [*insert*]. [*This exclusive grant must not conflict with any other grant of rights provided by ABC.*]

b. [*This is the main granting clause.*] Subject to the terms of this Agreement (including without limitation the approval rights and the restrictions on the use of the Player Attributes), ABC hereby grants to Sponsor, and Sponsor hereby accepts, for so long as this Agreement remains in effect, the exclusive right and licence in the XYZ Industry and in connection with the Products to (i) the designations as "Official Sponsor of XYZ"; "Official Sponsor of XYZ's National Teams"; "XYZ National Team Supplier"; and/or any other such other designations as the parties may mutually agree upon (collectively, the "Designations"); [*Set out each permitted designation in detail. Only these may be used by XYZ without further agreement.*] (ii) use, during the Term and within the Territory, the Licensed Marks, Designations,

Licensed Photo (subject to reasonable search and edit charges), and Licensed Footage (subject to reasonable search and edit charges) solely in connection with the advertising, marketing, promotion, and sale of Products. [*This section is where the controls on use are specified. Not all uses are typically permitted and any limitations on the use of the intellectual property that are intended must be inserted here.*] and (iii) conduct ABC Promotions. [*Insert here any limitations or restrictions desired in the conduct by XYZ of promotions using ABC assets.*]

c. During the Term, upon the request of the Sponsor at least ten (10) days in advance, ABC shall use efforts that are consistent with the provisions of ABC's athlete agreements to make ABC Players available for two (2) appearances on behalf of the Sponsor (at Sponsor's expense) for promotional purposes. Sponsor acknowledges and agrees that such Players are not expected to endorse Sponsor or the Products unless the Sponsor has entered into a separate agreement with the Player for such endorsement. [*This section illustrates the issue of "flow-through" rights—ABC may not grant to XYZ any rights that ABC has not received from the players in the ABC athlete agreement. It also confirms that a sponsor using an image of players is separate and distinct from an express or implied endorsement by the players.*]

d. By granting to Sponsor the rights and licences in this Paragraph 4, ABC shall not in any way be restricted from granting rights or licences to other persons or entities to use the Licensed Marks in connection with any products or services. ABC shall not license any person or entity in the XYZ Industry (other than Sponsor) the right to use the Licensed Marks in connection with the Products within the Territory during the Term. [*This section confirms the grant of exclusivity to XYZ in one industry and for one group of products but it expressly allows ABC to license the same rights to third parties in other industries and for other products.*]

5. RETAIL LICENSING RIGHTS

a. ABC hereby grants to XYZ, and XYZ hereby accepts, the exclusive worldwide right and licence to manufacture and sell at retail National Team uniforms, Authentic Competition Apparel, and replica Products that feature the ABC Marks with and/or without Player identification ("Licensed Products"). [*This clause allows XYZ to manufacture worldwide and to sell certain merchandise bearing the ABC trademarks. ABC is paid a royalty fee in return.*]

b. Throughout the Term, XYZ shall pay to ABC royalties, based on Net Sales of Licensed Product, at the rate of eight percent (8%) of Net Sales, except that when the Licensed Product features Athlete Attributes then the rate shall be eleven percent (11%). All amounts owed to ABC for royalties shall be determined quarterly, and any payments due shall be made within sixty (60) days of the conclusion of each such Contract Year. Within sixty (60) days following the end of each Contract Year, XYZ shall furnish ABC with a sales report setting forth the Net Sales of all Licensed Products sold during the applicable Contract Year by product type. ABC agrees that royalties shall be waived for any Licensed Products provided free of charge by XYZ to ABC for use by any Coach, Staff, and/or Team members. [*This clause specifies the royalty rate and when it is to be paid.*]

    c. XYZ guarantees that its aggregate annual royalty payments to ABC for each Contract Year shall not be less than the amounts set forth below: [*Insert annual minimums if this can be negotiated.*]

6. USE OF THE MARKS

Sponsor shall receive the exclusive marketing and promotional rights granted in section 4(a) and (b) on its own behalf [*Typically, the sponsor will be the only entity allowed to use and benefit from the rights granted to the sponsor by ABC. However, sometimes the sponsor will wish to have its related divisions, subsidiaries or retail partner's benefit from the grant of rights it receives from ABC. If ABC agrees that parties other than the sponsor may use its assets the following wording may ensure that the extended use will not encroach on other of ABC's sponsor's rights.*] and, subject always to the following conditions being satisfied, on behalf of its licensors or retail partners of the Sponsor that have been approved in advance by ABC, pursuant to section 7, which approval shall not be unreasonably withheld. In every case where the approval of ABC is sought, such approval is subject to the following conditions: (i) the marketing and promotional rights granted to the licensors or retail partner is used solely in connection with an ABC Promotion in conjunction with Sponsor, (ii) all use is subject to ABC's Marketing Guidelines, Schedule B, (iii) the licensors or retail partner's use of the marketing and promotional rights received through Sponsor do not result in ABC being in breach of any other sponsorship contracts, and (iv) Sponsor shall be responsible for all use of the marketing and promotional rights, and any damages resulting from such use, by the licensor or retail partner.

7. APPROVALS

All ABC Promotions authorized under this Agreement shall be subject to ABC's review and prior approval, which may be granted or withheld in ABC's good faith exercise of its sole discretion. In addition, Sponsor shall ensure that all materials utilizing the Licensed Marks shall be of high standards of quality and appearance and that the Licensed Marks will be accurately and faithfully reproduced. [*This ability to control and monitor issues of quality associated with the trade-mark is required when owners of trademarks allow third-party licensees to use them (See section entitled "The Intellectual Property Licence" on page 162).*] [*Insert details of how the review and approval will be managed.*]

• • •

11. USE OF PLAYERS

Sponsor acknowledges and agrees that the licence granted under this Agreement does not include, and shall not be used to imply, a testimonial or endorsement of any Licensed Products by any ABC Team player. Sponsor shall not use Player Attributes in any manner that may imply such a testimonial or endorsement without first obtaining written authorization from the subject player(s). [*Few athlete agreements go so far as to permit the sport organization to grant to their corporate sponsors a player's endorsement of a sponsor's product without the express consent of the player involved. Players typically seek extra payment for an express endorsement of a sponsor's product. Here are some typical provisions.*]

1. ABC Sponsors can use ABC player likenesses in their advertising and promotions if they either (a) have secured the particular player's consent or (b) have obtained, through their sponsorship agreement with ABC, the right to use ABC photos and footage. In the former case, ABC will require the Sponsor to confirm in writing that the particular player (or the player's representative) has reviewed and approved the proposed use of the player's likeness.

2. Under its athlete agreements, ABC has the right, subject to certain restrictions, to permit its Sponsors in advertising and promotions to use player likenesses that are contained in ABC photos and footage. To comply, ABC photos or footage may not be used in a manner that implies an association with any particular player or an endorsement by a particular player. ABC will make this determination at its sole discretion.

3. If ABC has granted a Sponsor the right to use player likenesses in ABC photos and footage, ABC will approve that Sponsor's proposed use of player likenesses provided that the photograph or footage depicts a "group" of players and such proposed use is consistent with ABC's rights under its athlete agreement. Whether such a use will be approved by ABC will be determined on a case-by-case basis. With respect to advertising and promotional materials, the "group" must include a minimum of three (3) players (not including any player-endorsers of the Sponsor) that are featured in equal prominence (e.g., no player may be featured or emphasized more than any other players), although certain uses will require more than three (3) players. [*See point 6. The larger the group the less likely there will be an implied association or endorsement made on behalf of a single player.*]

4. Use of attributes of any specific player on a "group" basis is subject to ABC's authority to grant the use of the player's likeness. For example, ABC may be unable to approve the use of a player with respect to a certain Sponsor because that player may have a business relationship with a competitor of such Sponsor.

5. Unless a Sponsor has separately obtained endorsement rights from a particular ABC player, the Sponsor may not use the likeness of a player in a way that implies or suggests, at ABC's sole discretion, an endorsement by the player depicted. Even if such endorsement rights have been obtained, the use of any ABC intellectual property in connection with the exercise of such right (e.g., depicting the endorser in a ABC uniform) is subject to ABC review and approval and player consent.

6. When using players in conjunction with promotions (e.g., posters or calendars), ABC, at its sole discretion, may require that a minimum number of players (greater than three or five) and/or ABC teams (men/women) be represented. [*The goal is to avoid a sponsor focusing on a single superstar and ignoring the rest of the athletes on the team or ignoring one of the men's or women's programs entirely. From the sport organization's perspective, the sponsor was licensed by ABC to promote its association with the sport and the National Team, not to focus on one or two athletes of a particular gender.*]

Appendix 8.4: Assignment of Copyright and Waiver of Moral Rights

In exchange for good and valuable consideration and the sum of $1.00, the receipt of which is hereby acknowledged, the undersigned hereby irrevocably assigns to [*insert the full name of the recipient*], its licensees, successors, and assignees, all of the undersigned legal and equitable interest, specifically including copyright, in [*describe fully and accurately the original work in which the copyright subsides—e.g., the graphic design of a stylized basketball or the 2007 level one coaching certification manual*], which is more particularly illustrated or described in Schedule "A" which is attached hereto, which the undersigned has authored or contributed to, either directly or indirectly ("the work").

By this assignment, the undersigned renounces and waives any and all rights to limit the use, distribution, modification, licensing, or sale of the work or any element thereof by [*insert the full name of the recipient*] or its licensees, successors, or assignees or to receive any compensation whatsoever by reason of any use, distribution, modification, licensing, or sale of the work or any element thereof by [*insert the full name of the recipient*], its licensees, successors, or assignees.

In addition, the undersigned, if an individual, specifically waives all of his or her moral rights in the work. [*Moral rights accrue only to individuals and may not be assigned, just waived.*]

Signed at this _____ day of _____ 2007.

_____

Author/designer of the work

_____

Witness

REFERENCES

Athans v. Canadian Adventure Camps Limited et al. (1977), 17 OR (2d) 425, 34 CPR (2d) 126 (HCJ).

Aubry v. Éditions Vice-Versa Inc., [1998] 1 SCR 591.

Bette Midler v. Ford Motor Co., 849 F. 2d 490 (9th Cir. 1998).

Carson v. Here's Johnny Portable Toilets Inc., 698 F. 2d 281 (6th Cir. 1983).

Charter of Human Rights and Freedoms, RSQ, c. C-12.

CIPO, list of wares and services associated with various trade-marks: http://strategis.ic.gc.ca/sc_mrksv/cipo/tm/tmdb/tmdb_help-e.html#criteria.

CIPO, *Trade-marks Journal*: http://napoleon.ic.gc.ca/cipo/tradejournal.nsf/$$ViewTemplate+for+TMJournal+English?OpenForm.

Copyright Act, RSC 1985, c. C-42.

Delores Rose Horton v. Tim Donut Limited and Ronald V. Joyce, unreported decision or the Ontario Court (Gen. Div.), file no. 95-CU-86126, 1997.

Gould Estate v. Stoddart Publishing Company (1996), 30 OR (3rd) 520 (Ont. Ct. (Gen. Div.)).

Joseph v. Daniels (1986), 11 CPR (3d) 544 (BCSC).

Krouse v. Chrysler Canada Limited et al. (1973), 1 OR (2d) 225, 40 DLR (3d) 15 (CA).

Ontario Assn. of Architects v. Architectural Technologists of Ontario, [2002] FCJ no. 813 (QL) (CA).

Patent Act, RSC 1985, c. P-4.

Registrar of Trade-marks v. Canadian Olympic Association (1982), 67 CPR (2d) 59 (FCA).

Trade-marks Act, RSC 1985, c. T-13.

Valiquette v. Gazette (The) (1991), 8 CCLT (2d) 302, [1991] RJQ 1075 (SC).

Contracts

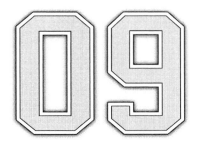

Introduction

Contracts are part of our everyday lives—we live with them and are constrained by them daily. Parents, children, partners, and friends enter into contracts every day. No business can operate without entering into contracts. Most everyone knows what a simple contract is—it is a "deal" we have agreed to and are expected to abide by. In other words, a contract is an expression of a mutual agreement by two or more parties who intend to be bound by their promises. Contracts may be formed orally or in writing and their terms can be express or implied. Written contracts may be short or long—depending on the nature of the agreement between the parties and the degree of detail the parties wish to include in the document. Because of the multitude of arrangements and fact situations possible, there is no single form of contract that can be used in every situation. So for those who might like the convenience of pulling a template out of a book, there is no such thing—at least, not in this book!

Understanding, creating, and interpreting contracts requires an interesting interplay between two distinct parameters: first, the underlying *legal principles* required to form a valid contract, and second, the unique *fact situations* that form the context within which the legal principles expressed in the contract are to operate. The legal principles that relate to contracts are few in number and easy to understand. In contrast, the fact situations that arise are infinite in number and can often be confusing, complex, and even conflicting. The best advice for understanding a contract, and from a more practical perspective, for drafting one, is to focus first on the legal principles and then to identify how they mesh with the relevant facts in a given situation.

> **BOX 9.1**   The Contract in Administrative Law
>
> Chapter 4, "Administrative Law—Fairness in Decision Making," explained that sport organizations are private tribunals that are self-governing through a contractual relationship that exists with their members. It further explained that this contractual relationship is expressed in the organization's governing documents such as its bylaws, policies, rules, and regulations. Although there is certainly some overlap between the principles of administrative law and contract law, we do not intend to suggest that a sport association's contract with its members is the same as a commercial contract such as those discussed in this chapter. This chapter outlines contract principles that apply primarily to business contracts. When a business contract is breached, there are usually damages that can be quantified in dollar terms. When there are breaches of the association–member contract discussed in chapter 4, the damages may not be financial. It is often said that "the currency of the athlete is competition," and when an athlete argues that his or her sport association has breached its duty to be fair, the remedy being sought is usually a competitive opportunity—in other words, a declaration that an athlete is eligible to compete, or an order than an athlete may compete by virtue of having been named to a team or restored to a team.

The legal principles serve as a form of "road map"—a steady and constant guide to the interpretation of every contract, despite the bewildering variety of facts that present themselves. A contractual "problem," whether related to drafting, contract formation, or contract interpretation, usually arises as a result of one, and at most two, fundamental legal principles. Thus, each analysis of a contract must start with a consideration of the legal principles. Because there is no absolute expression of "contract law" that dictates a result or an outcome, solutions to contracting issues are found in the continual interplay between the applicable legal principles and the relevant facts.

In this chapter we will present six legal principles that underlie and are applicable to every contracting situation. We will review a variety of contractual clauses and some unique contracts that are commonly encountered in the sport domain. Sample annotated clauses will illustrate typical issues and problem areas.

The Principles of Contract

Offer and Acceptance

For a contract to be valid there must be a definite offer made and a definite acceptance of that offer communicated in return. In this fashion, the parties, by their respective offer and acceptance, give evidence of their mutual intention to be contractually bound within the parameters contained in the offer. Because of the principle of mutual "offer and acceptance," it is simply not possible to form a unilateral legal contract. A personal "contract" or private undertaking may include a well-meaning promise to lose weight, make a charitable donation, or visit a sick friend; but, such intentions (if not fulfilled) are not enforceable by legal action. In contrast, a legal contract is a bargain entered into by at least two parties, with the bargain defined by the scope of the offer made and accepted. It is also required that all parties intend to be legally bound by their promises.

It seems a simple task to show the required offer and acceptance. Mary offers to sell her horse for $1,000 and Paul happily accepts. Paul pays Mary the purchase price and takes the animal. They have a legally enforceable contract. In this particular situation it can be said that the acceptance corresponds completely and exactly to the offer that was made. A contract is not made in this situation if Paul accepts Mary's offer but with a few adjustments (a saddle and bridle as well as the horse). This is a fundamental requirement for a valid "offer and acceptance" in contract law. Any acceptance of an offer must be clearly communicated because the acceptance "crystallizes" the exact offer that has been made and creates the binding contract. The principle of "offer and acceptance" serves to define the precise parameters of the contract that is being created.

In a more complex situation, it is not an easy task to formalize the exact parameters of an offer capable of acceptance from, say, several weeks' worth of discussion, negotiation, earlier drafts, and informal comments. The basic analysis should always be: Is the communication a formal offer? If so, am I clear what it encompasses, and if so, am I accepting it? Very few contract negotiations proceed as smoothly as Mary and Paul's—usually there is considerable give and take, offer and counter-offer between the two parties to the contract.

Consider the familiar pattern of negotiation between a home seller and a home buyer. The seller offers to sell at $100,000. The buyer does not accept but makes a counter-offer at $90,000 and inserts some conditions such as whether he or she can obtain financing, and the need to first sell the buyer's existing home. The seller replies with a counter-offer to sell at $98,000 but wants no conditions imposed. In return, the buyer makes an offer to pay $96,000 and waives his or her earlier conditions. The seller accepts. In this example the seller was the party making the initial offer (that could have been accepted) and yet in the end, the seller is accepting an offer from the buyer. They have a "deal" in which the acceptance corresponds completely and exactly to the latest valid offer that was made.

In the matter of offer and acceptance, it is important to remember these two rules: (1) a counter-offer is not an acceptance and (2) any change in an offer's terms on receipt of the offer is not an acceptance. The fundamental change made to an offer by imposing new terms or a counter-offer can result in no acceptance being possible.

Not every proposal is an "offer" capable of being accepted. What is often referred to in ordinary language as "puffery" is an offer that cannot be accepted but is only an *invitation to make an offer*—and perhaps to do business and enter a contract on the basis of that subsequent offer. For example, general comments made casually between friends about the condition of a car, how well it runs, and its value ("I'd pay $10,000 for that particular model" or "I'd sell this wreck right now for $100") are probably not capable of being accepted. These comments indicate only that the speaker is interested in seeing whether a deal is possible—that is, whether a formal offer may be forthcoming.

The distinction between a formal offer and an invitation to make an offer can become an issue in tendering situations when various bidders submit independent bids to an employer to perform some predetermined work. This process needs to be carefully designed so that the bids received by the employer are the actual offers capable of being accepted by the employer—if all preconditions are satisfied. Likewise, when a sport organization sends out requests for proposals or RFPs (which are often very detailed with regard to what is desired) and invites third parties to submit proposals as to how they would provide certain services, manage an event, or play host to an international competition, the RFP from the sport organization must be carefully designed so that it is not itself an offer capable of being accepted. Rather, the various proposals or bids that are received from the interested parties are in fact the offers that may or may not be accepted by the sport organization depending on whether the RFP conditions are fully satisfied. The point is this: Because contract law stipulates that a true offer can be accepted at any time—with the result of creating a legal and binding contract—it is prudent to control very carefully what offers are circulated to outside parties.

Consideration

The existence of "consideration" in a legal contract is absolutely crucial. Consideration was discussed in some detail in chapter 7 on work relationships. To create a valid and legally enforceable contract in Canada, there must be a "bargain" involving a promise made by one party supported by some "consideration" flowing to the party making the promise. At law, contracts are valid only if the parties to the bargain mutually promise to perform some act or undertake to perform some obligation for the other's benefit. In this fashion, the contractual promises are "bought" with the other party's reciprocal promises or with some additional inducement. Consideration is the legal term used to describe the means by which a contracting party's promise is bought. The consideration may be nominal but it *must* be present in every case. In addition, the consideration that supports a valid contract must be present *when* the contract is formed. Each side must stand to benefit to some greater or lesser degree at the moment of contract formation.

In British courts, where this legal principle of contract law was formulated, the transfer of a tiny peppercorn from the promisee to the promisor was held to be enough consideration to support a promise made and thus to create a valid contract. Without some element of consideration, no matter how small, the promise is not enforceable and the contract is not valid. In contract law, a gratuitous promise is unenforceable. A gratuitous promise is a promise freely made where only one party benefits (for example, to clean my room, to study three hours on Saturday, or even to donate $100 to a charity) without the promise being "bought." The reciprocity required is the need for the presence of some consideration that must be present at the time the contract was formed.

In most commercial contracts there will be consideration found in the mutual promises made by each party and set out in the agreement. For instance, the contract may specify that Sally, the website consultant, promises to do A, B, and C while Tom, the communications director, promises to pay Sally Y. Alternatively, products may be shipped by uniform supplier A and paid for by sport team B. The absolutely fundamental need for consideration to exist, and that it be present in every legal contract at the time the contract was formed, is shown by the inevitable phrases that find their way into most standard contracts. These two examples are typical: "For valuable consideration, the receipt and sufficiency of which is acknowledged, the parties agree as follows" or "In consideration of one dollar paid by each party to the other, the receipt of which is acknowledged, the parties agree as follows." These clauses, it is hoped, will prevent one party to the contract from ever arguing at a later date that there was no consideration present to support the promises made and that the contract was therefore invalid. What seems like a very odd phrase is, in fact, necessary to support the very existence of the contract.

Proper Parties

The parties to a contract often seem so obvious that potential problems can be overlooked. The applicable legal principle is that of "privity of contract." This principle holds that only the parties to a contract will be bound by it. This is consistent with the concept of a contract as a private bargain between two or more willing parties and that their respective mutual promises, which are set out in the contract, are bought with valuable consideration. As a result of this legal principle, if an individual person or a legal entity does not enter the contract, either by expressly signing the contract or otherwise evidencing an acceptance of it, it may be impossible to enforce the rights or obligations in the contract against that person or entity—despite an assumption that this party would also be bound by the contract's terms. The practical implications of privity of contract for the contract drafter are two-fold: first, always bring into the contract all potentially relevant persons and legal entities, and second, correctly identify who these parties actually are.

Because only the parties to a contract are bound by it, it is important to ask: Is there another individual or corporation that should be named as a party, but is not? Who is actually doing the work, and is this person bound contractually? Particular attention should be paid to the spelling of odd names and the proper corporate entities, and the actual form of business association being used (corporation, partnership, joint venture, etc.) should be correctly identified. A party to the contract should question whether the other party has the financial strength to honour its obligations or whether additional parties should be added so that payment will be assured. Could a parent company, a subsidiary division, or a related organization become a party to the contract to guarantee the obligations of the individual signing the contract? Should a director of an organization be forced to sign the contract in his or her personal capacity? This request will inevitably be resisted. The contentious issue of having directors and officers of a corporate party sign a contract in their personal capacity can be critical in a contract with an organization with very limited financial resources.

Another issue relating to privity of contract is whether the party has the proper authority to enter into a legally binding contract. See, in addition, the comments later in this chapter regarding factors that tend to limit contractual validity. For most adults this is not a major issue because any adult individual can sign an otherwise legal contract on his or her own behalf and will be bound by it. However, minors present very special considerations because most contracts are not enforceable against children under the age of 19 or 18, depending on the province or territory and how its laws define age of majority. As well, persons who are mentally handicapped (such as participants in the Special Olympics movement), and persons who are intoxicated or otherwise impaired, do not have the capacity to enter into contracts.

The question of legal authority to enter into a contract on behalf of a corporation or other legal entity is somewhat more difficult to evaluate. It would not be reasonable to have the janitor, parking attendant, or receptionist sign a legal contract that purported to bind a large corporation that employed them for millions of dollars in obligations. These persons simply do not have the power or authority to bind the corporation in this way—and no sensible person could claim to think that they did. But who can sign on behalf of an organization? This raises the related issues of *actual authority* and *ostensible authority*.

Actual authority is the authority that is expressly granted to a person to do certain things on behalf of a corporation. Individuals in accounting are expressly empowered to co-sign cheques up to a certain dollar amount. Vice-presidents are given authority by the board of directors to negotiate mergers and sign corporate documentation or long-term leases. Those with actual authority possess the power and authority to bind the company because this power has been delegated to them—despite what an outsider may believe or think is reasonable in the circumstances.

In contrast, ostensible authority is the perception held by an outsider that a certain person has in fact the "power to act" on behalf of a corporation by reason of that person's actions, demeanour, or words. The "holding out" of a certain degree of authority to act may be supported by an express grant for this specific power, but often it is not. In the result, a person with no actual authority but who "holds out" or represents that he or she has full power to sign a particular contract may be found to have ostensible authority if it is reasonable for the other contracting party to believe that this person had, in fact, the authority to act for and to bind the corporation. The corporation may be stuck with contractual obligations entered into by an individual who was not authorized to sign. The party who relied on the ostensible authority of this employee may be facing an argument from the corporation that it was not at all reasonable to assume, without checking, that this person had the authority to do what occurred. Either way the situation will be a mess, so be forewarned. All contracting parties should have the actual authority needed to bind the party on whose behalf they purportedly are signing the contract.

Contract Length and Renewal

For contracts that contemplate a single, discrete transaction, the issues of the contract's term and a potential renewal or extension are not relevant. These single-transaction contracts may be for the sale of an item, the provision of catering services for a party, or a speaking fee at a convention. The work is done and the contract is over. However, a great many contracts contemplate the provision of work or services over a lengthy period of time. Each party will be intending to grant rights and to perform obligations for a known time period. For all of these contracts it must be specified when the contract commences and when it will end or expire. The duration of the contract is usually a business decision rather than a legal issue. However, there are legal implications regarding a contract's termination and renewal.

If a contract is for a set term, it will expire on the stated termination date. Nothing further is needed for this to happen. The obligations of the parties defined in the contract will be at an end. If there is potential for the contract to be terminated by one or both parties before the set termination date, the contract should specify how termination will occur. The contract will typically contain clauses that identify defaulting events that can lead to early termination and will also provide any formal notice requirements and rights to "cure" any default that is alleged. Some contracts state that there must be arbitration prior to an early termination. In any event, if these mandated steps are followed carefully, the contract can be ended earlier than initially anticipated pursuant to its terms. Contract termination is not terribly complex: more troubling issues arise when the contract is intended to be extended beyond its anticipated term.

Some contracts are for a set term but they may be extended once or many times. Precisely how these extensions, or renewal rights, are expressed in the contract can have a critical impact on a party's long-term options and its flexibility to pursue other contracting opportunities with other parties.

It is certainly possible to provide for no renewal rights in a contract. In this event, the parties may still decide to negotiate with each other to try to reach a subsequent agreement to extend the contract on conditions that are mutually accepted. In such a case, the parties remain free to try to negotiate with each other, or with new partners, at the conclusion of the initial term. This model provides the greatest flexibility, but also the greatest uncertainty.

More typically, contracts feature provisions specifying exactly how and on what terms the contract may be extended involving the initial contracting parties. There are three common scenarios for extending a contract: a right of "first refusal," an "option to renew," and a "right to negotiate." There are significant legal and practical differences among these three scenarios.

Right of First Refusal

If a party has negotiated a right of first refusal in a contract (for example, a sponsor will typically try to insert this into a sponsorship contract), it means that the sponsor has the right to match and to accept any competing offer that the sport organization is prepared to accept at the end of the initial contract term. The critical issue with a right of first refusal is that the competing offer must be a complete and detailed proposal of the intended new contractual relationship. Very few potential new sponsors are interested in investing time and energy to negotiate a sponsorship agreement, knowing that an existing sponsor, who is possibly a competitor, can exercise its right of first refusal and accept any deal that the potential sponsor has just laboriously negotiated with the sport organization. The practical result is that rights of first refusal make it difficult or impossible to switch sponsors—even if the new sponsor is prepared to offer a significantly better arrangement or if the original sponsor's overall performance is poor.

Option for Renewal

An option is the right to accept, at a later date, terms and conditions that have been previously agreed. An option for renewal allows, for example, the sponsor to accept a renewed contract, on fixed terms, provided the option to renew is exercised within a defined period of time. Typically, the sport organization will want to be notified about six months before the end of the contract's term whether the sponsor is willing to renew on the previously agreed terms. The benefit of this option is that the terms of renewal are fixed and the only question is whether the option will be exercised. If the option is not exercised within the specified time period, the sport organization is then free to negotiate with any other sponsor or potential partner. The difficulty with renewal options is that conditions in the future may not have been accurately predicted when the terms in the option were negotiated— this can either help or hurt the organization, depending on its current negotiating strength and relative financial position.

Right to Negotiate

This right allows the parties a set period of time within which they agree to negotiate exclusively with each other regarding a decision to extend or renew the contract. Such negotiations must be undertaken in good faith. If the parties fail to reach an agreement within the time specified, each party will be free to contract with other parties with no restrictions or penalties. The main difficulty with this scenario is the obligation to negotiate in "good faith" and not simply "go through the motions." Some courts have taken the view that the promise to negotiate in good faith is too vague to be enforced.

The Substantive Content of a Contract

This legal principle can be stated simply enough: make your bargain and then express it clearly in the contract! Contracts mean precisely what they say—not what the parties later say they might have intended. If the parties do not express their arrangement accurately in the contract, it is the contract wording that will likely be enforced—not what the parties later claim they wished to have happen. It is not easy to capture on paper the entire deal or understanding between the parties. The substantive terms contained in the contract must demonstrate each party's clear intentions with regard to the offer and acceptance bargain they have made and it must specify their respective rights and obligations in sufficient detail. Contracts need not be long or complex—but in every case, no matter how short and simple, they must accurately describe the specific "deal" the parties have reached.

As we have seen, contracts can be created in writing, they can be created orally, or they may even be inferred from a person's conduct. However, it is far better to insist on having all important contracts expressed in writing. This creates certainty and becomes a record of the parties' intentions at the time the contract was formed. Parties who reach an agreement and fully intend to "do a deal" together typically agree on some (or most) major things, ignore much else, and perhaps disagree on a few items.

Unfortunately, parties often start to write up the legal contract before they actually understand or even agree on all aspects of their "agreement." Nothing wastes more time and money than this method of proceeding. It is absolutely essential that there be a fully formed and understood agreement first. Only after all the details are agreed on should the parties consolidate that agreement into a written document.

It is common for successful contracting parties to use a three-step process to formalize any type of complex or contentious deal. First, they verbally negotiate the broad structure of the deal or agreement. They address all the main points such as price, product quality, and delivery dates. If there is no broad agreement at this stage in the negotiations, there will be no need for a formal contract. Second, they actually write down the complete essential agreement in a form of shorthand using "deal points" or a "term sheet" so that the full agreement is fleshed out in more detail and all the implications can be fully understood. This second step should not be in a legal form nor should it use formal or legal language. This step allows the parties to focus on all parts of the deal in ordinary language and to determine whether the arrangement is sensible and conceptually coherent. This is the step where the inevitable kinks are worked out of the arrangement and issues that need to be addressed are inserted. Third, and only then, should the fully prepared and understood arrangement be drawn up as a legal contract.

Since every agreement reached is unique and specific to the parties involved, it stands to reason that each contract expressing an agreement should also be individually tailored to express the specific deal the parties have reached. Nowhere is it more true that *one size does not fit all*. In a perfect world, to continue with tailoring analogies, each contract should be perfectly "made to measure." The use of computers, word processing software and electronic sample precedents is a double-edged sword—they have allowed easy reproduction and sharing of voluminous contract material but at the significant cost of lost accuracy and context in the final product. There is an acute danger present when "cut and paste" drafting is substituted for a real effort to express carefully a unique contractual arrangement. To be sure, there are benefits to using standardized contracts, but those who use them must always be aware of their significant limitations. Sample forms should be used as a guide only—to help to identify topics and issues to include in a contract. Sample forms never contain the specific details that make a particular deal unique. That challenge remains to the contract drafter.

Damages

When a contract is broken, the injured party can be compensated for that breach of contract, but the range of relief available is quite limited. Payment of a sum of money in compensation for suffering legal damages is the usual remedy for a breach of contract. The intent of the law is to place the innocent party, through the payment of money, into as near as possible the same situation that party would have been in but for the breach of the contract. The awarding of damages, in the form of an order to pay a certain sum of money, is not intended to punish the party who is in breach but is designed to compensate the injured party for the loss of his or her bargain. The court will order that the party responsible for the breach pay to the other party the reasonably foreseeable losses that arose and flowed from the breach of contract. Of course, in many situations a sum of money (however large) is scant comfort for what has been suffered or lost. It is also hard to accurately quantify the sum of money that fairly represents what has been lost. In every case, damage awards are no more than rough approximations of this "value."

The relevant legal principle is that the damages suffered and compensated for must be caused by the breach of contract. In most cases the losses a party suffers are clear and it is perfectly obvious what caused them. Damages may be the lost profit from a joint venture, the value of a stock option never issued, or the refusal to pay a commission or bonus mandated in the contract on the occurrence of a triggering event. However, in some cases it is not easy to show that the breach of the contract actually caused the loss that is claimed. The concept of "causation" is used to identify what losses are caused by the breach of a contract. The notion of a "chain of causation" signifies that the causal links must not be broken and that the end result, where the "chain" eventually leads, can be foreseen.

Imagine, for instance, the expanding circles of ripples fanning out from a pebble thrown into a still pond. Near the point of impact it is clear the ripples radiating outward are the direct result of the pebble tossed. On the far side of the pond small waves lapping the bank may or may not have been caused by the thrown pebble— other events or factors may have intervened and influenced the water's motion that far from the point of impact: wind, a light current, a fish jumping, a small animal drinking at the water's edge, etc.

In summary, to be compensated by the payment of damage, the loss from a breach of contract must be, first, *caused* by the breach and second, the loss must be *reasonably foreseeable as a result of that breach* of the contract. As the chain of events

---

BOX 9.2　The Chain of Causation Can Lead to Strange Places

Bertha is a cook working at Sharp Ridges Alpine Resort. She is embroiled in a rocky working relationship with Spud, the dishwasher. After a recent fight at lunch, in a fit of spite, she made a big sign that said "Bite me!" and laid it on his dishwasher. Just then, Tommy, a tourist from out of province, drove into Sharp Ridges looking for directions to town. Tommy wears thick glasses and is somewhat visually impaired. He should not be driving at all—except this portion of his trip was out in the countryside on quiet back roads. He wandered beyond the Sharp Ridges office and into the kitchen, not seeing the "Staff Only" sign. As he entered, a gust of wind blew Bertha's sign from the dishwasher onto a plate of very hot chilli peppers. Tommy saw the plate of peppers and the welcoming sign. Thinking the peppers were a plate of beans, he grabbed a handful. A single bite caused him to gag and splutter, stagger backward, fall, crack his glasses, and bang his head on the floor. He was quickly revived by staff who sent him on his way with the directions he was looking for—feeling a bit woozy, eyes running, and very red in the face. The effect of the chillies returned within two minutes of his leaving. As he left the Sharp Ridges property, the sweat was running down his forehead and into his eyes. He also had a headache. His vision deteriorated. The cracked glasses lens did not help. The police later determined that he drove off the road and into an adjoining field where a fence was ruined, the car was damaged, and Art Frizzell's corn crop was flattened. In the process Tommy suffered mild whiplash and the car struck a student researching ethanol production as part of a summer research grant. As a result of her injuries, the student missed the first month of university and was not able to join the women's hockey team—thereby forfeiting her full four-year athletic scholarship to University of Minnesota at Duluth.

Did Bertha cause the damage to the glasses? Did Bertha cause the whiplash? Did Tommy cause the lost scholarship? Who should compensate Farmer Frizzell for his damaged fence and crop? Who or what caused what? What was reasonably foreseeable in this scenario?

---

resulting from the breach expands ever outward (like the ripples on the pond), it becomes increasingly difficult to maintain that certain losses were directly caused by the breach of the contract. Some events that occur in consequence of a breach of contract are just not within the reasonable foresight of the parties at the time of the breach. Even if there is an intact "chain of causation" leading to the damage claimed, meaning A led to B which led to C and then to D, the second question must still be addressed—were the damages at D foreseeable at the time of the breach? Only damages that are reasonably foreseeable as a result of a breach of the contract causing them may be compensated for.

There are only rare situations in Canada where *punitive damages* are awarded. This form of damage award is reserved for situations when the conduct of a breaching party is considered particularly outrageous and intentional. The intent of punitive damage is simple—to punish the wrongdoer and to send a strong message to future wrongdoers that this type of intentional conduct will not be accepted by the courts. Punitive damages, if they are awarded, are given in addition to any other damages intended to compensate a victim for direct losses flowing from the breach.

In our legal system an order for *specific performance* is also rather rare. Specific performance is an order of a court, or other decision maker, that despite the breach, the contract will be performed according to its terms. Canadian courts are generally reluctant to force contracting parties together to perform a bargain that has been breached. In many situations, the bargain expressed in the contract may no longer be workable or manageable, and the litigating parties are not likely to be happy to be ordered to continue to work and cooperate together. Orders for specific performance are rare because the courts do not want to assume the ongoing task of supervising the performance of private contractual arrangements. This is why the payment of money damages, despite its limitations, is by far the most common remedy awarded for a breach of a contract.

Several Factors May Limit Contractual Liability

Minors

The age of majority is defined in provincial/territorial legislation as either 18 or 19. Youth below that age are considered minors and at law are not responsible for certain contracts that they may enter into. Contracts that are primarily for the benefit of the minor are more likely to be considered valid and enforced despite their execution by a minor. Such contracts may be agreements to participate in an athletic

---

BOX 9.3   Professional Contracts and "Restrictive Covenants"

When there is a breach of contract between a professional athlete and a sports team, the financial damages to the team are difficult to assess and usually not what the team is looking for. As well, in such situations the courts are unlikely to order specific performance on the part of the athlete, nor would the team necessarily want this. However, such contracts often feature a specialized clause known as a "restrictive covenant," or a promise *not* to do something—in this case a promise not to play for any other team for a specified period of time, which usually corresponds to the term of the breached contract. The courts are typically prepared to enforce the restrictive covenant so that, although the athlete does not have to play for the team in question, he or she cannot play for any other team. (Restrictive covenants are discussed further below.)

or entertainment event or contracts in the nature of employment agreements. Athlete agreements are primarily for the benefit of the athlete but certain clauses may be resisted if they impose onerous obligations on the minor. Caution must be exercised in every case where a minor alone signs any contract that is intended to have legal effect (see *Toronto Marlboro Major Junior "A" Hockey Club v. Tonelli*).

Duress or Undue Influence

Contracts must be freely entered into if they are to be valid. Contracts are expressions of a person's intent to "deal" with another person. The "bargain" between the contracting parties must be mutual and the parties must mutually intend to be bound. If there is evidence of threats, force, or undue influence on a contracting party imposed by, or through, the other party to the contract, this improper conduct may be enough to invalidate the contract. The negative pressure to enter the contract must come from the opposite party because it is quite common for individuals to enter contractual bargains in rather dire straights—they may be under significant hardships or unfortunate influences, but of their own making.

Mistake

In some very limited situations, an honest mistake may serve to invalidate a contract. If there is a misunderstanding or misapprehension that goes to the root of the contract, it may be possible to claim that, if the true facts were known, the party would not have entered into the contract. The mistake could be made with regard to the subject matter of the contract (thinking it was red wine and not rum in the cask), a mistake as to title of an item sold (both parties may have believed Bill owned the horse that was for sale but in fact Mary did), or a mistake as to the quality of the product bought (a party paid for real pearls when they were actually cultured). In all cases of an alleged mistake where the mistaken party seeks to reject the contract, the law is technical and complex—far better to be certain of the true facts in advance.

Misrepresentation

A person who has been induced to enter into a contract because of a factual misrepresentation may be able to have the contract set aside and perhaps claim damages for the loss of the bargain. There is a general duty to inform the contracting parties of all material facts (as opposed to opinions) that might reasonably influence a contracting decision. An opinion may be that a car is attractive or it is reliable. The subject matter of the opinion is difficult to substantiate and it is also subjective. However, the fact that the car was in an accident needs to be disclosed. Misrepresentation, if it can be proven, may be innocent, fraudulent, or negligent, and the potential remedy varies in each case.

Illegality

On the basis of public policy, contracts for an illegal purpose are not valid. It is obviously not proper to go to court to enforce a contract between two drug traffickers who have a dispute about their transportation arrangements to import heroin into Canada and the payments owing to each other and to third parties. Contracts (otherwise valid) for any purpose that is illegal will not be enforced.

Particular Contracts

Releases and Waivers

Organizers of sport events, and participants in sport, sign waivers and releases every day. These are very specialized contracts that have only one narrow purpose—to confirm that the person signing the document will not make a claim against some identified group of people or organizations in the event an injury or damage occurs. Whether it is called a release or a waiver, the person signing the document is releasing any claims he or she may have, or waiving any right to start an action against named parties in certain defined and usually limited situations. The legal effect of signing a release or a waiver is obviously significant. If the person signing such a document is seriously injured or is killed at the event covered by the document, then the release or waiver, if upheld at a subsequent trial, will prevent any claim being made against the person or entity that caused the injury or death. The injured victim, or the deceased victim's family, is often left with no source to provide compensation for the injury or death.

As a result of the significant legal consequences that result if a release or waiver is deemed to be valid, the courts tend to scrutinize these contracts very closely to be sure they represent a truly informed bargain—an honest intention to give up important legal rights made by a person who was fully aware of the contract and of the consequences. Some waivers and releases are struck down, but it is not correct to say that "they are not worth the paper they are written on." People involved in sports sign waivers often, and it is a very common perception that they are worthless. However, this is not accurate: waivers *are* upheld by the courts. In principle, they are perfectly valid contracts if they are prepared and executed carefully; but they will always be closely reviewed to be sure all the formal contracting requirements are satisfied.

The key to understanding and drafting these documents is to clearly identify three things: (1) precisely who is being released; (2) for injury or loss, at what event or in what situation; and (3) caused by what and on the basis of what legal claims. If each of these three questions cannot be clearly answered there is a good chance the release or waiver will be struck down. It is understandable that a court will be worried if these fundamental issues are not clearly articulated and easily understood, because the person signing will not have understood the nature and scope of the legal rights being granted away. Appendix 9.1 gives a sample annotated form of release that identifies each of these three elements.

The three most common problems arising from releases and waivers, and the issues that regularly cause them to fail, are these: (1) the actual words used or the layout of the document; (2) the manner and timing of the presentation of the document, and (3) how it is signed and by whom. These three issues are addressed below. Our guidance in this section is drawn from an abundance of case law relating to waivers used in sport and recreation settings (see *Dyck v. Manitoba Snowmobile Association, Crocker v. Sundance Northwest Resorts Ltd., Delaney v. Cascade River Holidays Ltd., Karroll v. Silver Star Mountain Resort,* and *Blomberg v. Blackcomb Skiing Enterprises Ltd.*).

Words and Layout

The document must be clear, concise, and grammatically correct. It must say what it means. Those who are using waivers should try to have the content all contained on one page and should avoid using a tiny font. It is advisable to not combine the waiver or release with other information in the same document (for example, registration information or medical information). If information is combined, it will not be clear whether the signature at the bottom refers to the release or to the other issues. If the intent is to seek to have a released party's *negligence* waived, as well as all other conduct and causes of injury, including the inherent physical risks of the sport, then the word "negligence" must be expressly stated—generally in upper-case and bold letters so that it is brought to the attention of the person signing the waiver.

Presentation

The waiver or release should be provided to the person signing it well in advance of the activity. The sooner it can be delivered for a full and leisurely review by the person signing the better. Many commercial adventure-tour companies print the form of release they wish signed in the advertising brochure so it comes to the attention of the potential client as soon as possible—although it still must be presented to the client and signed by the client. In any event, the terms in the release must come to the attention of the person who is signing to accept its content. There must be time to review and reflect on it. Handing a client or participant a waiver to sign at the last moment before embarking on an activity, or once the participant has already travelled a great distance to attend the event, is not sufficient. Should this occur, the practical result is that the person is compelled to sign the waiver, thus it cannot be said that he or she entered into the bargain voluntarily and in an informed manner.

Signing

Despite the best wording, layout, presentation, and timing, the validity of a waiver can be undermined at the moment it is being signed. Often, a participant will ask questions at this time regarding what the document actually means. Although tempting, it is not advisable to interpret, explain, or summarize the document. The best response when queried by a participant is to say that the document means exactly what it says. Never dismiss or "explain away" the waiver with comments like these: "it's just a legal paper the lawyers fuss with—nothing to worry about" or "it's just a formality." The waiver is a formal and powerful legal document and an important risk management strategy. Sport organizers using waivers must make every effort to convey that impression and the seriousness of the contract when it is actually being signed.

As mentioned earlier under the discussion of factors that may limit contractual liability, minors are not bound by contracts, particularly those contracts that are not fully for their benefit. Any waiver or release involves the person signing giving up an important legal right (the right to seek legal redress for injuries), and the fact of doing so will never be construed as being to the benefit of a participant who is a minor. Furthermore, although parents and guardians can execute a limited number of contracts that are to the benefit of their children, a waiver of liability for negligence is not such a contract. It is unlikely that a waiver or release signed by a minor, or by the minor's parent or guardian, will be upheld by a court.

Indemnities

To indemnify means to "restore to its original condition." An indemnity is a legal term that means a party is making a promise to pay. An indemnification clause means that Bob agrees to compensate Carol, and perhaps others, for all claims, damages, or losses that Carol and others may suffer as a result of certain activities that relate to Bob and/or to the agreement Carol has made with Bob. Deciding whether to enter into an indemnification agreement is all about *managing risk*— identifying it, determining how to allocate it, and deciding who will be responsible for any resulting financial losses. Indemnities are very common in contracts, but are often written in such a complex manner that an ordinary person does not fully appreciate their meaning.

As such, an indemnity should be entered into by Bob only if there is little likelihood that those events that will trigger the obligation to pay will come to pass, and

Bob has money available to make the promised payment if the need arises. Few contracting parties appreciate that an indemnity agreement or clause represents a huge potential liability. Indemnities often form part of the standard clauses in contracts that no one really pays much attention to. Organizations should be very careful about entering into any form of indemnification in the contracts they sign. If the level of risk is unknown (as is often the case), such a clause has the potential to cost an organization a great deal of money. This is often referred to as a "contingent liability," or the liability that could arise if a certain event occurs. The best strategy is to avoid indemnities if avoidance is possible.

Much like a waiver or release, an indemnity contains three basic elements: (1) who is promising to pay; (2) who receives the benefit of the promise and may be paid; and (3) what events will trigger the payment. Appendix 9.1 provides annotated sample indemnity clauses that identify each element. The first two points are generally easy to define and constrain. The last point is most critical, and how it is worded can significantly narrow the scope of the contingent liability that an indemnity represents. Far too often the events that trigger a payment are too broadly stated. Depending on the fact situation underlying the contract, try to narrow and confine the causes of the losses that will have to be indemnified against. It is also possible to place a cap or a maximum limit on any indemnity payment.

In many agreements, mutual indemnities are inserted as a matter of course. The practice is justified on the basis that both parties are then in the same position, so they can hardly complain. Even so, try to resist this practice. It is rare that both parties are at the same risk of an event occurring that will trigger the demand to pay. Inevitably, the likelihood of both parties suffering the same measure of damages from the events defined in the indemnity is small. For example, because it is the sponsor who is greatly broadening the use and exposure of an organization's assets, the sponsor tends to face a greater risk of being sued and perhaps suffering significant losses. If the sponsor is sued, and has received an indemnification from the organization, the organization will be responsible for the sponsor's damages. A mutual indemnity with identical terms will not fairly balance and allocate the risks inherent in this situation.

If signing an indemnity is mandatory, and it often is, every reasonable effort to limit the scope of the "promise to pay" should be made. It is important that the indemnity is consistent with the agreement and with what the grantor of the indemnity has promised to do. Many indemnity clauses are "cut and pasted" from other agreements and have no reference to the particular situation described in the contract. An indemnity should be provided only against events that can be controlled and thus guarded against, and this is typically no more than a promise not to breach the agreement within which the indemnity is found. If the scope of a triggering event is dependent on either the conduct of a third party or some other external factor, making this promise to pay should be strongly resisted.

Remember that an indemnity is just a promise to pay. As such, it may be worthless if the triggering event occurs and the grantor of the indemnity, in fact, has no funds to pay it. The person seeking to be paid pursuant to an indemnity must, on his or her own initiative, take the steps required to collect on the promise and enforce the indemnity agreement. Those who might be seeking to rely on an indemnity should consider seeking some form of financial security to bolster the bare promise to pay that an indemnity represents. This can be done by inserting other grantors into the indemnity (such as a parent company or an affiliate) or, more aggressively, insisting on a mortgage, a registered security interest, or a personal guarantee from someone with sufficient funds to secure the payment.

Finally, indemnities may also give rise to insurance-related problems. Executing a contract with an indemnification clause means that the organization or person who is granting the indemnity is taking on an unknown liability, which may constitute a "material change" in the insurer's risk. Such a risk should be reported so that the insurers can confirm that the limits of the insurance policy are sufficient to cover any potential claim that might arise out of the indemnity.

Restrictive Covenants

A "covenant" is a promise. Restrictive covenants comprise a class of contracts that limit, or restrict, the rights of an individual, typically an employee, to engage in certain conduct. Historically, restrictive covenants have been used in property transactions to prevent the purchasers of property from later doing certain things—including selling their property for undesirable uses or to undesirable purchasers. The most common restrictive covenants in the sport domain are in the employment area, and include non-competition agreements, non-solicitation agreements, and confidentiality agreements. Their scope, or how broadly they are drafted, will have an effect on whether they will be enforced. A restrictive covenant that has an excessively broad scope, imposing unreasonable restrictions or prohibitions, will likely be struck down by the courts. The key to writing a restrictive covenant clause is to strike a balance between protecting the legitimate business interests of one party with the right of the other party to continue to work and earn a living in a field for which he or she is trained or has experience. Restrictive covenants may not be used to completely eliminate competition, but they can be used to protect against improper competition so long as the restrictions are reasonable and are constrained to a limited geographic area and for a limited period of time. The biggest danger with restrictive covenants is that the restrictions tend to overreach—if the restrictions are unreasonable, and are not directly tied to a legitimate interest demanding protection, the covenants will likely fail.

In terms of non-competition agreements, the geographic area where the restrictive covenant applies must be reasonable and should be linked to the previous sphere of activity for an employee. For instance, an employee who worked exclusively in one neighbourhood should not have a geographic restriction imposed covering all of a province or even an entire city. The duration of any restrictions imposed also must be reasonable. The duration should be linked to the degree of influence the employee has over his or her former customers, and to an estimate of the length of time that influence might last. Another factor to be considered might be the period of time necessary for the employer to hire and train a replacement employee. A restrictive covenant with no area or time restrictions applied to it may be interpreted as being unlimited in scope and will likely not survive any scrutiny by a court.

The party seeking to rely on a restrictive covenant must show that there is a legitimate business interest that needs protection. The overriding principle with restrictive covenants is that an employee should not be unreasonably restricted in the practice of his trade. Canadian courts will refuse to enforce these clauses if they are considered to be in restraint of trade. All such agreements will be enforceable only to the extent that they are reasonably necessary to protect a legitimate interest of the employer. The less restrictive the obligation, the more likely the clause will be upheld. For non-competition agreements to be valid there must be a realistic danger existing to the business from the ongoing activities of a former employee. This might be the case if the departing employee was a key person or because the employee's specific expertise or extensive public or industry contacts were the principal force behind the enterprise. In every case, the restrictions imposed must focus on the particular threat posed by a particular employee to the business's commercial interests and must not result in a general bar from employment in that field in every capacity.

The restrictions imposed must go no farther than absolutely necessary to address the legitimate threat identified. There is real danger in a "one-size-fits-all" use of precedents or templates when creating restrictive covenants. Each relationship and each business interest is unique and these must be considered on a case-by-case basis. To make a non-competition covenant seem more reasonable, one option to consider might be to have the covenant effective only if the employee resigns or is terminated for just cause. A court may be more likely persuaded to find a restrictive covenant reasonable if the employee has freely left his employment to actively pursue a new opportunity at the employer's expense. In contrast, it may be considered unreasonable for an employer to impose severe restrictions on an employee's future livelihood when that employer has just terminated the employee's employment without cause.

Non-solicitation agreements restrict an employee from soliciting the suppliers, customers, or employees of the employer while employed and for a period of time after the employee has left his or her employment. Non-solicitation agreements should not be inserted solely to prevent the otherwise voluntary departure of employees. Non-solicitation agreements that prohibit a departing employee from soliciting the customers of a business are often a less restrictive way to protect a legitimate business interest of the employer than a non-competition clause. These should be encouraged.

The Ontario Court of Appeal in the case of *Lyons v. Multari* reviewed the non-compete restrictions imposed on a departing employee. The employee was a dental surgeon. The restriction was as follows: *"Protection covenant—3 years—5 miles."* The court confirmed that the factors to evaluate as to the reasonableness of the restrictions were whether there was a proprietary interest of the employer worthy of protection, was the scope of the restrictions too broad (as to location and time), and whether the covenant restricted competition generally. The court found that the non-competition clause was too broad and was not actually needed to protect the employer given the role of the employee at the clinic and his relationship with the clinic's patients. The court stated that because the least restrictive method of protecting a business interest was desired, in this particular case prohibiting the direct solicitation of patients of the clinic would adequately protect the legitimate interests of the clinic; but apart from this, it was the court's view that the departing dentist could continue to practise dentistry with no other restrictions. Many subsequent court decisions have reiterated the principle that in the face of a legitimate proprietary interest demanding protection, only the least restrictive covenant addressing this interest will be upheld.

In the course of employment, employees often gain access to information of the employer, or of the employer's clients or customers, that is private and confidential. If employers wish to protect this information, they can obtain a covenant whereby the employee agrees not to pass the information on to any third party during or after the term of employment. The information must be unique and particular to the business that is caught within the scope of such an agreement. This could be trade secrets, customer lists, supplier pricing lists, intellectual property, or business or marketing plans. Some agreements define separately *business information* and *confidential information* and impose different levels of protection on each class of information. Information that is in the public domain and that is readily available from other sources is not confidential and should not be included within the scope of this covenant.

The greatest danger with confidentiality agreements, in terms of interpretation and compliance, is being able to identify precisely what information is caught within the scope of the restrictive covenant. Some confidentiality agreements state that information to be included must be expressly marked "Confidential." This provides certainty but is difficult to adhere to consistently over time. Other versions of confidentiality agreements simply say that general business information is caught or that information relating to a particular project or service provided to a party is all deemed confidential. Some agreements actually say that all confidential information of the association is deemed "confidential"—this of course is no help at all! Those drafting such restrictive covenants should strive to make crystal clear what information is included and what information is excluded from the scope of a confidentiality agreement. One party will inevitably seek to have the inclusions as wide as possible, and the party making the promise will try to narrow the scope of the promise. Once the nature and extent of the information that is covered is understood, it becomes a rather simple matter of managing the flow and access to that information for the required time period.

Other concerns with these sorts of promises include how to allow for limited disclosure of the confidential information for work-related purposes. Often the confidential information is used daily to perform usual work functions (for example, a membership database), and so all staff with access to this information may be required to sign similar covenants to ensure the complete protection of the information received. In some work situations an organization does not want to receive information because it could taint a project—for instance, proprietary software development must not include any third-party materials—and so the control of this sort of information flowing *into* a company is critical. A document that is conceptually similar to a confidentiality agreement is a *non-disclosure agreement* and this form of agreement can be used to prevent the flow of particularly sensitive information both in and out of an organization.

One final point must be stressed. Will the employer be able to detect a breach of the employee's covenant not to disclose certain information and, if so, will the employer be in a position to enforce the clause? All restrictive covenants imposed in a contract or agreement must be self-enforced, and so obtaining a promise without a mechanism to check compliance and insist on enforcement will be meaningless.

Appendix 9.1 provides annotated samples of each type of restrictive covenant discussed above.

Multiparty Hosting Agreements

This form of contract is often used in connection with sport-event management and sponsorship-selling arrangements. "Hosting contracts" are typically multiparty agreements where an event owner (typically a sport governing or sanctioning body) decides to allow one or more other parties the right to host the event, manage the operation of the event, use certain intellectual property of the owner, and perhaps sell various sponsorship properties to that event. This basic contract structure is used for all major international sporting events, including the Olympic Games, the Commonwealth Games, and sport-specific world championships. There is in every instance a grant of rights flowing downward, as in a chain, commencing with the owner of the various commercial and athletic properties.

The starting point for this grant of rights is of course the owner of the event (whether the International Olympic Committee [IOC], an international federation, a national federation, or a scholastic sports body). As owner, the organization decides how best to exploit and generate revenue from this asset that they own. Typically, the first-level grant is made down to a local organizer or organizing committee who is charged with actually presenting the event—subject always to a great many conditions imposed by the owner. That local organizer is, in fact, usually a group or a committee and is the "host." The host has responsibility for presenting the event on behalf of the owner. The host then typically enters into a wide variety of further contracts with managers, service providers, and suppliers who each have specific roles and responsibilities. This concept is not dissimilar to the comments on licensing found in chapter 8. As in a licensing arrangement, where it was stressed that a licensor of intellectual property must grant a licence only to a licensee covering what he or she actually owns or controls, the same principles apply in a multiparty contractual arrangement.

The unique feature of all such vertically structured hosting agreements is the "flow-through" nature of the rights that are granted. Gaps or breaks in this chain of rights being granted can be hugely problematic because mistakes that are made continue to flow to other parties down that line of contracts. Great care is required to be sure that each tier is operating on a permitted basis. What this means, in practice, is that A, as the owner of the event and the owner of all rights associated with the event, starts the process with the complete bundle of rights associated with the event. A decides, perhaps through a bidding process, that B will be the event host. A may retain some rights to exploit itself (perhaps media broadcasting or the right to sell sponsorships in a certain product class) and then grants the majority of the rights associated with the event along to B, the host of the event. In the grant from A to B there are inevitably many restrictions and conditions that A will impose on B—and also on anyone with whom B decides to contract to fulfill the obligations of B contained in this initial, top-level grant. It is critical for B to assess and ensure that whatever rights it may subsequently grant onward to its managers, service providers, suppliers, sponsors, or contractors are actually received from A, and are consistent with what A is allowing B to do. Any recipient of rights from B will be constrained precisely by what B is permitted to do or is prohibited from doing by A. This same analysis continues down the chain to any potential grants made to C and even onward to D.

Appendix 9.1 gives two examples of this style of multiparty contract. Sample #6, with just the recitals included, is intended to show the variety of relationships that are possible and the contracts involved in hosting a major international event. Sample #7, the Major Cup contract example, is taken from an actual event arrangement to demonstrate how the host must be aware to ensure that the rights it grants downward (in the example provided, to the manager) have been received by the host and are permitted in the initial grant to the host.

Despite the unique "flow-through" of commercial rights, these hosting contracts are otherwise rather usual—there must be consideration, a clear expression of the deal reached, and, of course, the correct parties named. The trick is to track very closely what is being received, and thus what can be passed along, to be sure no contractual promises are made that are not allowed or that cannot be kept.

Typical Contract Clauses

The following clauses, because they create certainty and also provide flexibility, are often included in contracts.

Arbitration Clause

Any private agreement that allows the parties to settle disputes through arbitration or mediation will be quicker and more cost effective than litigating the dispute in court. The topic of alternative dispute resolution is discussed in chapter 10. Here is a sample arbitration clause:

> In the event that a dispute between the parties remains unresolved, then the parties may agree that the dispute be arbitrated and, in that event, this section of this Agreement shall be considered "an arbitration agreement" and the arbitration shall be an arbitration conducted under the *Arbitration Act*, 1991, SO 1991, c. 17, as amended ("the Act"). The parties hereto further agree that the arbitral tribunal shall consist of a single arbitrator. A request for arbitration shall be invoked as follows: one of the parties hereto shall file a photocopy of this section of the Agreement with the Arbitration and Mediation Institute of Ontario ("AMIO") together with a written request (with a copy of same to the other party hereto) that AMIO provide to the parties from AMIO's membership a list of three proposed arbitrators, each of whom is experienced in [*insert the nature of dispute*] arbitration. In the event that the parties are unable to

agree on one of the three proposed, then AMIO shall select a further fourth arbitrator as the appropriate arbitrator and AMIO's selection is binding upon the parties.

The arbitration shall be heard at such time and place as selected by the arbitrator in consultation with the parties. In the event that the parties are unable to mutually agree on a time and place, then the arbitrator's decision as to the time and place of the arbitration is final and binding on the parties and not appealable by any party hereunder. The conduct of the arbitration shall be pursuant to the provisions of the Act, although the arbitrator may, with the consent of the parties, dispense with any requirement of the Act, save and except that no party shall be deemed to have contracted out of the provisions of section 3 of the Act.

The parties agree that the arbitrator shall have full discretion, as if he were a judge, to award to a successful party interest on any monetary award together with the successful party's costs of the arbitration and, in determining the costs that a successful party is to be awarded, the arbitrator shall, after issuing his Award, receive and consider any offers of settlement and compromise exchanged between the parties in exercising his discretion as to any award of costs and the scale of costs. Any Award issued by the Arbitrator shall be final, conclusive, binding, and non-appealable.

Severability Clause

This provision allows one part or a single section of a contract to be struck down without the entire contract becoming invalid. For example, if one section of a non-competition clause were to be struck down because the geographic scope was deemed to be too broad, the remaining parts of the clause and the rest of the contract would survive. Including a severability clause is a good idea in any contract, because it will protect the remainder of the contract if some small part of it is invalid, for whatever reason. And even if only one part of a clause is struck down, the remaining parts of that clause will be saved, provided the substance of the clause remaining has not been radically changed. Here is a sample:

> Every provision of this Agreement is severable. If any term or provision herein is held to be illegal, invalid, or unenforceable for any reason whatsoever, such illegality, invalidity, or unenforceability shall not affect the validity of the remainder of this Agreement or any other provision.

Governing Law

This clause specifies which law will apply to a dispute or the interpretation of the contract, as in Canada, each Canadian province or territory and the federal government controls a separate legal jurisdiction. This is an important clause to include when, for example, a national organization with a head office in British Columbia hires an employee residing in Nova Scotia to work for it in both Ontario and Manitoba. In the Canadian sport system, it is typical to have activities subject to a contract carried out in more than one jurisdiction. Note in particular that in Quebec the provincial *Civil Code* (based on the *Napoleonic Code*) is significantly different than the common law applicable in the remaining provinces. Here is a sample:

> This Agreement shall be governed by and construed in accordance with the substantive laws of Ontario, Canada. Any dispute arising under this Agreement shall be resolved through the courts of Ontario, Canada and the federal and provincial laws applicable thereto.

Entire Agreement

This clause prevents one party from attempting to rely on verbal representations or "side deals" not expressed in the formal written contract. Even though many issues may have been discussed and discarded in the course of negotiating the contract, only the terms contained in the final written agreement should be binding on the parties. For example, in the process of negotiating a sponsorship deal, many issues are raised, discussed, and discarded. The final written document should fully and completely express all the terms and conditions agreed by the parties. An entire agreement clause in a contract will make it difficult for a party to allege that the real contract or understanding is part oral and part written. It is good practice to have a single agreement capture every aspect of a contractual relationship. Here is a sample:

> This Agreement constitutes the entire agreement between the Parties with respect to their contractual relationship. As of the date of execution of this Agreement, any and all previous agreements, written or oral, express or implied between the Parties or on their behalf relating to the subject matter of this contract are terminated or cancelled and each of the Parties forever releases and discharges the other of and from all manner of actions, causes of action, claims, or demands whatsoever under or in respect of any such earlier agreements.

Independent Legal Advice

No contract should be forced on an unwilling or intentionally naive party. A party must understand the full legal implications of the contract if the contract is to be binding on that party. This may be an issue particularly for the types of contracts that typically enforce unequal bargaining power among the various parties—for example, employment contracts, financing arrangements, and athlete agreements. Courts want to see that the contracting party against whom the bargain is being enforced was given the opportunity to have the implications of signing the contract explained by a lawyer. It is advised that sport managers encourage this type of legal review because it protects all parties to the contract. Alternatively, the party signing a contract can expressly waive the opportunity to review the contract with a lawyer, while acknowledging that he or she was given the chance to do so. Here is a sample:

> The Employee confirms that it has been recommended to the Employee that she consult a solicitor and obtain independent legal advice prior to the execution of this contract. The Employee confirms that she has obtained independent legal advice or has voluntarily declined to seek independent legal advice despite being given every opportunity to do so. The Employee confirms that she has signed this Agreement voluntarily and with full understanding of the nature and consequences of the Agreement.

Waiver

This type of clause creates flexibility for both parties without either party losing rights that have been negotiated for and are included in the contract. In essence, a waiver establishes that a party does not have to enforce strict compliance, in every instance, with a particular term or condition in the contract. However, a waiver used once or twice does not preclude that party from insisting on strict compliance with a particular term or condition at any time in the future. Here is a sample:

> The failure at any time of A or B to demand strict performance by the other of any of the terms, covenants, or conditions set forth herein shall not be construed as continuing a waiver or relinquishment thereof, and either party may, at any time, demand strict and complete performance by the other party of such terms, covenants, and conditions.

Note that the use of the term "waiver" here is not the same as in a "waiver of liability" or "release of liability," discussed earlier.

Assignment

Some contracts contain provisions that prohibit the parties from assigning their particular interest in the contract to others. This is common in independent contractor agreements. If the party's relationship with a particular sponsor or contractor is largely dependent on trust and personal contact, the organization should ensure that the contract cannot be assigned to someone else.[1] Failure to do this may result in the contract being assigned to a new contractor or to an entity or sponsor with whom the organization has no interest in being associated, or worse, a sponsor the organization cannot be associated with because of other contractual commitments. This particular problem can be dealt with by including a clause in the contract that states that the contract cannot be assigned without mutual consent, and that consent will not be given if any other contractual relationship will be jeopardized by the assignment. Here is a sample:

> This Agreement and the rights and obligations of A hereunder are personal to A and shall not be assigned or delegated by A. The rights granted to Y by A hereunder are personal to Y and shall not be assigned, delegated, or passed through by Y without A's prior approval, which approval shall not be unreasonably withheld.

Force Majeure

These clauses describe events that are beyond the reasonable power of a party to control. If the events listed in the clause do, in fact, occur, and if as a result certain obligations remain unperformed, the party who fails to perform is not deemed to be in breach of the contract. Here is a sample:

> None of the parties shall be in breach of this Agreement if the performance by that party of any of its obligations hereunder is prevented or pre-empted because of acts of God, civil or military authority, acts of public enemy, war, accidents, fires, explosions, earthquakes, floods, the elements, strikes, labour disputes, or any cause beyond the party's reasonable control. However, in no event shall any act or omission by or on the part of any party, or any inability on the part of any party hereunder to pay any amount owing hereunder, constitute or be deemed to be considered any event beyond the reasonable control of such party.

---

1   Of course, exactly the opposite can be found in many professional athlete contracts where a clause is inserted expressly to allow a team to trade, or assign, a player to another team.

Appendix 9.1: Sample Contract Precedents

This appendix contains examples of excerpts from various actual contracts. These examples are not templates—they are for illustrative purposes only. We do not recommend that readers cut and paste these examples into their own contracts. In all the examples set out here, text in *italics* is annotation provided by the authors, and does not form part of the contract excerpt.

Sample #1: Waiver and Release

In consideration of [ABC] agreeing to allow me to participate in [*Insert here the event activities including any pre-event or post-event activities where appropriate*] (all of which are hereafter "the Event Activities"), and for other good and valuable consideration, the receipt and sufficiency of which is acknowledged, I hereby agree as follows:

TO WAIVE ANY AND ALL CLAIMS that I have or may have in the future against ABC, its Directors, Officers, employees, agents, volunteers, independent contractors, subcontractors, and representatives (all of whom are hereinafter referred to as the Releasees) [*This sets out precisely who is being released.*]

and to RELEASE THE RELEASEES from any and all liability for any loss, damage, expense, or injury, including death, that I may suffer or that my next of kin may suffer as a result of my participation in the Event Activities, [*This defines at what event or activity.*]

due to any cause whatsoever, including NEGLIGENCE, BREACH OF CONTRACT, BREACH OF ANY STATUTORY OR OTHER DUTY OF CARE INCLUDING ANY DUTY OF CARE UNDER THE *OCCUPIERS' LIABILITY ACT* ON THE PART OF THE RELEASEES AND FURTHER, INCLUDING FAILURE ON THE PART OF THE RELEASEES TO SAFEGUARD AND PROTECT ME FROM THE RISKS, DANGERS, AND HAZARDS OF THE EVENT ACTIVITIES. [*This sets out the cause of the claim.*]

I further agree to hold harmless and to indemnify the Releasees from any and all liability for any property damage or personal injury to myself or to any third party resulting from my participation in the Event Activities. [*This is a positive promise to pay rather than a release, which is a promise not to sue.*]

I agree that this Agreement shall be binding upon my heirs, next of kin, executors, administrators, and assigns in the event of my death. I agree that this agreement shall be governed and interpreted in accordance with the laws of the Province of [*insert*] and any litigation involving the parties to this Agreement shall be brought in [*insert*]. In entering into this Agreement I am not relying on any oral or written representation or statements made by the Releasees with respect to the safety of the Event Activities. I further acknowledge that I have read, understand, and agree to be bound by the terms of this waiver and release and that I am signing it voluntarily without duress or undue influence.

Sample #2: Indemnification

Version 1

The undersigned, ABC Inc. [*This is who will be responsible for paying*] hereby agrees to be solely responsible for and to indemnify and save harmless XYZ [*Insert who or what company and, if a company, its respective Directors, Officers, shareholders, employees, and agents*] ("XYZ Parties") from and against any claims, demands, losses (but not anticipated profits), causes of action, or damages, including reasonable lawyers' fees (collectively, "Claims") arising out of or in any way relating to [*Insert here precisely what the promise to pay relates to. Try to limit this as much as possible, for example: all ABC Inc.'s advertising and promotions in connection with the Agreement dated; the conduct of ABC Inc. at a certain event; breach of a certain Agreement by ABC Inc.*]

Version 2

Supplier shall indemnify and hold ABC harmless from and against any and all claims, liabilities, losses, and expenses (including reasonable attorney fees) arising out of any third-party claim or action arising from: (i) any statements and/or representations made by Supplier or its employees with respect to the Products or (ii) any acts or omissions of any Resellers appointed by Supplier pursuant to this Agreement or (iii) any breach of this Agreement by the Supplier.

Sample #3: Confidential Information

Employee acknowledges that ABC possesses and will possess in the future certain "Trade Secrets," which include the following (whether any or all are in tangible, intangible, magnetic, digital, or other form or media whatsoever, and whether or not identified as confidential): [*This example does not require that the information be specifically marked confidential.*]

[*Insert exactly what is to be treated as confidential—examples are given below.*]

a. all computer programs (source and object code); software design, maintenance, and user documentation; data; product and system designs and specifications; screen displays; operation methods and processes; equipment designs and specifications; product and/or service information; all concepts, methods, techniques, formats, patterns, compilations, programs, devices, designs, technology, equipment, formulas, algorithms, processes, packaging, testing, information, data, systems, operations, ideas, research, improvements, inventions, discoveries, and know-how;

b. information relating to ABC's customers, accounts, suppliers, distributors, marketing activities or plans, business plans, distribution, pricing, financial matters, financial statements, and product and service performance, reliability, and other test or benchmark results (Trade Secrets listed in this subsection (b) are hereinafter also referred to as "Business Information");

c. information generally regarded as confidential in the industry or business in which ABC is engaged, which are or shall be owned, developed, used by, related to, or arise from ABC, its businesses, activities, investigations, work of its employees or agents, utilization of equipment, supplies, facilities, or information, now or in the future, whether or not published, patented, copyrighted, registered, or suitable therefore; and

d. any information, item, or material that is revealed to ABC by third parties under any confidentiality agreement, understanding, or duty.

Exceptions: Notwithstanding the foregoing, the term "Trade Secret" does not include information that is

a. generally known to or readily ascertainable by the public through proper means;

b. properly and lawfully obtained from a completely independent source; or

c. required to be disclosed by court order or applicable law (provided that ABC shall be given notice and an opportunity to obtain a protective order against such disclosure).

Restrictions: Employee acknowledges and agrees that all rights to Trade Secrets are and shall remain the sole property of and in the control of ABC or its licensors. Employee agrees not to use or disclose any Trade Secrets, other than Business Information, at any time in the future, except as necessary to perform his/her duties for ABC. Employee also agrees not to use or disclose any Business Information until five (5) years after the termination of his/her employment, except as necessary to perform his/her duties for ABC. Notwithstanding the foregoing, Employee agrees not to use or disclose any information received by ABC from a third party for the period required by any confidentiality agreement, understanding, or duty between ABC and the relevant third party.

Sample #4: Non-Competition

[*This example is from a contract for a highly specialized software engineer.*]

For a period of one (1) year following termination of Employee's employment with ABC, Employee will not become employed by, consult with, or become involved in any way with any Competing Business of ABC. "Competing Business" means: (1) any business which develops, markets, or sells [*Define business; widgets or records management software, etc.*] or services that compete with those developed, marketed, or sold by ABC during Employee's employment and/or for one (1) year after the termination of Employee's employment; and (2) includes, without limitation, [*List specific competitors*] and such other competitors as ABC identifies from time to time in its business planning documentation as its direct competitors. [*Note there is no geographic area limitation since work in this field is done worldwide. The focus is on who specifically* not *to work for—all other employers are acceptable.*]

Employee acknowledges that the terms of this Agreement are reasonable under the circumstances in that they represent the least restriction on Employee's future employment and ability to earn a living that are consistent with protection of ABC's Employee Inventions and Trade Secrets.

Sample #5: Non-Solicitation

During Employee's employment and for one (1) year afterwards, Employee will not solicit or recruit any other individual who is an employee of ABC [*This is the promise to not solicit employees*] or who has been an employee of ABC at any time during the period of one (1) year after the termination of Employee's employment, to perform services for another employer. During Employee's employment and for one (1) year afterwards, Employee will not influence or attempt to influence customers of ABC either directly or indirectly, to divert their business away from ABC. [*This is the promise not to solicit the customers of the business.*]

Sample #6: Hosting Agreement Recitals

AGREEMENT made as of the date:

AMONG:

Her Majesty the Queen in Right of Canada
(hereinafter called "Canada"),
as represented by the Minister of Canadian Heritage
(hereinafter called "the Federal Minister"),

- and -

The Minister of Municipal Affairs, Sport and Recreation and the Minister of Canadian Intergovernmental Affairs and Native Affairs for and on behalf of the Government of Quebec
(hereinafter called "Quebec"),

- and -

The City of Montreal a legal entity under public law
(hereinafter called "the City"),

- and -

The Société des internationaux du sport de Montréal, a legal non-profit entity,
(hereinafter called the "SISM")

- and -

The Aquatic Federation of Canada,
(hereinafter called "the AFC"),

- and -

The XIth FINA World Championships—Montreal 2005 Organizing Committee, a legal non-profit entity
(hereinafter called "the Organizing Committee").

Whereas:

The Fédération internationale de natation (FINA) is the sporting organization that governs all international competitions in synchronized swimming, open water swimming, swimming, diving, and water polo and, as rights holder, has entrusted the AFC and SISM with the rights to hold the XI FINA World Championships (Championships);

The AFC is the member representing FINA in Canada;

Following the selection of Montreal by FINA as the host of the Championships in 2005, the AFC, SISM, and FINA have concluded the Host City Agreement, which sets out the nature of the undertakings and obligations of each Party and establishes the terms and conditions under which these Championships will be held, including the constitution of an Organizing Committee;

The Organizing Committee is an integral part of this Agreement and is empowered by the AFC and SISM to organize the Championships at Jean Drapeau Park in Montreal in July 2005, comprising the planning, preparation, financing, and staging of these Championships;

The Parties to this Agreement recognize that the Championships will be an event of international importance that will be a source of pride to the sport community and the general public;

Canada, Quebec, and the City have already made commitments to support the organization of these Championships;

The City shall undertake facilities projects to renovate the Pavillon des Baigneurs and the construction/reconstruction of three permanent outdoor swimming pools at the Île Sainte Hélène Aquatic Complex for the purpose of holding the Championships;

To this end, the City will receive a financial contribution from the Government of Quebec as part of the Quebec municipalities infrastructures program, and has concluded a memorandum of agreement in this regard;

The holding of the Championships will leave a legacy for the sport community and the general public, including the permanent facilities built or renovated for the Championships, as well as the equipment and technical, electronic, and computer material required to hold future international and national competitions in synchronized swimming, swimming, diving, and water polo;

FINA has authorized the Organizing Committee, SISM, and the AFC to sign this Agreement, as set out in Annex 11;

This Agreement has been approved by the Government of Quebec as per decrees ... dated... .;

The Parties to this Agreement wish to record the conditions governing their respective contributions to the organization of the Championships and establish the general conditions of their cooperation.

NOW THEREFORE, each Party agrees as follows:

Sample #7: Hosting Agreement

MAJOR CUP AGREEMENT

BETWEEN:

ABC
(hereinafter—"Manager")
- and -
XYZ ATHLETICS
(hereinafter—"Host")

WHEREAS the Host has been granted the right to host the Major Cup in 2007, to be played at a site acceptable to the owner of the Major Cup ("Owner"), acceptable to the Host and subject to the negotiation by Manager of an acceptable facility rental agreement;

AND WHEREAS Manager wishes to manage the Major Cup on behalf of the Host and Owner in 2007;

AND WHEREAS the parties wish to enter into an agreement regarding their respective rights and obligations associated with the management of the Major Cup for 2007;

NOW THEREFORE this Agreement witnesses that in consideration of the mutual covenants and agreements herein contained, and other good and valuable consideration (the receipt and sufficiency of which are hereby acknowledged), the parties hereto covenant and agree as follows:

RIGHT TO MANAGE

1. The Host has agreed with Owner, the owner of the event, and the owner of all intellectual property associated with the Major Cup to host the Major Cup in 2007. [*This refers to the initial grant from Owner to Host.*]

2. Host hereby exclusively grants to Manager, for so long as this Agreement remains in effect, the right to manage, on its behalf and on behalf of the Owner, the Major Cup and any property specifically affiliated with the Major Cup in 2007 listed in this Agreement. This grant of rights to Manager is conditional on the obligations contained herein being satisfied and on the agreement between Host and Owner not being terminated. [*This clause passes along to the Manager the obligations the Host undertook when it accepted the rights as Host.*]

3. Manager will work with Host to develop a working committee, including a chairperson, for the 2007 Major Cup. The purpose of this working committee will be to assist Manager and the Host to ensure the management and operation of the Major Cup is consistent with the terms and conditions contained in this Agreement and in the agreement between Host and Owner. [*It is critical to be sure all that the Manager does is consistent with the initial grant to the Host.*] However, Manager will be responsible for day-to-day operational decisions regarding the management of the Major Cup.

OTHER AGREEMENTS BINDING ON MANAGER

1. Manager agrees that the following agreements plus attachments and addendums, all of which are attached hereto, form part of the Agreement:

   a. The Agreement between Host and Owner dated X (the "Owner Agreement"). [*In this way the obligations imposed on the Host by the Owner are passed along to the Manager.*]

2. Manager hereby agrees to adopt, assume, and be bound by all of Host's restrictions, financial obligations, and covenants contained in Section 1 and Schedule "A" of the Owner Agreement, with the exception of Sections 1.3 and 1.9. [*This will vary in each case because the Host may decide to remain responsible for some of the rights it received from the Owner but decide to pass on to the Manager the balance of these responsibilities.*] Manager further agrees to strictly follow all of the requirements to obtain consents, permissions, or approvals from Owner and other parties as specified in the Owner Agreement and all attachments. The Host, as provided in the Owner Agreement, is specifically relying on Manager to satisfy the Host's commitments in the Owner agreement as aforesaid, and failure to do so shall be considered a breach of this Agreement.

3. All benefits accruing to Host pursuant to Section 2 of the Owner Agreement shall, when and if received, be passed on to Manager by Host. [*This generally will refer to the right to sell sponsorships and raise money, granted by Owner to the Host—which the Host is passing along to the Manager.*]

INTELLECTUAL PROPERTY RIGHTS

1. The following are the *only* Properties, owned by Owner, that may be utilized by Manager for the purpose of marketing, licensed merchandise, and sponsorship sales pursuant to this Agreement: [*These are all that were provided to the Host by the Owner.*]

   - The word mark [*insert*]
   - The word mark [*insert*]
   - The word mark [*insert*]
   - The Major Cup trade-marked logo

   All licensed merchandise revenues generated using the word marks and logos listed above shall accrue to Manager for the duration of the term of this Agreement. Manager confirms that no TV broadcasting rights to the Major Cup are being granted to Manager by Owner or Host. [*The Owner did not grant these TV rights to the Host so the Host cannot pass them along to the Manager.*] However, obligations directly associated with Owner's TV broadcast rights for the major Cup are being imposed on Manager in this Agreement.

2. The following are the *only* Properties, owned by Host, that may be utilized by Manager for the purpose of marketing and sponsorship sales pursuant to this Agreement: [*Host needs to define which of its intellectual property may be used by the Manager.*]

    • The Host trade-marked logo

    • The word mark "Host Athletics."

3. Host hereby grants to Manager, for so long as this Agreement remains in effect, a royalty-free, Canada-wide, non-exclusive licence to use the Owner Properties and the Host Properties to fulfill its marketing and sponsorship obligations in this Agreement. The grant of licence to Manager is expressly made subject to the following restrictions and conditions: [*The actual assets that may be used by the Manager have been defined in paragraphs 1 and 2—this is where any restrictions on the use of the assets can be inserted.*]

    a. All use of the Owner Properties and the Host Properties shall be consistent in all respects with the Owner Agreement, including Schedule "A" and the Owner Guidelines contained in the Owner's Operations Manual. [*This specifies restrictions on use.*]

    b. All use of Owner's word mark and logo, all Major Cup sponsors' promotional materials, and the Event Title Sponsorship shall be consented to and/or approved by Owner. [*The consent of the Owner for some use is demanded.*]

    c. All use of the participating teams' logos or other intellectual property shall be consented to by the respective teams.

    d. The Owner's word mark and logo must always be used in conjunction with the name, year, and location of the Major Cup.

    e. Manager's use of the Owner's word mark and logo, the Owner Properties, and the Host Properties shall: [*These are standard trade-mark controls and restrictions.*]

        • be in accordance with their respective trade-mark registrations, if any, including limiting all use to the wares and services with which the trade-mark may be properly associated.

        • be consistent with public morality and business practices which do not compromise or reflect unfavourably on the good name or good will of the Owner or Host.

        • be a faithful and accurate reproduction of the various Properties in accordance with the graphic standards established by the Host and the Owner from time to time.

        • not use any unapproved form of the Properties, adopt a confusingly similar trade-mark or merge any Properties with any trade name or other marks, or use the Properties as part of a trade, business, or corporate name or style.

        • subject to the right of the Host and Owner to monitor and inspect the use being made of the Properties to control the character and quality of the wares and services with which the trademarks may be properly associated.

REFERENCES

Blomberg v. Blackcomb Skiing Enterprises Ltd. (1992), 64 BCLR (2d) 51 (SC),
where an operator took reasonable steps to bring the content of a waiver to
the attention of the plaintiff, who chose not to read it.

Crocker v. Sundance Northwest Resorts Ltd., [1988] 1 SCR 1186, where a waiver was
not upheld: the injured party was intoxicated when executing the waiver.

Delaney v. Cascade River Holidays Ltd. (1989), 44 BCLR (2d), 24 CCLT 6 (BCCA),
where a waiver was upheld, although the court was concerned with the
timing of the presentation of the waiver for execution.

Dyck v. Manitoba Snowmobile Association, [1985] 1 SCR 589, where a waiver was
upheld; the injured party acknowledged not actually reading the waiver.

Karroll v. Silver Star Mountain Resorts Ltd. (1988), 33 BCLR (2d) 16 (SC), where
the court held that the content of a standard-form waiver need not be
brought specifically to a party's attention.

Lyons v. Multari (2000), 50 OR (3d) 526 (CA).

Toronto Marlboro Major Junior "A" Hockey Club v. Tonelli (1975), 11 OR (2d) 664
(HCJ).

Dispute Resolution Systems

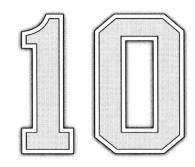

Introduction

In chapter 4 we saw that members of sport associations can always take their disputes to the courts, but that what the courts can do is quite limited. On occasion athletes (and others) have pursued their grievances through judicial review, or have asked the courts to grant injunctions or court orders to force organizations to take certain actions, or to cease certain actions that relate to a sport dispute. Although

an application for judicial review or an injunction will produce a "winner" in the outcome, it is often said that no one wins in litigation because the personal, organizational, and financial costs are great indeed.

Some additional options for resolving conflict that are often more appropriate and desirable than litigation include techniques of alternative dispute resolution, also known as ADR. There are a wide range of ADR techniques that can be used for resolving common disputes ranging from business matters to divorce and custody issues to neighbourhood disagreements. The following two ADR techniques are the most common and are being used more and more frequently for resolving disputes in society generally, and in sport specifically:

Mediation—a process whereby an independent, neutral third person helps parties in a dispute reach a mutually agreeable settlement by facilitating negotiations between them; and

Arbitration—a process whereby the parties refer their dispute to a mutually acceptable, knowledgeable, independent person to determine a settlement. The parties usually agree beforehand to be bound by the arbitrator's decision.

There are also other techniques of dispute resolution occurring along a continuum from informal, conciliatory, and private on the one end to formal, adversarial, and public on the other. Avoidance, negotiation, conciliation, facilitation, administration, adjudication, legislation, and even violence are all methods of resolving disputes, but when the term "ADR" is used in ordinary language, it usually refers to mediation and arbitration. Arbitration is used more frequently in the sport context than any other method of ADR, and it is the primary focus of this chapter.

Advantages of Arbitration

The advantages of independent arbitration over litigation of sport disputes have typically been identified as the ability to obtain a timely hearing, to incur lower costs than in litigation, to have access to an independent "expert" adjudicator to hear the dispute and, overall, to work within a dispute resolution process that is sport-specific and sport-sensitive.

For example, many disputes involving selection issues inevitably arise on the eve of a competition, leaving little time for the parties to seek redress. Last-minute hearings, although not necessarily the most desirable, can nonetheless be accommodated by an independent arbitration process—and indeed have been.[1] Rules for arbitration typically allow for the abridgement of timelines, and hearings can be accommodated by telephone conference call if needed. A pool of expert adjudicators are typically available on short notice and, in the case of a major multisport event such as the Olympic Games or the Pan-American Games, adjudicators can be located at the site of the competition.[2]

Often costs of arbitration can be much less than costs of litigation. Of course, there are many variables to consider when adding up the costs of arbitration—the complexity of the matter, the number of parties involved, the time spent in the hearing process, whether legal counsel is used, the format of the hearing, to name but a few factors. And although costs may be less than those of litigation, this does not mean

---

1   It is always possible to obtain last-minute injunctions from the courts; however, the process can be difficult to navigate and virtually impossible to initiate without legal counsel, and can rarely accommodate the geographic separation of many of the parties, particularly when they are in final preparation for a competition.

2   In the case of the Olympic Games, an ad hoc court of arbitration for sport (CAS) mechanism is located on-site to hear matters throughout the games. This practice has also been recently introduced at the Canada Games—a multisport national competition held every two years in Canada, where representatives of the Canadian sport arbitration program are now located on-site.

the arbitration process is necessarily inexpensive, particularly for athletes who have limited incomes.

A significant factor affecting the ability of sport organizations to resolve disputes within the organization through their own internal mechanisms is the inherent bias, whether perceived or actual, of the organization's appeal process. Within the context of the selection of an athlete to a team, it is typically the organization that establishes the selection criteria and process, it is the organization that makes the selection, it is the organization that establishes the appeal policy, and it is the organization that manages the appeal hearing. The athlete who may be appealing some aspect of a selection decision sees himself or herself battling a decision of the organization using the process of the organization, often before decision makers appointed by the organization. Independent arbitration goes a long way to minimize the perception that the entire process is tipped in favour of the organization and against the athlete.

In an ADR system designed specifically for sports disputes, arbitrators can be selected for their legal expertise as well as their knowledge of the sport system and sport-related issues. When sporting matters go before the courts, there is often limited understanding among judges of the culture, ethos, and practical realities of the sport domain. Thus, decisions are being made by courts in isolation of the environment in which the decision is to be implemented. Issues to which adjudicators need to be sensitive include timing of the hearing, particularly where competitive timelines loom; power imbalances between parties including coaches, athletes, and organizational representatives; earlier sport decisions of a similar nature; the technical challenges of team selection using objective and subjective criteria; the expertise of coaches and others in decision making; and the role of discretion in decisions, among others.

BOX 10.1   Make the Forum Fit the Fuss

Techniques of alternative dispute resolution, or ADR, are being used everywhere—in business, institutions, and government. These techniques are also being used more frequently in the non-profit world and specifically in the sport sector. In its simplest form, ADR is a collection of diverse procedures to prevent, manage, or resolve disputes. The primary purpose of ADR is to reduce the costs and other negative consequences of disputes. The literature on ADR is vast, and these techniques have become so mainstream that the term *alternative* may no longer be accurate. In sport settings, the better term may be *appropriate* dispute resolution. The challenge for the sport system is to find the dispute resolution process that is most appropriate for the parties and the dispute at hand: in other words, "to make the forum fit the fuss."

For all these reasons, the case for a system of arbitration to deal with the increasing number of disputes being raised in sport is powerful and has, in large part, been borne out in practice as measured against the factors mentioned above. Arbitrations, on the whole, have been carried out quickly, relatively inexpensively, and by expert arbitrators.

ADR in Sport

Sport is organized hierarchically from the level of the local club, to the regional level (or in Canada, to the provincial/territorial level), to the level of the national sport federation and finally, to that of the international sport federation. Dispute resolution mechanisms are a part of that hierarchical structure and can operate independently within a particular level or can overlap between levels. For example, at all levels of operation, sport organizations typically have their own internal dispute resolution mechanisms in the form of hearings and appeals, such as those described in chapter 4.

Now emerging at the national level in many countries is a system of independent, third-party dispute resolution that allows disputes to be referred outside the sport organization. The earliest such system was put in place in the United States under the *Amateur Sports Act of 1978*. This legislation called for certain types of disputes to be referred to independent third-party dispute resolution through the American Arbitration Association. In 1995, China incorporated provisions for dealing with disputes as part of the *Sports Law of the People's Republic of China* (see Nafziger and Wei, n.d.). The United Kingdom, Australia, New Zealand, and Canada have all recently introduced independent systems.[3] Independent arbitration in sport has been described as a "growth industry," and observers say the emergence of the Europe-based International Court of Arbitration for Sport (CAS) is one of the most important developments in sports law in recent years (see Nafziger, 2001).

The CAS is the final body for dispute resolution at the international level. Established in 1983, CAS provides an independent, third-party process for disputes that arise either within or between international sport federations. CAS is also available for nationally and internationally ranked athletes once they have exhausted appellate opportunities within their national sport federations. Referred to by some as the "Supreme Court of World Sport" (see Carter, 2004), CAS is now recognized as the legitimate and established arbiter of international sport disputes. As evidence of

---

3   The Sports Dispute Resolution Centre of Canada (SDRCC) was created by legislation in 2003 after being introduced on an ad hoc basis in 2002 just prior to the Winter Olympic Games in Salt Lake City.

𝔹𝕆𝕏 𝟙𝟘.𝟚   Order of Presentation in a Hearing

Some sport managers will find themselves responsible for overseeing an internal hearing to resolve a dispute. As we saw in chapter 4, procedural fairness occurs along a spectrum, and hearings can range from simple and informal to complex and formal. For most internal hearings, the following procedure will usually be appropriate.

Typically, the party having the burden of proof goes first. Thus, in a disciplinary hearing, the organization has the onus of proving that there was a breach of the code of conduct (or whatever policy document applies) and should present its case first. In an appeal, the individual bringing the appeal has the burden of proving that the original decision was made in error, so that individual should present his or her case first.

The party responding to the party that has the burden of proof should go second, and any affected parties should make presentations after that.

Typically, each party presents its evidence through the introduction of documents, other records such as videotape, audio tape, or oral testimony from themselves or from other witnesses. This is called the "evidence" stage. The other parties may be given an opportunity to ask questions or seek clarification of evidence. In a formal hearing, this would be called "cross-examination." Cross-examination can occur in a number of ways—for example, by means of questions through the panel chairperson or questions directly to the witness. The purpose of cross-examination is to "test" the evidence—that is, check it for consistency and completeness.

Once all the parties have presented their evidence and have been questioned on it, then each party must be given an opportunity to tie all the evidence together in the most persuasive way possible. This is called the "argument" stage. Lay people usually don't have a clear understanding of the difference between evidence and argument, and sometimes evidence and argument merge together in a hearing involving lay people. If lawyers are involved, there will be a clear distinction between these two phases of a hearing.

Finally, the party having the onus of proof has an opportunity to respond to anything raised by the other side or the other parties in either their evidence or their argument. This is called the "rebuttal" stage. No new evidence should be allowed at this stage.

Once all the stages have been completed, the hearing can then be adjourned for the panel to make its decision.

this, and emerging from the expanding number of CAS decisions, is a body of legal precedent that can guide decision making across all sport, throughout the world.

Although there is considerable variation in the design and function across each of these third-party systems of dispute resolution, the basic methods of dispute resolution are similar: arbitration and mediation are the primary methods within several national systems, and are added to variously by ombuds services, investigative services, referrals to legal representatives, and resource centres offering dispute prevention and education resources. For example, the Sport Dispute Resolution Centre of Canada (SDRCC) offers a newsletter, templates for policies, best practice guidelines, an annotated jurisprudence database, and other useful links and publications (see SDRCC services and programs).

Across all systems, arbitration has been the initial mechanism offered. It quickly became the core mechanism, and this largely remains so today. Although mediation is included in each of these systems, it has tended to be little used in sports disputes.[4] As well, mediation is by definition a confidential process, so even if it were widely used, applicable cases would not be reported. This pattern of reliance on arbitration as a core ADR mechanism is not surprising given the nature of the disputes that predominate at the international and national levels of sport. The majority of disputes coming to arbitration have been related to doping, team selection, and eligibility. For example, in the first full year of the SDRCC program in Canada (2004—the year of the Summer Olympic Games in Athens), of the 22 disputes that went to arbitration, 18 were Olympic or Paralympic-related and all 18 dealt with competitor selection issues. These are the kinds of issues for which there is very little, if any, middle ground for the parties. Such disputes are necessarily rule-based and rule-driven, and thus lend themselves to arbitrated outcomes.

Even where a rule allows some flexibility and mitigating circumstances may be argued in an attempt to lighten a penalty (as in the case of the sanctioning provisions under the current World Anti-Doping Code), organizations may wish to use the dispute resolution process to obtain a public outcome that will serve as a deterrent to other offenders. The confidential and "compromising" (in the meaning of seeking a middle ground, or compromise between two views) nature of mediated settlements may not be appropriate in such situations. Indeed, the CAS rules of mediation[5] explicitly exclude disciplinary and doping matters from mediation, perhaps in recognition of the fact that the CAS does not want to become engaged in internal, policy-based decisions of sport bodies. However, the fact that in his first four years as US Olympic Committee (USOC) Ombudsman, John Rugers handled over 800 files, suggests that there is a role for interest-based, as opposed to rule-based, dispute resolution in sport (see USOC). As well, the rules of the SDRCC in

---

4   In the first four years after the introduction of mediation into the CAS framework in 1999, only a handful of matters were mediated. The same can be said within the SDRCC system, although use of resolution facilitation and mediation is growing in Canada.

5   CAS Mediation Rules, art. 1: "CAS mediation is provided solely for the resolution of disputes related to the CAS ordinary procedure. A decision passed by the organ of a sports organization cannot be the subject of mediation proceedings before CAS. All disputes related to disciplinary matters, as well as doping issues, are expressly excluded from CAS mediation."

𝔹𝕆𝕏 10.3 The Matt Lindland Case

Formal systems for dispute resolution within sport are a fairly recent phenomenon. An interesting and little-studied topic is how the structural design of such systems influences their efficiency, as well as their effectiveness in achieving the objectives or purposes that motivated their creation in the first place. The maxim "form follows function" could not be more true in this situation, because the structure of a dispute resolution system (and, in particular, the procedural rules that guide it) should be created so as to fulfill its intended function.

The case of American Olympic Wrestler Matt Lindland stands as a clear example of a case where form did *not* follow function. This case gave rise to significant unintended consequences including over a dozen judicial or quasi-judicial interventions, and created chaos for everyone involved (see Thompson, 2001). During the course of the 2000 US Olympic wrestling trials Mr. Lindland sought to appeal the outcome of one of his matches. He was denied at two levels of appeal within the US Wrestling Association and, as a result, his opponent was named to the US Olympic Wrestling Team, which had the effect of bringing into the dispute the US Olympic Committee, or USOC. Lindland subsequently applied for independent arbitration of the matter, as he was entitled to do under section 205 of the US *Amateur Sports Act*. Unfortunately, the rules of arbitration did not allow for the affected athlete, Keith Sieracki, who had now been named to the Olympic team, to be a party to the proceedings. Sieracki thus initiated his own arbitration in a wholly independent proceeding from that of Lindland. Lindland was successful in his arbitration, as was Sieracki. Each then applied to the courts to have his arbitral decisions upheld. The US Wrestling Association and the USOC now found themselves in the untenable position of being faced with two completely incompatible and mutually exclusive decisions as a result of a multiplicity of different proceedings in different jurisdictions. Eventually, the two matters were consolidated and a single outcome achieved, but only after this dispute had played through a total of 15 different proceedings, all compressed into a very short period of time just before the staging of the 2000 Summer Olympic Games.

The case clearly highlights the need to consider and define carefully what sort of decisions ought to be reviewed (or not reviewed) and by whom, who the parties to an adjudication should be, whether there should be any limitations on the scope of a review by an adjudicator, whether the adjudicator should be able to substitute his or her own decision, and whether the adjudicator should be able to modify, either directly or indirectly, the underlying policies of the organization from which the initial decision flowed.

Canada have been revised recently to require all parties to attempt to mediate all disputes (except doping matters) before an appointed "resolution facilitator" (see Van Rhijn, 2007). This has enabled some settlements but, even where settlement is not the result, the step of resolution facilitation has helped some parties to better clarify the issues in dispute.

Sport Arbitration in Canada

The Sport Dispute Resolution Centre of Canada was created by the *Physical Activity and Sport Act* in 2003. Its mission is to provide to the Canadian sport community a national alternative dispute resolution service for sport disputes, and expertise and assistance regarding alternative dispute resolution. The goals of the SDRCC are

- to ensure access to independent ADR solutions for all participants in the Canadian sport system;
- to strengthen the transparency and accountability of the national sport system and national sports organizations by clarifying their responsibilities to athletes, coaches, and other stakeholders;
- to ensure that independent ADR processes are equitable for all participants; and
- to offer a low-cost mechanism throughout Canada in both official languages.

These policy objectives very much reflect what are generally perceived to be the advantages of arbitration of sport disputes over other avenues of recourse and, in particular, litigation. Until the creation of the SDRCC, the typical dispute resolution process employed by the Canadian sport community involved three levels of decision making: an initial decision guided by organizational policy; a second level of decision involving a challenge of the initial decision through an internal appeal; and finally, where there had been an error of law or jurisdiction, a narrow application to the courts for judicial review.

Under the SDRCC, a mediation and arbitration component has been introduced to operate between the second and third levels of decision making. Although such mechanisms cannot completely oust the jurisdiction of the courts, it is certainly understood and expected that any arbitration outcome is considered to be final and binding on the parties. This arbitration mechanism of the SDRCC also contemplates a full hearing *de novo*[6] of the original matter, thus giving the arbitrator

---

6   The term "hearing *de novo*" means literally a "new hearing." This means that the arbitrator may hear the substance of the matter all over again from the very beginning, as opposed to simply reviewing a decision from the perspective of procedure. This is provided for in s. 6.18 of the Code, which states: "The Panel shall have full power to review the facts and the law."

very broad decision-making powers.[7] In many cases, the arbitrator may have a greater scope of review than the appeal panel that made the decision he or she is reviewing. As well, the rules of the SDRCC do not specify the "standard of review" to be used in arbitration.[8] However, it appears that a standard of "reasonableness" has prevailed in cases before the SDRCC, particularly those cases that relate to disputes over team selection, where "reasonableness" means that the arbitrator will not interfere with a decision in which the decision maker has interpreted the organization's policies fairly and has applied discretion without bad faith or arbitrariness.[9]

At the time of writing this book, about 75 sport disputes have come before the SDRCC and certain trends are emerging. It is clear that the rules of procedure for the arbitration of disputes in Canada are broad in nature and give the arbitrator wide authority to review earlier decisions, as well as wide discretion in crafting remedies, even to the extent of influencing the policies of the organization. However, in reality, it is clear that the 20 or so arbitrators appointed to work within the program have been reluctant to go so far. They have limited their reviews and have looked only at whether or not organizations have followed their own policies and have exercised their discretion properly. They have not ventured so far as to alter the policies of organizations, even where they have taken issue with such policies.

---

7   Section 6.18 of the SDRCC Code goes on to say that "[i]n particular, the Panel may substitute its decision for: (i) the decision that gave rise to the dispute; or (ii) in case of Doping Disputes, the CCES's assertion that a doping violation has occurred and its recommended sanction flowing there from, and may substitute such measures and grant such remedies or relief that the Panel deems just and equitable in the circumstances."

8   The term "standard of review" refers to what threshold must be met to allow an appellate body to overturn another body's decision. This threshold can be viewed along a continuum with "correctness" at the low end of the threshold, "patent unreasonableness" at the high end, and "reasonableness" representing a middle ground between the two extremes. A standard of reasonableness infers that the decision maker must apply and interpret the organization's rules reasonably and fairly, and apply discretion without bad faith or arbitrariness. In light of such a standard, even if an appellate body might have exercised its discretion to reach a different decision, it should owe considerable deference to the expertise reflected in the original decision maker.

9   In the decision *Boylen v. Equine Canada et al.* (Arbitration Award, ADR-Sport-RED Ordinary Division, July 11, 2004), the arbitrator elaborated on this standard and wrote: "I believe the correct standard in these circumstances to be that of reasonableness and would be reluctant, absent full argument on more explicit facts, to set the standard of patent unreasonableness before I could intervene. Furthermore, I believe that sufficient deference is warranted to decisions made by expert bodies, absent clear misdirection, [and] that mere correctness is too low a standard for overturning such decisions." This standard has been confirmed in subsequent cases related to selection.

Overall, decision makers in the SDRCC program have respected the authority of the sport organization to determine its own policies and rules so long as such policies and rules have been made properly and in good faith. Arbitration decisions rendered under the SDRCC since its inception in 2003 are now forming a substantial body of jurisprudence and are informing—and perhaps, it might be said, constraining—the rules of procedure of this new system of sport arbitration in Canada.

REFERENCES

Amateur Sports Act of 1978, 36 USC 371.

Carter, James H., "The Law of International Sports Disputes," presented at the Second International Conference on International Law, New Delhi, November 14 to 17, 2004.

Nafziger, J.A.R. and L. Wei, "China's Sports Law" (n.d.), IV(2) *International Sports Law Journal* 129-65.

Nafziger, J.A.R., "Arbitration of Rights and Arbitrations in the International Sports Arena" (2001), 35(1) *Valparaiso University LR* 357-77.

Physical Activity and Sport Act, SC 2003, c. 2.

SDRCC services and programs, http://www.adrsportred.ca.

Thompson, Steven J. "Olympic Team Arbitrations: The Case of Olympic Wrestler Matt Lindland" (2001), 35(1) *Valparaiso University LR* 407-30, at 407.

USCO, Independent Commission of the United States Olympic Committee (Public Session), April 25, 2003, at 15 and 16.

Van Rhijn, Judy, "The Shine Is Off the Apple: Arbitration Becoming a Process of Last Resort" (April 16, 2007), *Law Times* 22.

Risk Management

Introduction

Risk is an integral element of sport. Sport without risk would cease to be sport. Although in some businesses a manager's objective is to eliminate all risk to the extent possible, in sport the objective may be more properly characterized as minimizing unacceptable risks but maintaining a balance among those risks that are considered reasonable, acceptable, and in many cases, integral to the sport activity. This unique aspect of sport must be factored into any discussion of risk management within sport organizations, facilities, programs, and events.

A second unique aspect of risk management in sport is that the overwhelming majority of opportunities to participate in sport in Canada arise out of the efforts of private,

voluntary organizations. Governments may fund sport and may provide facilities, and private businesses may own professional teams and operate professional sport facilities, but participation in sport in this country is almost entirely the domain of the non-profit sector. Within the total non-profit community in Canada, sport and recreation account for the second largest segment, just behind the social development sector but well ahead of the religion, arts/culture, health, environment, and international communities. There are presently over 33,000 sport and recreation organizations in Canada, over half of which report annual revenues under $30,000 and over three-quarters of which have no paid staff whatsoever, relying solely on volunteers to oversee and manage their programs (see Corbett, 2007). This enormous unpaid volunteer component creates challenges for any sport manager.

This chapter describes a practical and sensible risk-management approach that can be implemented in any type of sport organization. The chapter also concludes this book and hopefully ties together the many ideas and concepts presented previously. Risk management is about taking this knowledge and applying it in the day-to-day management of sport organizations. At its core, risk management is about minimizing loss, harm, and liabilities—but it can also serve as a more positive tool to help sport leaders manage resources wisely, lead and govern effectively, make decisions soundly, and project positive images toward sponsors, government funders, and the public.

One word of caution for the sport manager—there is no magic formula for risk management. There is no cookie-cutter or checklist that can be used to manage risks in a league, team, organization, or facility. Although there are universal concepts and common approaches, there are no black and white rules to risk management. One organization's risk-management program will be very different from another's, depending on the sport discipline, the nature of participants, the organization's

---

BOX 11.1   Failing to Plan Means Planning to Fail

The adage "failing to plan means planning to fail" applies to risk management. Many sport organizations have learned the hard way that they might have benefited enormously from having planned ahead to deal with a sudden incident, emergency, or crisis. An important risk-management tool for any sport manager is an "emergency response plan." Such a plan should identify clearly the appropriate steps to be taken when a serious incident occurs. The plan should address not only what needs to be done to respond to an emergency and to ensure the safety and well-being of the parties involved in an incident, but also what messages should be communicated and by whom, to members, the public, and the media. Terms such as "crisis management plan" and "issues management plan" may also be used to describe how an organization should respond to the public and to the media in an emergency. Emergencies can range from serious injury to public scandal to a doping incident. These have the potential to cause enormous harm to the brand and image of the organization. However, that harm can be mitigated through thoughtful, appropriate, and well-timed responses and communications. It is better to plan these responses ahead of time, rather than making them up in the heat of the crisis. It is now standard practice in Canada for national sport organizations and national teams to prepare emergency plans and crisis management protocols in advance of departing for international games and competitions.

tolerance for risk, whether or not the organization operates a facility, its structure and mandate, and its relationship with its members. The key to managing risk well is to understand a practical methodology and to know the underlying law, and then to integrate this knowledge systematically and in a common sense manner within the organization's daily business operations.

The Sport Organization's Risks and Responsibilities

From the perspective of risk management, there are three important areas of responsibility for every sport organization:

- The sport organization's first responsibility is to provide a safe and secure environment for participants. This means having policies and standards that promote safe programs in safe facilities, overseen by qualified personnel and trained volunteers. This responsibility was addressed in chapter 2, where concepts of negligence, liability, and standard of care were discussed. Chapter 3 on violence and chapter 7 on work relationships also elaborated on the sport organization's responsibilities to promote a secure environment for its members and participants.

- The sport organization's second responsibility is to make decisions fairly, especially decisions that affect members. This means having and following proper policies and procedures when making important decisions and handling disputes among members. This responsibility was addressed in chapter 4, where principles of administrative law and the responsibilities of private tribunals were discussed, as well as in chapter 5 on doping in sport and chapter 6 on discrimination. Chapter 10 elaborated further on conflict and provided some tools for improving decision making and dispute management.

- The sport organization's third responsibility is to properly care for and protect its assets and resources, including money, equipment, facilities, and intangible property such as data, corporate image, and marketing rights. Chapter 8 on intellectual property touched on some legal issues relating to identification and protection of intangible assets.

Failing to meet any one of these responsibilities can lead to unwanted consequences, some of which have a legal aspect. For example, injury or harm to a participant can lead to a lawsuit that will cost the organization money, time, and very possibly higher future insurance costs. Poor conflict management and decision making can lead to appeals, arbitrations, and lawsuits that will take an emotional toll on individuals as well as cost money and take time. Even if legal action is not the result of bad decisions, these disputes will harm important relationships, burn out volunteers, and tarnish an organization's goodwill and public image. Finally, failure to take care of assets (whether tangible assets such as physical property or intangible assets such as intellectual property) is simply bad business management, and this in turn can have harmful financial and legal consequences for the sport manager.

Approaches to Risk Management

Much of this book has addressed the essential question "How does the law expect me to behave?" The sport manager today requires a core of legal knowledge to do his or her job—knowledge that might not have been so important in the past. He or she needs to understand negligence, liability, standard of care, administrative law, contract law, criminal law, dispute resolution techniques, and human rights law. Having described these responsibilities in this book, the next question for the reader is "How do I behave responsibly?" The answer lies in risk management.

There are three general steps in risk management that are applicable to any context: risk identification (asking the question, what are the risks?), risk assessment (determining how significant the identified risks might be), and risk treatment (identifying what measures should be taken to address significant risks). These steps can be summarized as "identify—measure—control," and they apply equally to all organizations ranging from a local soccer club to a for-profit, multinational corporation. The definitions used by all risk managers are also consistent.

So, what does *risk* mean for the sport manager? Traditionally, risk has been defined as *the chance of injury, damage, or loss*. For the sport organization, this can be extended to mean "the chance of *injury* to your members or participants, *damage* to your property or property of others that you may be responsible for, or other *loss* to your organization, directors, volunteers, members, or to someone else." Ultimately, the effect of risk is financial: the injury, damage, or loss is going to cost money. And often, this cost is incurred because the risk has resulted in some form of legal action or dispute.

Risk management has been defined traditionally as *reducing the chances of injury, damage, or loss by taking steps to identify, measure, and control risks*. Risk management is sound business practice, and undertaking risk management is not necessarily complicated. It does mean that the sport manager and others within the organization must make a concerted effort to think about and identify potential risky situations, decide which situations or circumstances might pose serious risks, and then determine what practical steps they can take to minimize or mitigate those risks. The common ingredient in all these tasks is common sense. This task is also made easier when there is a culture within the organization that promotes safe and prudent conduct by all staff and volunteers.

Some examples of traditional risk-management measures used in sport organizations are

- designing a system whereby sports equipment and facilities that are used on a regular basis are inspected thoroughly according to a fixed schedule;
- establishing and following a policy with regard to minimum qualifications for instructors, coaches, or other staff—for example, determining as a matter of policy that all coaches in programs will have level II certification and will be members of Coaches of Canada;
- carrying adequate property and liability insurance for an office, facility, or programs,
- ensuring that proper and progressive coaching techniques are used in elite development programs;
- implementing a system of screening when hiring summer program staff who will be working closely with children in unsupervised settings; and
- ensuring that policies and criteria to evaluate and select a provincial team are clearly written, properly implemented, and transparently communicated to coaches and athletes.

The terms "tradition" and "traditionally" have been used in the above text because in recent years there has been an evolution in how the issue of risk management is approached within the non-profit sector generally, and within sport organizations specifically. Historically, risk management in sport involved taking steps to ensure that activities were safe, that appropriate insurance coverage was acquired, and that the necessary paperwork in the form of signed waivers and releases was in place. This describes the efforts of most sport managers in the 1980s. Through the 1990s it became apparent that sport organizations routinely face risks related to a wider array of legal issues: the main concern was no longer injury prevention, but liabilities arising from decision making, member complaints, breaches of contract, human rights, team eligibility and selection, harassment and conduct matters, and incidences of violence. Risk management thus broadened in the 1990s to incorporate measures to address all forms of loss exposure faced by the organization. The evolution did not stop there—today, risk management is emerging as a comprehensive management technique to improve organizational performance through effective leadership and governance, efficient planning, and relevant programming.

Much of this recent evolution stems from the development of an Australia/New Zealand risk-management standard (AS/NZS 4360) that has been promoted through the Australian Sports Commission (see Standards Australia International). A similar standard (CSA Q850) is beginning to take root in Canada, primarily in federal government circles. The Australia/New Zealand standard has been adapted for testing through a pilot project in Canada with eight national sport bodies.[1] This project differs from traditional applications of risk management in Canadian sport in a number of ways: risk management is seen as a tool to promote social change and values-driven sport, risk is defined very broadly (risk is *the chance of something happening that can have an impact on the achievement of objectives*), risks are identified in relation to the strategic objectives of the organization, and the resulting risk-management measures are incorporated into the organization's strategic and business plans. As well, this new approach recognizes that risk management must be comprehensive and integrated into all levels of management of the organization. As a result, responsibility for risk management is evolving from a committee function overseen by volunteers within the sport organization to a day-to-day responsibility of management and staff.

A Practical Methodology for Risk Management

As noted above, there are three steps in risk management—identify risks, measure risks, and control risks. Most sport managers do some risk management some of the time, usually intuitively. The challenge is to make that implicit and ad hoc process more explicit. Put more succinctly, risk management is an organized and systematic process of asking the following three questions about a sport program, facility or event (refer to Appendix 10.1 for a useful worksheet to guide this process):

- what are the possible things that can go wrong? (this is the task of *identifying* risks);

- how likely is it that these things will go wrong, and what are the consequences if they do go wrong? (this is the task of *measuring* risks); and

- what can we do to keep things from going wrong? (this is the task of *controlling* risks).

---

1   The risk-management pilot project is a multiyear project of the True Sport Secretariat, which is carried out under the auspices of the government of Canada's *Canadian Strategy on Ethical Conduct in Sport*, approved by all federal, provincial, and territorial sport ministers in 2001. The organizations participating in this pilot project include Diving Plongeon Canada, Athletics Canada, Swimming Nation Canada, Gymnastics Canada, Speed Skating Canada, Skate Canada, Canoe Kayak Canada, and Field Hockey Canada.

The first step in any risk-management exercise is thus to identify the major areas of risk facing the sport organization. These "risk areas" can be defined as potential events or occurrences that could lead ultimately to loss or harm for the organization:

- liability losses (resulting from the sport organization being sued);

- failure to comply with existing standards or funding requirements;

- damage to property (either the sport organization's own property or the property of others for which the sport organization has responsibility);

- loss of revenue or earnings;

- loss of members or participants;

- loss of key personnel (staff as well as volunteers);

- loss of brand value and public image; or

- failure to be able to deliver on critical strategic objectives.

It is possible to bring some order and method to the task of identifying risks by keeping in mind that there are four main *sources* of risk and three main *types* of risk facing any sport organization. The four main *sources of risk* are

- *facilities*—the buildings, fields, offices, and other venues where the sport and its related activity occur;

- *equipment*—this includes equipment used by athletes, coaches, and officials within the sport activity itself, and equipment used by the organization in the provision of sport services and programs;

- *program*—there are physical risks that are an inherent part of the sport itself, some of which are desirable and thus reasonable while others are not; and

- *people*—this is the human element and includes participants, staff, volunteers, directors, and spectators, all of whom can be unpredictable in their behaviour and can make mistakes in carrying out their duties.

The three main *types of risk* for a sport organization are

- *physical injury*—this is the risk that a participant will be seriously hurt;

- *wrongful actions*—this is the risk that an individual will experience a loss of rights or opportunities for which there is a legal remedy and for which the sport organization may be responsible; and

- *property loss or damage*—this is the risk that property owned or controlled by the sport organization, or for which the organization is responsible, will be lost, stolen, or damaged. Intangible property losses include such things as traditional sources of intellectual property (copyrights and trade-marks) as well as public image and goodwill.

The second step of the risk-management process is to measure the risks that have been identified in terms of their potential seriousness. The seriousness of any particular risk depends on both its *frequency* (a measure of how often it might occur) and its *severity* (a measure of its consequences if it does occur). The terms *possibility* and *consequences* can also be substituted to reflect these two categories. While this evaluation can become a complex exercise in probability and mathematics, it doesn't need to be. Although detailed injury statistics are available for certain popular and high-risk sports, and these in turn permit detailed calculations of frequency and severity, most sport situations require only an informed judgment as to whether a particular risk is low, moderate, high, or very high. On this basis, the sport manager can then determine which risks are more important and thus warrant taking measures to control them.

Once significant risks are identified, the third step of the risk-management process involves finding practical, affordable, and reasonable ways to manage them. Typically, the organization will already be taking a number of steps to deal with the identified risk, so this step often involves identifying further measures that can be taken and deciding which, among those, the organization might commit to over the longer term.

As noted in the introduction to this chapter, there is no magic formula for controlling risk—the measures that a sport manager will select and implement will depend on the factors and unique circumstances of the sport club, organization, facility, or event. However, there are four generic strategies that are used to control risks:

- *retain* the risk (the risk is minor and inherent in the sport activity, and the sport manager is thus willing to accept the consequences—so does nothing about it);

- *reduce* the risk (the risk is significant enough for the manager to do something about it—he or she does things to reduce the likelihood of events occurring, or the consequences if they do occur, by careful planning and organizing, preparing and educating staff and volunteers, and by inspecting and monitoring facilities and equipment, etc.);

- *transfer* the risks (the risk is significant enough that the sport organization doesn't want to take it on itself, so it transfers the consequences of the risk to others through contracts, insurance, or waivers); or

> # BOX 11.2   Measuring Risk
>
> In the risk-management pilot project being undertaken in Canada, the following definitions have been successfully used to gauge the significance of risks facing national sport organizations.
>
> The possibility of a risk can be
>
> - "unlikely"—less likely to happen than not;
> - "possible"—just as likely to happen as not;
> - "probable"—more likely to happen than not;
> - "almost certain"—sure to happen.
>
> The consequence of a risk on the achievement of objectives can be
>
> - "minor"—it will have an impact on the achievement of the objective that can be dealt with through internal adjustments;
> - "moderate"—it will have an impact on some aspect of the achievement of the objective that will require changes to strategy or program delivery;
> - "serious"—it will significantly affect the achievement of the objective;
> - "catastrophic"—it will have a debilitating effect on the achievement of the objective.
>
> These measures are then considered in combination to determine whether the risk is low, medium, high, or very high. This is essentially a subjective judgment that involves consideration of the organization's mandate, its strategic objectives, and its tolerance for risk. For example, where the sport organization's programs cater to children or youth, any risk that presents a severe consequence, no matter how remote its possibility, will likely be a risk that the organization cannot tolerate. On the other hand, organizations that serve skilled adult participants may find that they have a higher tolerance for risk and can accommodate a greater range of risky activities. In all cases, it is critically important that the organization have the explicit discussion about risk: what it can tolerate, what it cannot tolerate, and that there is consensus about the outcome of these discussions.

- *avoid* the risk (the risk is potentially so severe that the sport manager doesn't want anything to do with it, so he or she decides to avoid doing whatever creates the risk in the first place).

As a general rule, there is a relationship between the seriousness of the risk and the preferred strategy, where *retain* and *reduce* strategies are used for low and moderate risks, and *transfer* and *avoid* strategies are used for higher risks. As a general rule, it is also a good idea to mix and match a variety of strategies, rather than to rely on just one or a few. It should also be noted that strategies to *transfer* risks do nothing to reduce the possibility or consequence of a risk, but merely transfer to another entity the ultimate liability associated with the risk. As such, transfer measures do not make a sport program, facility, or event any safer. Strategies to reduce or avoid risk, on the other hand, can go a long way toward promoting the safety of sport participants and the effective governance of a sport organization.

Under each strategy, there are numerous tools and techniques to choose from, as illustrated in the next section. The choice of measures, and how they will be combined and implemented, will depend on a host of factors that are specific to the sport organization and its circumstances. It is also important to note that risk-management activities will occur at different levels depending on the mandate of the sport organization, as expressed in its constitution, objects, and bylaws. A local sport club or sport facility that offers direct programs to individual members or participants can adopt a narrow approach to risk management, which means the organization manages risks only for those program activities it engages in directly. On the other hand, a sport organization that is the governing body for sport activities within Canada or within a geographic area such as a region, zone, province, or territory of Canada must manage risk for its own activities as well as for those activities carried out by others who are under its purview by virtue of its mandate as a governing body.

For a sport governing body, risk management occurs for three types of activities:

- *Direct activities*—These are the activities that the organization undertakes directly for itself (governing the organization through the board of directors and committees, running a provincial office, employing staff, certifying coaches and officials, disciplining members, and possibly operating a high-performance program involving a provincial team, coaches, staff, and officials who will train, compete, and travel to events outside the province). The fact that very few sport governing bodies possess or control facilities means that responsibility for this significant area of risk and responsibility falls to others.

- *Indirect activities*—These are the activities that fall within the indirect jurisdiction of the sport governing body through its "oversight" function of a sport discipline. Most sport governing bodies issue a "sanction," or other form of recognition, to competitions organized and hosted by others but nonetheless within the sport discipline. Typically, only competitive results from sanctioned events are recognized by the sport body. Sport governing bodies are not in a position to control these activities, but they can exercise indirect control through establishing and enforcing standards. All sport governing bodies should identify the appropriate risk-management standards that will govern sanctioned events, and in turn monitor these events to ensure that these standards are maintained.[2]

- *Supported activities*—These are the activities carried out by local sport clubs that are typically member associations of the sport governing body. A sport governing body has an important leadership role to play in terms of influencing the activities of its member sport clubs, which means providing suitable risk-management assistance, resources, and tools to help local associations and clubs in their own risk-management efforts. The use of these tools can be encouraged by linking them to participation in a club quality-assurance program, or to eligibility for insurance coverage or other benefits of membership.[3]

Examples of Risk-Management Strategies

The following are simple illustrations of techniques commonly used to manage risk. This information is not presented with the intention of serving as a checklist. Although some sport managers may believe that following a checklist is sufficient, the authors of this book are of the view that risk management is a process of analysis and judgment to be applied in a systematic fashion in each situation. The risk-management measures and commitments that are the outcome of that analysis will vary from one organization to another.

---

2   It is strongly recommended that all sport governing bodies put into force and monitor risk-management guidelines for all sanctioned events (surprisingly, only a minority of sport governing bodies presently do this). These guidelines should address issues such as: insurance requirements including naming the sanctioning organization as an insured; preparation of an emergency response plan; orientation and training for all volunteers including security personnel; implementation of alcohol management guidelines for social events associated with the sporting event; provision of appropriate first aid and sport medicine services; and pre-event inspection of all facilities, grounds, and equipment. It is also suggested that the sanctioning organization designate an official representative to work with the host organization in advance of the event, and to be on-site during the event to monitor compliance with risk-management guidelines.

3   Many sport organizations have used insurance programs quite effectively as a risk-management incentive. For example, in some sports strict compliance with rules about eye guards, mouth guards, and other protective equipment is a prerequisite for the participant to be covered by the organization's insurance programs. Other organizations use their insurance program as a lever to ensure that member clubs, leagues, and associations maintain their status as "member in good standing."

Most measures to reduce risk involve planning, organizing, and influencing human behaviour. This is an area where sport organizations have the potential to exercise the greatest control and where there are the greatest number of options to manage risk. At the same time, this is probably the area to which sport organizations devote the least amount of time and the fewest resources when undertaking risk management.

The illustrative examples of measures to *reduce* risk listed below are grouped according to the *source* of risk.

Where the source of risk is *facilities and equipment*, sport managers should

- design and follow a regular maintenance, repair, and replacement program for their facilities and equipment;
- design security measures to protect office equipment and data, such as careful control of keys and regular schedules for data backup;
- strictly enforce the use of prescribed safety and protective equipment at all times—no equipment, no game!

Where the source of risk is *people*, sport managers should

- provide all new board and committee members with detailed orientation materials and consider a mentor or "buddy" system for new volunteers;
- comply with any existing policies or legislation with regard to the screening of staff and volunteers;
- carefully recruit, select, and train volunteers, particularly those who will be working directly with children, youth, or other vulnerable persons;
- prepare written job descriptions for all staff and volunteer positions and approve a personnel policy that provides clear procedures for handling personnel matters;
- help staff pursue professional development so that they can remain current with trends in the sport and the industry;
- support ongoing certification of coaches and officials, and training of volunteers so that they remain up to date on new safety practices and other innovative techniques;
- develop and implement codes of conduct, discipline, and dispute resolution policies that will enable the sport organization to better handle controversial decisions and disputes;
- for major events, develop emergency response plans that identify key roles and responsibilities in the event of an injury or other incident.

Where the source of risk is *program*, sport managers should

- follow approved food preparation and alcohol management practices in facilities and at events;
- educate participants and parents about inherent risks of the sport through verbal messages, signage, and printed materials such as informed consent agreements;
- well in advance of selection events, develop sound criteria and a process for applying the criteria to make selections;
- post appropriately worded rules and warning signs in prominent places throughout the facility;
- incorporate relevant standards and guidelines from higher-level sport governing bodies (national and international) into the sport organization's operating procedures, and encourage member clubs and associations to do the same.

These are illustrative examples of measures sport managers should take to *transfer* risks:

- insist that adult participants sign a waiver of liability agreement (if the organization has decided philosophically that it wishes to use waivers in its programs—the complex topic of waivers is discussed in chapter 9);
- review all insurance needs and purchase insurance coverage that is appropriate in scope and amount for all activities as well as all paid and volunteer personnel;
- contract out discrete work tasks such as instructional clinics, event management, catering, bartending, and transportation to outside parties;
- ensure that there are proper indemnification provisions in all contracts signed by the organization, including those relating to rental of facilities, contracts for services, and licensing and sponsorship;
- if putting on a major event jointly with other organizations, create a partnership agreement that defines and shares the risks among the partners.

These are illustrative examples of measures sport managers should take to *avoid* risks:

- decide to simply not do something, because the risk is too great;
- suspend or postpone events in dangerous conditions;
- not travel to competitions in bad weather;

- restrict novice participants and lower age groups to lower-risk activities;
- purchase high-quality equipment that meets all safety standards;
- do not serve alcohol at functions where there will be families or minors;
- adhere strictly to all the organization's bylaw provisions, policies, and rules.

All of the above examples can also apply to risk management for those activities undertaken by other entities over which the sport governing body has some influence. For example, risk-management guidelines for a sport body's sanctioned events may include

- requiring that the host organization provide a certificate of insurance with suitable levels of coverage and naming the sanctioning organization as an insured;
- ensuring the site or venue provides access to emergency vehicles;
- designating in advance a *call person* (the person who contacts 911 in an emergency) and a *control person* (the person who takes charge of the situation and directs others) to handle serious incidents;
- ensuring volunteers are adequate in number, are identifiable by a badge, cap, or t-shirt, have assigned duties, and have undergone an orientation session;
- ensuring there are proper first-aid supplies and persons trained in delivery of first aid on-site at all times;
- if crowd control is an issue, ensuring that the host organization has made proper security arrangements, using either professional security personnel or trained volunteers;
- if there is a banquet or other social event, ensuring that all health code requirements are met, and that alcohol is being served in accordance with approved alcohol management guidelines;
- ensuring that the venue or site has been properly inspected for safety hazards before the competition; and
- having the sanctioning organization designate a representative to meet with the host organization in advance to explain the risk-management guidelines, and be on-site during the event to monitor compliance with the guidelines.

Sanctioning guidelines may also include measures that are specific to the sport discipline, such as those that might be required by the international governing body for the sport.

𝔹𝕆𝕏 𝟙𝟙.𝟛 Insurance Is a Common Risk-Management Tool

There is little debate that insurance is one of the most common risk-management tools in sport. Insurance is a method of spreading financial risks and costs among a large group, so that the losses of the few who experience them are shared with the many who do not. Insurance allows a sport organization to substitute a small and defined expenditure (a premium) for the possibility of a large, although uncertain, future loss. Although insurance does not reduce the possibility or consequences of risk, it provides protection against possible future catastrophes, and is an essential business tool.

The following are some general recommendations regarding the sport organization's insurance policy:

- The organization should carry a limit of at least $2 million of general liability insurance. Government funders and owners of facilities may insist on higher limits.

- "Named insured" and "additional insured" should include the directors, officers, and employees (which are standard in most policies) *as well as* volunteers, members, athletes, players, coaches, instructors, and officials.

- The policy should include a *severability of interests* clause (also known as a *cross-liability* clause). Without such a clause, an insurance policy covers only liability in relation to third parties—that is, those parties *outside* the organization. Liability to other parties *within* the organization (the organization's own members, volunteers, coaches, players, officials) would not be covered, even though such liability situations could, and do, occur in sport. For example, the negligent actions of another participant or a volunteer may cause injury to an athlete, and without a cross-liability clause, the organization's liability insurance would not provide coverage for a legal claim made by that athlete against the other participant or volunteer.

- Organizations should consider purchasing directors and officers liability insurance. Some general liability policies will also include errors and omissions coverage for the wrongful acts of directors and officers, and this provides similar protection.

- In addition to the insurance clause described above, organizations should ensure that rental agreements for use of another operator's facility contain an appropriate indemnification clause, whereby the facility operator promises to indemnify the renting organization for losses it might incur as a result of their actions, or as a result of events that are their responsibility and not the responsibility of the renting organization. Conversely, if the sport organization rents out its facility, it should ensure that rental contracts contain appropriate indemnification and insurance clauses. Indemnification clauses are discussed more fully in chapter 9.

In terms of providing risk-management support to member associations, the various resources and tools to assist member clubs in their own risk-management efforts can include

- providing member clubs with up-to-date copies of all relevant written policies, manuals, and minimum standards that they are expected to follow when delivering their sport programs;

- referring member clubs to outside resource persons and experts when needed;

- compiling and distributing a discipline-specific risk-management awareness kit for directors, volunteers, and staff of clubs;

- compiling and distributing insurance information so that clubs are aware of the scope of coverage, and providing them access to the insurance broker if they have questions;

- helping clubs design proper agreements, registration forms, and waivers or, where appropriate, providing standard-form documents for their use;

- putting on a risk-management seminar in conjunction with the annual meeting and encouraging club members to attend; and

- providing nominal staff assistance to those clubs who want to develop and implement their own risk-management programs.

Conclusion

The information in this chapter has provided a general approach for undertaking risk management, and has given some examples of risk areas that face sport organizations and facilities, along with suggestions for measures to control these risks. Keep in mind that there is no uniform template or generic checklist that can be used to do risk management within a club, league, program, or facility. Risk-management decisions require some basic legal understanding, background experience in the sport, and good judgment. The right risk-management decisions will depend on each sport organization's circumstances.

It is also important to remember that managing risk is an ongoing process. The fundamental steps in risk management don't change, but the sport organization's circumstances do, and the legal responsibilities of the organization may also change, although usually more gradually. For example, as little as 10 years ago there were few expectations that volunteer sport organizations would screen all their volunteers; today, the sport organization that does not undertake some form of personnel screening is likely no longer achieving a reasonable standard of care in the eyes of the law.

In closing, risk management is not rocket science—it is organized common sense, where common sense is the sum of knowledge and experience. The chapters of this book have provided most of the information that is needed for the sport manager to make a smooth transition from doing risk management in an ad hoc manner to doing it in an organized manner. Organized and systematic risk management means that the sport manager undertakes a comprehensive risk assessment to ensure that all sources and types of risk are considered and all legal responsibilities are fulfilled. Risk management, like the law, does not expect perfection. As a result, a sound risk-management plan is an appropriate, reasonable, and affordable mix of strategies, suited to the sport organization's needs, circumstances, and resources. And while risk management is largely about preventing the negative, it can also serve to promote the positive. Risk management done well will help the sport manager to improve membership development, performance success, financial viability, organizational capacity, and community image.

Appendix 11.1: Risk-Assessment Worksheet

The following worksheet was developed for use in the risk-management pilot project of the True Sport Secretariat of Canada.

Risk-Assessment Worksheet

CATEGORY OF RISK *(This is usually linked to the organization's high-level strategic objectives, for example: high performance, growth and development, holistic athlete development, financial viability.)*

IDENTIFICATION OF RISK *(The chance of something happening that can have an impact on achieving desired outcomes.)*:

Assessment of Risk

1. The *possibility* of this risk occurring is: ___ unlikely (1)   ___ possible (2) ___ probable (3)   ___ almost certain (4)

2. The *consequence* if this risk occurs is: ___ minor (1)   ___ moderate (2) ___ serious (3)   ___ catastrophic (4)

3. The *significance* of this risk is: _____ (a value from 1 to 16 determined by multiplying possibility score and consequence score)

4. Describe what *current controls/measures* are presently in place for this risk.

5. Are these *controls/measures* adequate? Why?

OPTIONS FOR TREATMENT OF RISKS

1. Can this risk be *accepted* as is, with the current controls in place?
   ___ yes   ___ no
   Provide rationale, if answer is "yes" (if "yes," remaining questions do not need to be answered)

2. Can this risk be *avoided* altogether?   ___ yes   ___ no
   If yes, how?

3. Can this risk be *transferred* to others?   ___ yes   ___ no
   If yes, how and to whom?

4. What are other treatment measures we can use to *reduce the possibility* or *reduce the consequences of this risk*?

FURTHER COMMITMENTS

Based on the significance of the risk, existing measures that are in place, and capacity of the organization to implement new measures, additional commitments are identified and responsibilities and timelines assigned.

Once implemented, this worksheet is revisited annually or more frequently to make adjustments as appropriate.

REFERENCES

Corbett, Rachel, "Encourage Good Sports for Better Sports" (May/June 2007), *Law Now* 27-30.

Standards Australia International, AS/NZS 4360 (Sydney, Australia: SAI Global, 1999).

Glossary

ADR

An acronym that means "alternative dispute resolution." These are techniques for resolving disputes that are alternatives to litigation. They include: negotiation, facilitation, mediation, and arbitration, among others.

adverse effect discrimination

A rule or practice that appears neutral on its face but that may unintentionally single out particular people identified by a prohibited ground, thus resulting in inequitable treatment.

affirmative action program

A provision in human rights legislation that makes exceptions for "special programs" that might otherwise be seen as discriminatory but that are intended to break historical or systemic patterns that have worked to disadvantage certain groups of people.

appeal

A review of an original decision. Sport organizations often permit their members, within certain parameters, to challenge decisions by referring them to a different body than the one that decided the case in the first instance. The appeal body typically reviews the decision to determine whether there were any procedural errors.

arbitration

A process where the parties refer their dispute to a mutually acceptable, knowledgeable, independent person to determine a settlement. The parties usually agree beforehand to be bound by the arbitrator's decision.

athlete assistance program (AAP)

A federal government financial assistance program for high performance and developmental athletes performing at the national level of sport in Canada.

balance of probabilities

Civil standard of proof for the complainant (or plaintiff) who must prove that over 50 percent of the believable evidence is in the plaintiff's favour. Often expressed as "more likely than not."

beyond a reasonable doubt

A criminal standard of proof. Reasonable doubt is sometimes described as proof to "a moral certainty." The decision maker must have no reasonable doubt that the defendant committed each element of the offence before finding in favour of the Crown.

bias

This concerns the impartiality and independence of a decision maker. Bias occurs where a decision maker is predisposed to decide a certain way, and is unable to consider other views or possible outcomes. Bias is said to be actual (the decision maker truly is influenced to favour one side or the other) or perceived (the decision maker may be impartial, but the circumstances, as viewed by an outsider, would appear to indicate otherwise). Procedural fairness requires that a decision be free from either type of bias.

blood boosting

A performance-enhancing technique whereby an athlete's blood is withdrawn and then reinjected. It was developed by researchers in response to concerns that the health of athletes participating in the

1960 Mexico City Olympic Games would be jeopardized due to performance at such high altitudes. The procedure was openly condoned and used by athletes up to the time the IOC published its first list of banned substances and practices in 1983 and included it as a prohibited method.

bona fide occupational requirement (BFOR)
A provision in human rights legislation that allows a party to argue a reasonable justification for a discriminatory practice. For example, even though human rights legislation throughout Canada specifically prohibits discrimination on the basis of a person's "record of convictions," discrimination based on a record of convictions may be allowed if the employer can demonstrate a good faith and reasonable requirement that a conviction for a certain offence is fundamentally incompatible with a specific position of employment.

burden of proof
Refers to the legal responsibility of a party to prove that their version of the facts is true. The burden can change: in other words, one party may have the original burden and once that party has met their burden it switches to another party.

civil law
An area of law dealing with matters between private citizens.

comfortable satisfaction
A civil standard of proof somewhere between the civil standard of "a balance of probabilities" and the criminal standard of "beyond a reasonable doubt." It sometimes is used in a civil case where the consequences to the defendant are very grave and greater scrutiny of the evidence is deemed appropriate. This is the standard of proof required under the World Anti-Doping Code.

common law
A set of legal standards or principles that have emerged from hundreds of years of judicial decision making. Common law is also known as "judge-made law."

consent
To accept or approve. Consent may be implied by circumstances or expressed, either orally or in writing.

consideration
To create a valid and legally enforceable contract there must be mutual promises supported by some benefit or "consideration" flowing between the parties. Consideration is the benefit received by one party to notionally "buy" the other party's promise. At law, contracts are valid only if all parties to the bargain mutually promise to perform some act or to undertake to perform some obligation for the other's benefit. Consideration must be present at the time of a contract's formation. In an employment situation, the classic "bargain" consists of an employee's promise to accept the position and do the work expected in return for the employer's promise to pay the wages and provide the benefits that have been agreed to.

constructive dismissal
A unilateral action on the part of the employer that, if it represents a fundamental breach of a major term of the employment relationship, may allow an employee to claim that a "constructive dismissal" has occurred. In this situation, the employee is "dismissed" at law as a result of the actions of the employer, who may not intend the employment relationship with that employee to end. It is the employee who treats the employment relationship as terminated as a result of the actions of the employer.

contributory negligence
A finding by a judge that an injured person should, due to his or her own conduct, assume some responsibility for his or her injuries, thus lessening the proportionate liability of the defendant. In the United States, the term "comparative negligence" may be used.

criminal law
The area of law that deals with matters of public interest between individuals and the state (represented by the Crown prosecutor) as set out in the Canadian *Criminal Code*.

custom
A long-established course of conduct that has the explicit consent of the majority of the population.

defence
An argument made in answer to or by way of justification of an allegation. Some, but not all, defences are accepted at law as a proper answer to the allegation and thus constitute a full repudiation of the allegations.

direct discrimination
Refers to the direct, or overt, and usually intentional differential treatment of another person, or group of persons, characterized by a prohibited ground.

discrimination
A distinction based on grounds relating to personal characteristics as opposed to merit, which impose a burden or have an adverse effect on those to whom it is applied.

doping
The use of a substance or method that appears on a list of prohibited substances and methods.

duty of care
The legal duty of person A to act responsibly toward person B, because person A can reasonably foresee that person B may be affected by person A's actions. Duty of care arises as a result of relationships (parent–child, teacher–student, coach–athlete) or by virtue of proximity between two parties.

employee
An employee performs general duties for an employer in return for a regular salary, with income taxes, employment insurance premiums, and government pension plan contributions withheld by the employer and remitted to the government in regular installments. An employee may participate in the employer's benefits and pension program. The period of employment for an employee is typically open-ended.

hearing
The opportunity given to a person to make representations before a decision maker. Hearings can range along a continuum of flexibility and formality. The most formal hearings occur in a courtroom; at the other end of the continuum, a hearing can be as simple as an exchange of documents or a conversation.

independent contractor
An independent contractor provides his or her services to an employer for an agreed upon fee to perform specific tasks. When these tasks are completed the employer pays the independent contractor the full amount of the contract according to the agreed-on payment schedule and does not withhold taxes or other payments. Independent contractors receive no benefits. The term of employment lasts for as long as it takes to perform the specific tasks.

insurance
A method of spreading financial risks and costs among a large group, so that the losses of the few who experience them are shared with the many who do not. Insurance is a financial tool that allows a sport organization to pay a small and defined expenditure in the form of an annual insurance premium in return for an insurance company assuming liability for a possible large and uncertain future loss.

intangible property
A subcategory of personal property that has no physical existence (i.e., cannot be seen or touched), such as trade secrets, patents, copyrights, and trademarks. Intangible property is the rights and interests that a person can acquire through the ownership of a copyright, for example; although valuable and important, these rights and interests exist only as concepts.

intellectual property
The broad category of "intangible" property that has commercial value and that consists of human knowledge and ideas.

intention
A person intends a consequence when that person foresees that his or her conduct will likely produce the consequence if the conduct is continued, and he or she continues the conduct anyway.

judicial review
An application to a court to review the procedural aspects of a decision made by a tribunal.

jurisdiction
The doctrine (or rule) that determines what the court has authority over and the strength or scope of that authority.

just cause
Conduct that represents a fundamental breach of the employment relationship, or conduct that is incompatible with the duties the employee must perform in fulfilling the employment relationship. If there is just cause, the employer can terminate the employment relationship without providing any notice of the termination.

law
A set of rules or principles established through previous decisions, authority (e.g., legislature), custom, or agreement and enforceable through some civic authority. The law sets out the rights and obligations of those subject to it.

lex sportiva
A distinct and universal body of legal principles of sports law.

lieu days
Days off given in compensation for hours or days worked that exceed the statutory requirements in provincial legislation. Instead of being paid for overtime worked, the employee can be compensated by receiving days off at the same rate.

mediation
A process where an independent, neutral third person helps parties in a dispute reach a mutually agreed on settlement by facilitating negotiations between them.

natural justice
An established principle that an individual standing to be adversely affected by a judicial or quasi-judicial decision is entitled to notice, an opportunity to make representations, and an unbiased decision maker.

negligence
Behaviour or action that falls below a legally determined, reasonable standard of care. There are four distinct elements of negligence, all of which must be proven for there to be a finding of negligence and corresponding liability. The four elements are: (1) a duty of care is owed, (2) the standard of care imposed by that duty is breached, (3) harm or loss results, and (4) the breach of the standard caused or substantially contributed to the harm or loss.

objective test
A test that looks at what would be in the mind of a reasonable third party in contrast to the "subjective test," which looks at what is in the specific individual's mind.

pay in lieu of notice
A lump-sum payment provided to the employee on termination instead of receiving advance notice of termination. Pay in lieu of notice eliminates the working notice period. The lump-sum payment must correspond to the value of compensation (salary and benefits) the employee would have received over the full notice period.

police records check (PRC)
A search, with the employee's or volunteer's consent, through police databases for records of criminal convictions for which a pardon has not be granted. A standard police check provides a search result from the Canadian Police Information Centre (CPIC) database.

precedent
The doctrine (or rule) that requires a judge to follow the decision in a previous case with similar facts.

prima facie
A Latin term meaning "at first look" or "on its face" —a matter is self-evident without closer inspection. At law the term has a more specific meaning. A *prima facie* case is one that addresses the allegations made, and that, if believed, justifies a verdict in the complainant's favour in the absence of a response from the respondent.

private tribunal

Bodies that are autonomous and self-governing and that have the power to write rules, make decisions, and take actions that affect their members, participants, and constituents. Most non-profit sport organizations are private tribunals. The term "administrative tribunal" means the same thing.

procedural fairness

An evolution of the principle of natural justice to encompass administrative tribunals as well as judicial and quasi-judicial tribunals, and to impose on them a duty of fairness that includes the right to a hearing and an unbiased decision maker.

product liability

A liability to a manufacturer, supplier, distributor, or retailer that might arise from defective or poorly designed equipment or products.

prohibited ground

A characteristic explicitly listed in human rights legislation on which discrimination is forbidden.

proximate cause

The fourth and final element of negligence, this refers to whether there is a sufficiently strong causal link between a breach of a standard of care by one person and the injury or harm that ultimately occurred to another. Negligence may be established if a failure to achieve a standard either caused, or substantially contributed to, an injury or other loss.

reasonable notice

The advance notice of the termination of employment that the law presumes will be provided to a terminated employee. The length of the reasonable notice given to an employee depends on many factors. The presumption that an employee receives reasonable notice on termination can only be rebutted by clear words in an employment contract.

reckless

Conduct that one knew, or ought to have known, would likely cause serious injury to another, but for which they were nonetheless indifferent to the risk and carried out the conduct anyway.

resignation

The voluntary leaving of a position of employment when the resignation has been formally accepted by the employer.

risk

The chance of injury, damage, or loss that ultimately has negative financial consequences for an organization or business. More recently, some sport organizations are interpreting risk more broadly to mean "the chance of something happening that can have an impact on the achievement of objectives."

risk management

A formal exercise that involves identifying and assessing risks, and devising and implementing measures to address risks by either avoiding them, reducing them, mitigating their consequences, or transferring the liability for risks to other parties.

screening

The ongoing process of investigation and research on the part of the employer, with the employee's consent, of the various factors and information that will demonstrate whether the employee is personally appropriate for the job or task he or she is going to be asked to perform. Screening can continue throughout the employment relationship. Volunteers may also be screened.

sexual harassment

Defined at law as conduct of a sexual nature that is unwelcome and that detrimentally affects the work environment or leads to adverse job or service-related consequences for the victim of the harassment.

standard of care

A legal expectation of what constitutes reasonable behaviour in the circumstances where a person owes a duty of care to another. Standard of care is influenced by four factors, none of which is alone determinative: applicable written standards, unwritten standards, previous case law (or precedent), and common sense.

standard of proof

The level of certainty and the degree of evidence necessary to establish proof in a proceeding.

stare decisis

The doctrine (or rule) that requires a court to abide by previously decided cases made by a higher court.

statute law

The body of laws passed by a legislature.

statutory liability

Liability that might arise from the breach of a duty as defined in a statute. This is in contrast to a breach of duty that is set out in common law.

strict liability

A principle of liability that finds a party is responsible, or liable, regardless of the party's intent.

subjective test

Looks at what is in the specific individual's mind in contrast to the "objective test," which is measured against what would be in the mind of a reasonable third party.

systemic discrimination

Discrimination that stems from the operation of a system of procedures, rules, and attitudes over time that, perhaps unintentionally, has the effect of disproportionately affecting a particular group.

tangible property

A sub-category of personal property that includes assets that can be seen and touched.

trespasser

Someone who enters a premises without permission, or someone who enters a premises lawfully but then does not stay where he or she is supposed to stay. The duty of care that an occupier of a premises owes to trespassers is defined in occupiers' liability statutes.

vicarious liability

Means that a party is held legally responsible even though it has done nothing wrong. An employer is responsible (or "liable") for the wrongful acts of employees acting within the scope of their employment duties. The employer and employee are considered associated parties in the ongoing business of the employer's organization. The employer is held responsible for damages caused to others by the employee while the employee is performing the work of the organization.

volenti non fit injuria

Latin phrase meaning "harm does not come to one who consents."

voluntary assumption of risk

Based on the legal principle of *volenti non fit injuria*, this presumes that an injured participant voluntarily accepts the inherent risk in a situation and assumes legal responsibility for it.

waiver of liability contract

A binding legal agreement in which a participant in an activity agrees beforehand not to pursue any legal action against the organizers of the activity, should the participant be injured. In other words, the participant waives his or her legal right to sue for damages.

working notice

Working notice arises when a notice of termination is given to an employee in advance so that the employee knows that her employment will end on a set date in the future. For the intervening period, until the predetermined termination date, the employee continues to work for the employer on the same terms and conditions.

wrongful action

A term used to described unlawful acts of directors of corporations. Directors of non-profit organizations have statutory duties that arise from their role as "trustees" or stewards in representing the interests of the members of the organization.

Index